So far, so good

So far, so good

The Autobiography
of a Wandering Minstrel

ROGER AND NATALIE WHITTAKER

TEMBO PUBLICATIONS COMPANY
NEW YORK, NEW YORK

This book is for our children, who have patiently put up with the antics of their parents.

We would like to thank Milton J. Shapiro, without whose help this book would have been finished two weeks earlier!

Acknowledgements are also due to B. Kipkoriɪ for permission to reproduce the extract from KENYA'S PEOPLE – *The People of the Rift Valley* at the beginning of Chapter Two.

All text copyright © 1986 Natalie Whittaker
All music copyright © Tembo Music Ltd.

First published in the United States by
Tembo Publications Company
15 Oakland Avenue
Harrison, New York 10528

Printed in the United States of America

ISBN: 0-938177-00-1 paperback

Library of Congress Catalog Card Number: 86-50373

Chapter 1

I   was   born   to   sing   the   songs   for   you

ALL I HEARD was a slight intake of breath. The hair on my neck
bristled and the sweat trickled down my spine. I realised with
horror that I was unarmed, my only weapon the paint brush I
was clutching.

Without moving, I said to the figure behind me,

'Don't be a fool!'

The breathing was harder now and, after a moment that
seemed a lifetime, I turned to face our African gardener. His
eyes were bulging and glazed; his mouth worked spasmodi-
cally, foaming with spittle from the frenzy into which he had
worked himself. His hands clutched the machete used for
clearing small trees from the undergrowth, so sharp and strong
that it would have needed very little effort to end my mortal
days.

'Drop it! And don't be an idiot,' I said quietly in Swahili,
feeling the greater idiot myself with my defenceless bluster, and
knowing that at any moment my head could part company
from my shoulders.

The seconds ticked by and then, as I plucked up the courage
to take two steps towards him, to my immense relief he
dropped the weapon, turned and walked slowly away.

I sat down on the verandah steps that I had been painting,
shaking like a leaf and quite unable to call for assistance. By the
time I had recovered my equilibrium he had disappeared from
view. Later I heard that he had been found and imprisoned. I
never saw him again. I was not called as a witness, not even
questioned as there was no trial. This was the time of the
'troubles' in Kenya, or 'Mau Mau', and our gardener was a
suspected Oath Administrator. Therefore, under the Emergency Powers, mere suspicion meant automatic imprisonment.

The year was 1954 and I was an eighteen-year-old school boy. On the day in question I had snatched a few hours away from preparing for my final exams to paint the front of our house. During those difficult years, we kept guns to hand at all times. Even in school we older boys were armed in order to protect the younger children in the event of an attack on the school itself.

Mau Mau was a poor translation by the British of a Kikuyu phrase describing Kenya's fight for independence from British rule. As with so many nations, Kenya suffered a bloody and painful birth before emerging as the modern African state it is today. Determination by the European settlers to maintain control of what they saw as the fruits of their labours clashed with national pride and a desire for self-determination on the African side – often with brutal fury.

How I, of northern British ancestry, happened to be there in the first place is where this story really begins . . .

* * *

My father was born in 1905 in the town of Basford, Staffordshire, to a family widely respected in the grocery and bakery trades, who owned a large chain of stores throughout several counties. His family were both musically artistic and adventurous. When not working, the three sons all played musical instruments (my own father playing the violin) and developed their own band, whilst my Aunt Doris became an accomplished ballet dancer.

My grandfather obviously influenced this musical environment as I have in my possession a card printed in 1895 advertising the Glee Club with which he sang. These were 'barber shop' groups that went from house to house entertaining on festive occasions, taking requests from a list printed on a card.

As I said, they were an adventurous family, and my uncles who did not follow in grandfather's footsteps took to travel. Arthur joined the merchant navy; Harold emigrated to America to seek his fortune. My father, Edward, was the one who stayed at home to learn the family business and serve his seven years statutory apprenticeship.

In another part of the county, Woolstanton, my mother, Viola, was born in 1906. Hers was a family of high powered educationalists and administrators in the school system. Her father was a highly respected deputy headmaster of Hanley School and almost her entire family were involved in the profession.

As one of eight children, with a very determined mother, it seemed unlikely that her future would ever lead anywhere but in the footsteps of her family. It seemed even more improbable that my father's and her paths would ever cross. But Fate has a strange way of intervening in this life and on a visit to her sister Elaine's house in Basford (after many weeks of being seriously ill with diphtheria) the two girls popped into one of the Whittaker stores where my father was working at the time.

I believe he asked my mother to join him after choir practice one day, and that was the start of their romance. At the time, they were nineteen and twenty respectively. I was never told whether it was 'love at first sight'. All I do know is that nothing was ever to separate them. Their relationship met with immediate difficulties, for in those days the academic and trade way of life seldom mixed. To this day, I do not know fully why my maternal grandparents disapproved of my father, but I suspect my maternal grandmother for one felt that my father and mother had little in common.

However, my mother had inherited one vital aspect of her personality from her mother – an iron-willed determination; nothing was going to part her from the man of her choice. When they decided to actually become engaged, my maternal grandparents were furious. The pressure brought to bear was intense, but the strongest of loves are often those forged in adversity and in fact the young couple were to be faced with a far more serious drama in the weeks that followed, one that was to test their affections and strength to the ultimate.

Although on the surface a quiet man, in his youth my father had the normal wild streak many young men seem to possess before they finally settle down. His little 'fling' took the form of an extremely high powered motorbike which he loved. But, however capable the rider, motorbikes will always be far more dangerous than cars and then, as now, there was always the danger of meeting a careless idiot on the road. In my father's

3

case, it was a gentleman very much the worse for drink driving a large car.

Usually my mother went everywhere with him, but fortunately that day she was not riding pillion. The car hit my father head on, dragging him for hundreds of yards under the vehicle. It apparently took some time before the befuddled driver finally realised that the rider of the bike was underneath his car. By the time he brought the vehicle to a halt, my father was barely alive.

His face was cut to shreds, the skin of his scalp hanging from his head and his nose smashed beyond recognition. Both his legs were broken, as was his pelvis, his back, and, it was only discovered fifty years later, his neck.

He sensed very little of the frantic dash by ambulance to the hospital as he was semi-conscious at the time. But in the casualty department of the hospital, he recalls hearing through the haze the nurses frantically rounding up the surgical team and advising the operating staff that there had been an extremely serious motor accident. He heard, too, the gruesome details that 'bones were protruding through the skin of the patient'.

Initially, in the race to save his life, the medical staff concentrated on putting him back together as best they could. However, once his life was no longer in danger, his injuries were investigated more fully and the local surgeon decided that one leg, badly broken and a mass of steel pins, was developing gangrene. He could see little hope of saving it and decided the only answer was amputation.

Understandably, my grandfather was reluctant to give his permission. However, if only amputation could save my father's life . . . the decision would have to be taken. Just at that moment, a miracle, as it were, appeared on the scene in the person of my uncle Harold, returned to England from America. He fought my grandfather's decision to allow the amputation, making him promise to seek out a second and even a third opinion before allowing surgery to take place.

With time of the essence, a rapid and frantic search was undertaken, resulting in my grandfather finding a surgeon willing at least to take a look at my father's condition. This was Dr. Eric Young, who had his own nursing homes in

4

Birmingham and Newcastle-under-Lyme. This eminent man drove from Birmingham at breakneck speed to the hospital where he examined my father and agreed to take on the case – but he actually saw little hope of saving the leg. For the moment, at least, he patted my father's face and said,

'Don't worry, lad. I am not going to agree to them taking your leg off tonight.'

My father's impression was that the resident staff was not all that happy with Dr. Young's diagnosis and plans; nevertheless an operating room was made available.

Much of all this my father perceived only hazily. He was heavily sedated and trussed up like a mummy, practically unable to move, talk or even open his eyes. It was assumed by the nurses that he was also deaf and thus, to his consternation, he overheard them placing bets at five shillings a time on whether or not he would have to have the leg amputated anyway, no matter what Dr. Young did.

The operation went ahead. My father does not recall any sense of panic or distress; he was too sedated for that. If anything, he was in a blissful state of drug-induced euphoria. But when the operation was over and he began to come out of the anaesthetic the first thing he did was reach down to feel for the leg, remembering stories told by amputees of how they could still 'feel' the amputated limb. It was not until later, fully conscious, with a nurse holding a mirror for him to see for himself, that he was convinced he was still in one piece.

The specialist's handiwork was undoubtedly unorthodox. He had made a dozen or so incisions on the top side of the infected leg and then corresponding cuts underneath. Then for several excruciating days, father suffered strong antiseptic solution being washed through the wounds. With these washes and tender nursing, he began to heal.

When it was apparent that my father's leg was saved, the resident doctors looked at the withered multi-fractured poor appendage and said,

'Well he still has his leg – for all the good it will do him!'

My father still remembers bitterly this traumatic remark fifty years later and I think this may well have been what gave him the necessary courage to carry on.

After many months in hospital, although his spine and pelvic injuries were sufficiently healed for him to sit up and move around, my father's spirits were at a very low ebb and he was unable to look to the future with much optimism. My mother used to visit him daily and wheel him around in the wheelchair for long 'walks', trying her best to boost his morale. But, inevitably, on one of her visits he suggested to her that she would be better off with somebody fit and whole and that she should therefore consider their engagement at an end. My mother, being my mother, would not even listen to such a suggestion, let alone break their wedding plans.

Fortunately, Nature has a wonderful way of mending the spirit as well as the body. With my mother behind him, with my grandfather's faith, with his brother Harold and the rest of his family supporting him, my father started to fight back.

As soon as he was fit enough to leave hospital, my grandfather sent him off to Devon, where he had a friend with a farm by the sea. As my mother pushed his wheelchair to the train, I don't think even she could envisage the next thirteen months or my father's determination to walk again.

The fresh air and good country food boosted his general health and before long his renewed strength gave him fresh courage. He refused the use of the wheelchair and had the local doctor strap his legs in irons. After a while he couldn't stand the irons, which hurt almost as much as the injuries, and persuaded the doctor to let him try crutches. Day after day, falling and pulling himself up again, he got stronger and steadier. When the time came to return home, the crutches had been thrown away and replaced by sticks. He had steadfastly refused to give in to his injuries and had conspired with the farmer not to tell the family of his mobility.

My grandfather had, of course, regularly received reports from his friends concerning my father's general return to health, but the secret had been so well kept he had no idea that he was now almost able to walk. Meeting the train from Devon with the wheelchair, he cried unashamedly when my father lowered himself onto the station platform and, albeit somewhat shakily, walked with the aid of sticks to meet his family.

Their immediate reaction was one of utter delight but, following a visit to Dr. Young, who was equally astounded, this turned to apprehension for after a thorough examination he felt he had to advise my father that he would never really recover his health unless he left the damp cold weather of England. The ideal climate for him was somewhere at a high altitude with a dry atmosphere. His two suggested locations were Brazil or Kenya. As my father had no knowledge of the Portuguese language and Kenya was English speaking, it was the obvious choice. The year was 1929.

Tourists see it as it is today, one of the most beautiful places on earth. It's a land full of life and colour; a land full of startling contrasts: rugged mountains, wild bush, lush valleys, salt flats, vast lakes and near deserts. Along the coast, the crystal blue sea and shimmering white sands dotted with modern hotels make it a holiday paradise.

In the 1920s, it was very different. It was still largely unpopulated and the small pockets of European communities were joined by a network of rough dirt roads, washed away with monotonous regularity by every bi-annual rainfall. Inland the only sure way of getting to and from the coast was by train Only buildings in the cities of Mombasa and Nairobi were vaguely representative of European architecture. Most settlers outside the cities lived in wooden houses similar to the 'Wild West' with corrugated iron roofs purpose built for the climate.

But it was a country being opened up fast by people who followed the traditions of previous settlers in wild, untamed lands everywhere else in the world; people like my father and mother, with little money but a great deal of courage, foresight, ambition and energy with which to forge a bright future.

Still, in those early days back in England when they had to decide on their plans, it must have been quite an awesome proposition, especially to my mother who had never so much as crossed the channel to France. They read as much as they could about the different possibilities open to them, and talked to many people who knew the country, seeking their advice. Finally, my father decided to continue doing what he knew best – the grocery grade. Farmers and other settlers living in the bush as well as the city dwellers would always be in need of supplies and it seemed the obvious choice. He contacted the owners of a chain of departmental stores in Nairobi called Servicestores and they agreed to take him on.

My maternal grandparents' initial annoyance at their

7

daughter's engagement now turned to absolute rage. How dare this young man, a physical wreck, have the effrontery to want to marry their daughter, let alone think of whisking her away to a foreign, uncivilised country, with no prospects and no future except certain danger and deprivation. Mother, fiercely proud of father and his achievements, completely lost her temper, and there followed a terrible and traumatic family row, mainly involving my grandmother and culminating in my mother spending a lot of time at the Whittaker household.

She found comfort in her future in-laws, who took her to their hearts during the time my father was preparing for his departure.

So with a job under his belt and some small financial assistance from my grandfather, he said his goodbyes to his family and of course to my mother, who was to follow in three months when he had settled in. They agreed they would be married as soon as she arrived.

Many of the passengers on the four-week sea journey were settlers who had been on leave, so my father and the other young men who were new to Africa were able to glean valuable first-hand information. Isolated on the boat, as the trip wore on the prospect must have become increasingly more daunting as the 'tales' became increasingly wilder. However, apart from the stories of hardships, wild animals and diseases, my father also began to assemble a much better idea of the openings and prospects for a newcomer to the land.

On his arrival at Mombasa, he made plans for his wedding in three months time, then took the train inland to Nairobi to start to piece together his new life.

Meanwhile, back in England, aided and abetted by her future mother-in-law, my mother gathered together the necessities that every young bride should possess, including her wedding gown. Her parents still hated her leaving and did their best to persuade her to stay.

That cold, grey December day of her departure must have been quite heart-breaking for her. Whilst all the other passengers waved goodbye to their relatives and friends on the East India dock, there were only two faces she knew in the crowd to bid her farewell – her brother Mac, and her sister Elaine. I can imagine how she must have wept when she recalled her mother's words on the day before her departure:

'Today I buried my daughter in the churchyard!' Whereupon she took to her bed for three weeks.

However, she was a young woman of much strength and, luckily, a great sense of humour. Within hours she had met up with Ethel, the only other lady on board and to hear her tell it, it was quite a trip. Two young ladies and a boatload of men! Some in Government, some army personnel and others just like themselves, leaving home to start a new life. But in spite of all the joviality and fun, she was heartily glad to see the docks of Mombasa harbour gleaming white in the hot African sun.

As the ship manoeuvred to the dock, she could see my father down on the quay. He cupped his hands and kept yelling to her. At first she was too far away to hear what he was saying, then finally she deciphered the message.

'Have you got the ring?'

'The ring? What ring?'

'The wedding ring!'

Father's last instructions to her had been to buy one that would fit her finger. What a thing to forget! The other passengers gathered on deck could not fail to overhear this exchange and seeing mother's confusion, roared with laughter, which didn't help her predicament.

As the gangway was placed in position and father rushed up to help her and the porters with the baggage, urging her to hurry, she realised that his promise 'to marry her as soon as she arrived' literally meant just that.

Her bags were rushed to the hotel and then my father promptly dragged her through the streets to find a jeweller. At last, in an alleyway, they found an Indian jeweller's shop, but alas they had not got a wedding ring her size, only one that was too small. While father paced up and down glancing repeatedly at his watch, urging the man to hurry, mother watched as the old man quickly filed down the ring, all the time thinking,

'All my gold! There goes another bit!'

The ring was now just big enough, and there was another mad dash back to the hotel to change into their wedding finery.

By now, mother was hot and bothered, her head swimming with the rapidity of events and, as father dashed off to the cathedral to join the best man, she only had a few moments in which to change into her wedding dress.

The dress, having been packed in a box for over a month, was neatly creased in the exact shape of the box, but there was no time in which to have it pressed. Near to tears and wondering if she had done the right thing, she donned the crumpled garment, shoved her feet into the matching shoes and, grabbing her handbag, ran to the cathedral, pulling on her gloves as she went.

My father's best man, Jack Hunt, was a friend he had met on the train down to Mombasa who was also getting married – to Ethel, my mother's travelling companion.

As mother rushed into the church to join them, she caught the heel of one shoe in the grating at the beginning of the aisle and it came off. Most brides dream of that elegant gliding entrance to join the man of their dreams at the altar, but not so poor mother! She was crumpled and dishevelled, her hair plastered to her flushed face, now limping as she proceeded down the aisle. She vainly attempted to get rid of the shoe altogether by shaking her leg as if fending off a snapping dog. The group at the altar turned to see a hopping, kicking apparition bearing down the aisle towards them. Just as she drew level, the shoe flew off and she collided with father in her effort to maintain her balance, nearly sending the others down like ninepins.

With a valiant attempt at dignity, she managed to calm herself for the actual ceremony, but the final straw came when she found that her hands were so hot that she couldn't get her glove off, let alone the ring on!

Most women at this point would have collapsed in hysterics, but not my mother. She started to laugh. The clergyman, who up until then had been looking somewhat askance at the entire spectacle, joined in, and with much tugging by all the offending garment was removed and the marriage vows finally made. This was one bride who would never forget her wedding! To this day, she relishes the telling of the tale.

The wedding over, mother was really looking forward to a few days alone with her new husband – but it turned out there was to be no honeymoon. No such luxuries, just hard work from then on. They spent the night in a hotel, but the next morning they were on the train for Nairobi for my father had to work on the following day. After the comparatively civilised views of Mombasa with its Arab influence, its mosques and minarets, and the city's magnificent cathedral, the African skyline and panorama seen from the train must have been quite fascinating to my mother.

Any visitor to Africa will tell you that the initial impression is one of heat and dust, quickly followed by colours bright and clear, and as the senses assimilate details – sound!

Africa is never quiet. During the day the birds whistle and call, the crickets chirp and the air is alive with the buzz and whirr of the wings of millions of tiny insects. From somewhere comes the cough of a leopard. An elephant trumpets, a warthog snorts, a lion roars, a hyena yelps. There's a cloud of dust and the thunder of a thousand hooves as a herd of wildebeest or zebra is scattered by a marauding lioness.

At night the sweet-smelling air, tinged with the aroma of cedarwood smoke, is filled with strange screeches and whoops and from the bush come the menacing grunts and roars of the big cats.

So, as the train chugged through bush, across plains and through endless African townships, mother was seeing the real Africa for the first time. In those days it was easy to glimpse wild game such as elephant and giraffe from the rail track as well as the seemingly endless herds of various antelope and zebra. As the train stopped at the stations, Africans selling a multitude of items would gather around, chattering loudly.

Wide beaming smiles in ebony faces surrounded her, addressing her in languages she could not understand. But the message in their happy smiles struck her instantly, although what she was experiencing was far different from anything she could have imagined back in England. She felt immediately at ease. My father had picked up a smattering of Swahili (the universal language of most East African tribes when talking to foreigners) and was able to translate simple phrases.

In those days Nairobi was a bustling but small city with a couple of good hotels, namely the Norfolk and the Stanley, as the rich and the well-travelled had already discovered the excitement of hunting safaris. Fortunately, today, safaris are purely photographic, In the early days, however, before hunting, poaching and encroaching farmlands meant the endangering of many species, these safaris were all big game hunts. The hotel lobbies held famous faces by the score and the farmers and ranchers would come into town for supplies and a few days socialising before returning to their far flung homesteads.

My father worked intensely hard and very long hours, saving every penny he could with obsessive zeal. My mother immediately went to work as a secretary for a firm of lawyers to help fill the family coffers for they were saving towards a business of their own.

Although her introduction to Africa had not been a total culture shock, nevertheless mother found it quite hard to accept some of the deprivations, the sanitary conditions and the lack of many luxuries she had been used to back home. She admits readily that there were times when she could cheerfully have got on the next boat back to England. None more so than the first time they managed a holiday after about a year of marriage.

A friend very kindly offered to let them use his 'country cottage'. No honeysuckle and neatly kept lawns there, just a mud and wattle house deep in the bush and perched on the edge of a ravine, spanned by a bridge to the African servants quarters and the kitchen.

There is a lovely story I must tell at this point that has become part of the 'Settlers Lore' in Kenya. It concerns an Englishman preparing his house for his first visitors, and in particular, a young and tender memsahib from England. Whether it was my parents or somebody else I will never know, but apparently the young man, realising that his houseman never wore any clothes at all, called this servant to one side and tried as tactfully as possible to persuade the man to wear some covering, because 'young English ladies were not accustomed to seeing naked men'. The man beamed and walked away. The guests duly arrived and when unpacked sat down on the verandah in the mellow evening sun for a drink. The bell was rung for the servant who quickly appeared. But to the consternation of his employer, the amusement of the men and the blushes of the young lady, his covering was in the form of a discarded Colgate toothpaste box, neatly held on by a piece of string around his waist!

12

I doubt this probably apocryphal story was about my parents, but I do know that their host left the morning after they arrived to allow the young couple the privacy of a belated honeymoon.

My mother, always having been very independent and after receiving a lesson on the working of the wood burning stove from the old cook, subsequently informed the staff that she would cook the dinner, and they were dismissed for the evening.

Sunsets so near the equator do not linger and night sets in within an hour. Of course, as there was no such luxury as electric light, mother set off to the bridge spanning the ravine clutching a hurricane lamp. The entire length of the bridge was set with cupboards holding all the cooking utensils.

As she browsed through the pots and pans making her selection, she smelt a strange musty odour. Simultaneously, she heard the sound of rasping breathing. Remembering all the advice she had been given about not making sudden movements with animals and not knowing what was making the sound, or where it was, she nonchalantly reached for a pan on the top shelf of the cupboard. As her hand went up, the breathing turned to a deep growl. Suddenly the pan and others on the shelf flew in all directions with a clatter and a banging that could be heard way down the valley. A full-grown leopard launched itself from its hiding place, fortunately over mother's head and not at her throat.

As the leopard disappeared like a ghost into the night, she screamed at the top of her voice. My father and all the servants came running. She managed to make herself heard and understood amongst the babble, but received scant sympathy for her experience. The servants merely smiled and my father calmly remarked,

'Well, this is the African bush and it's full of animals.'

Leopards, unlike other big cats, will kill for fun as she was to discover later. I think she would have had a heart attack if she had known that at the time.

In any case, the drama of the wedding, the strangeness of her surroundings and the months of very hard work now took their toll. The confrontation with the leopard was the final straw and for the first time mother did have hysterics and vowed to return to England. My father's only comment was that he was staying and if she went, she needn't expect him to join her. He finally calmed her enough to persuade her to remain until morning. She stayed, and was to have many other unexpected meetings with wildlife in the future.

By now they were learning, as I did constantly although born there, that you don't live 'in' Africa, you live 'with' it. I find this hard to explain to friends that have never experienced life in Africa. You develop a resignation to events and you never expect, just accept, and somehow it just all falls into place.

About this time, 1930, my father and mother built their first house in Groganville. This was an area just outside the town of Nairobi named by Grogan, the famous explorer who walked from the Cape to Cairo at the turn of the century, and consisted then of a few houses clustered at the edge of the Nairobi River valley. This new home was my parents' pride and joy and holds one of the clearest recollections I have of my early youth. They planned every detail and it had, wonder of wonders, the first flush loo in Nairobi. Friends and neighbours gathered on 'Moving-In Day' to attend the ceremony of the 'First Flush'. A rousing cheer heralded this advent of modern plumbing. The nagging question of what would happen should the water pump to the valley seize was momentarily forgotten.

The house at Groganville holds a very warm place in my heart. It was set in an acre of garden planted with wonderful trees – the best of which was a big fig tree. Because of the climate most of the year the grass is parched brown, but the moment the rains come it recovers to lush green velvet. As for the flowers, well, they were and always are a florist's dream. All year round a rainbow of colours surrounded me and, although English gardens are magnificent, they are sedate and I sorely miss the sharp brightness of my childhood surroundings. The house was small, built of stone, with a large red polished stone verandah that looked down the garden to the valley and river below.

Our neighbours were far enough away for privacy but close enough for companionship and the valley teemed with wildlife in those days. Game still came in sufficiently close to give mother the occasional heart-stopping moment, such as the morning she and her African cook were hanging out washing and a full-grown lion quietly wandered across the grass, glanced at them totally unconcerned, and then disappeared into the valley.

To this day large monkeys raid the fruit trees in the garden and are very savage, often trying to kill household pets. But above all, the snakes were, and still are, an enormous problem. Snakes, scorpions and deadly spiders have adapted to the encroachment of buildings, people and civilisation in general and survive in perfect symbiosis.

It was with one of these that mother had her nearest brush with death. One night the electric lighting having failed, which it did with monotonous regularity, she decided to take a bath by lamplight. She put the lamp on the bathroom floor and in the gloom reached to turn the taps on. As she did so, the tap started to hiss and thinking there was the usual air lock in the water system, she called to father,

'Teddy! I think the system's got an air lock. You had better come and fix it.'

She proceeded to undress whilst waiting for the water to trickle into the bath. My father came in and asked her to hold the lamp higher while he attacked the offending pipe with his spanner. As he did so, they both froze, because there, wrapped around the tap, was a black mamba whose bite is inevitably fatal. Mother managed to hold the lamp steady as it uncoiled itself and rose into its position of threat. Father took an almighty swing with the heavy spanner with all the strength he could muster, nearly decapitating the snake.

It sounds all very calm, collected and matter of fact when you read it now, but I can assure you they both retired to the drawing room for a very large drink to steady their nerves, all thoughts of bathing forgotten until the gardener took the body away the next day. In fact, they shut the door and wouldn't go back in case it wasn't quite dead! Snakes have a clever way of playing dead while merely stunned, only to come frighteningly to life again and reappear in the most unlikely places. One lesson you soon learn is to always make sure the snake is really dead.

By 1933, Dad realised that he had saved almost enough money to raise a mortgage to buy his own store and after looking around found the ideal location on the outskirts of town at a place called Westlands. An existing store owned by his present employers was up for sale along with quite a bit of land surrounding it which could be built on later, so the prospects were very good indeed. By now they were about to become parents for the first time, and in the summer of that year my sister Betty was born. This was as good a time as any to move on, so summoning up all their energy, they took the plunge and bought the store.

Now tied to the home by a new baby, my mother could no longer work independently, so whenever the infant permitted, busied herself with doing the book-keeping for my father's first business.

So now they were settled in their own home, with a bonny child and a thriving business. All in all, everything was rosy until the morning of March 22nd, 1936, when the peace was shattered. I arrived! Seven pounds of me!

Mother says that she knew that from the moment I was born that I was going to be difficult, different and awkward. When I ask why she says,

'Your arrival was extremely difficult and I thought I was going to die. However, you were considerate enough to arrive at 7.45 on a Sunday morning.'

'How do you know it was 7.45?' I ask.

'Well, Dr. Anderson smacked me on my rump and said, "Good girl, now I will be in time for morning service!" '

The story of my arrival home from hospital is quite amusing because, typically, Betty was the apple of my parents' eye, and from the moment I arrived I disturbed the status quo. She walked up to my cot and said,

'Take him back! We don't want him!'

Then she spied a pink elephant in my cot and demanded it.

'That's Roger's dear,' said my mother, 'you can't have it.' A few minutes later my mother went out to check on her favourite son and found a large dog-eared book on my stomach and the elephant gone.

'Well, he said he wanted it,' said Betty.

I am really forced to say that our relationship was an abrasive one for many years with my sister being given the responsibility of looking after her young brother, which to my mind she did with far too much zeal most of the time.

For the first couple of years I was the ideal baby, happy and placid with a hearty appetite that quickly led to my resembling the 'Michelin man' in no time at all. Mother began to believe that her first impression of her son had been wrong, but one person had seen through my deception – Betty. If only she could have told them that what I was doing behind my angelic facade was sitting and assimilating, listening and learning.

Another factor was my enormous size. I probably found it hard to get around! However, by the time I was three, that baby fat had begun to disappear and with my increased mobility I became a mini-tyrant, thinking up the most dreadful antics, turning my mother's hair grey, but eventually warming my sister to me. She could now let rip and get up to no end of mischief, whilst using me as the eternal scapegoat!

Chapter 2

I had a lot of growing to do

'WHY ARE THE sun, moon and stars up in the sky, whilst Man and the animals are on the earth?'

'Once the sun, moon and stars were on the earth with Man and the animals, but they became frightened and went away. You see, they once all slept together, motionless, on their sides. All except Man. One day Sun noticed him turn his head, and he grew suspicious. Soon afterwards Man turned right over. Sun, Moon and Stars were alarmed, and decided to go away into the sky to see what would happen. When they had gone, Man got up and walked away. He made himself weapons from stones and he killed small animals for food, and larger animals to provide him with skins to cover his body. He made a boat and caught fish. The animals began to be afraid of him. Elephant and the other big animals realized that it was too late to escape into the sky, so they hid in the forest, and they have been hiding from Man ever since.'

This was the kind of story I grew up with. No 'Aladdin and his Magic Lamp' or 'Jack and the Beanstalk'. With the onset of war in Europe, my mother had to return to work and Betty and I were brought up by African nannies, or 'ayahs' as they were known. Our ayahs were predominantly Nandis and, as all Africans, loved children dearly. In the absence of our mother, we were considered their children and they loved us as their own. We, in return, loved them and my memories of those ladies live with me to this day. All Africans are highly tolerant of children, believing that all experience gleaned in those early years makes the adult person and that the mother, in particular, holds the key to the child's development.

We spent all our time with them, often going to their quarters, romping and playing around their homes. Consequently Swahili became my first language. One of my earliest memories is of squatting around a cooking pot while the ladies gossiped and boiled goats' heads for us to pick clean later. I remember, too, rolling in the dust with all the other children and playing games with pebbles, and above all the comfort of a warm black breast for me to cuddle and fondle when hurt or distressed. It is the most natural thing in the world for an African woman to give her breasts to an unhappy child – any child – and that practice only stopped as I grew older and mutual modesty developed. This was my first appreciation of the wonders of the female anatomy!

It was also around their homes that I first started to take an interest in musical instruments; the African guitar made and played by all villagers was the first instrument I ever came across. This was a box or can over which was stretched taut a hide – usually goat-skin. The framework came in the form of an arm with six or eight wire strings from the bottom of the box and pulled tight to the top of the arm, with cloth tuning pegs attached to the top, which were twisted when the instrument needed tuning. The bottom of the box had a sound 'hole' cut in it. Many of the songs I learnt then I use in my stage act today, and the rhythms and method of strumming make it hard for my Western musicians to follow.

Naturally we saw our parents at weekends and in the evenings. Less so my father, as he was rapidly becoming a workaholic, spending every moment, including Sundays, in his shops. I say 'shops' as the land he had bought with the original store was now fully developed and he could be considered a property developer at that stage. I cannot say in all honesty that I was close to my father in my childhood. He was an extremely stern man, but to this day a man universally admired for his enormous integrity, placing importance on honesty and truth above all, and highly intolerant of incompetence. He has always judged others by his own elevated personal standards and finds it hard to accept normal human weaknesses. Later in my early adult life, I did become close to him, but that was only after he had retired from business. It was almost as though he gave a great sigh of relief and turned around and said,

'Now I can get to know you all!'

In that respect, the fates have been extremely kind to us

19

both. I treasure dearly the relationship we have today and appreciate the fact that we eventually had a chance to get to know each other.

My mother is a beautiful woman with wonderful bone structure, always vivacious and full of stories, fun and laughter, but with a long memory and an explosive temper. She is what the Africans call 'kali' and the Americans call 'don't mess with . . .' She has a powerful personality and when I was a child it appeared that she ruled us all with a rod of iron. Whether my father actually permitted the supposed domination or just pretended in order to keep the peace, I will never know. All I do know is that they loved each other to distraction.

My impression is that at one point my father was so embroiled in forging his business that he had to make a choice between his children and his wife. With the little energy and time he had left over after business, he quite understandably chose his wife and during my childhood I saw very litle of him. Now, as I race around the world in pursuit of my own career, I can understand and appreciate the drives, conflicts and frustrations he experienced. But as a child I was resentful of his absence and hurt by his apparent lack of affection.

In spite of the limited parental company, that was a golden period: lovely wild days with no sense of time, feeling the sun on our bodies, romping and rolling in the grass. We were so happy with our African 'mothers, brothers and sisters'. By European standards we were thoroughly undisciplined, but to the Africans we were learning by the experiences of Mother Nature to do what came naturally and with no thought to the dangers. The Africans accepted the hazards that we met daily with a philosophy totally unacceptable to us in the West.

By the time we started school, the hours spent in the class-room proved only an irritating interruption that prevented us from spending all our time at play. Our playground was the valley and the river beyond. We never wore shoes. In fact, our shorts were our only clothing. Down to the river we'd go, through a winding natural path amongst the rocks, where scorpions and snakes lay hidden, and although our dogs were frequently stung or bitten, it never occurred to us that we might disturb them and be in danger. We merely avoided them.

The river itself, though free of crocodiles, held other hidden dangers. Bilhartsia was the unseen enemy in the waters – a revolting nematode worm whose larvae are found in their millions floating in the rivers and lakes, and which bore through the skin, develop in the urogenital system and eventually kill.

I clearly recall in later years seeing in a medical laboratory (in what was then Salisbury, Rhodesia) the preserved kidneys, bladder and ureters of a victim who had died from an infestation of Bilhartsia.

The bladder was parchment thin from the constant loss of tissue, torn away by the excretion of microscopic eggs which attach themselves by the million to the walls of the bladder by means of hooks. The ureters were cotton thin and how the man had survived for as long as he did was beyond me. The autopsy revealed a salt cellar full of the tiny eggs. I well recall the shudder that went through me when I realised that as children we had all swum in the rivers and had never been tested for Bilhartsia.

But we had no knowledge or thought of that as we dived and swam; our only fear was of becoming tangled in the weeds and drowning. Many large animals came down to the river to drink, but I suppose we made such a noise that they never wanted to come too close.

One of our neighbours was a man called Lester who had a son, David, who although older than my sister (so about eight years older than me) was soon to become my best friend. At first, when he was presented with this obnoxious cocky little kid from next door (and I was!) he did everything to avoid me. I hero-worshipped him, and realising that he thought me too young for his more adventurous gang games, I took to doing something that nearly gave my mother a heart attack. I would carry live scorpions around in my shorts pockets!

At the time I was a tough little five-year-old, but this act of foolhardy bravery was enough to make the older fellas sit up and take notice. They felt that if I could do that, then I was ready to join them in their favourite game . . . tarantula fights. Now, in England, small boys have chestnut 'conker' fights, but we played with live tarantulas and trapped the spiders that lurked in the burrows under the grass of the lawn.

David, Betty and I would spend hours winkling these creatures out of their lairs with a stick. As they grabbed the stick, we would flick them into tin cans, the idea being that you would finally have a champion capable of taking on all comers. But sometimes the spiders felt kindly towards each other, so we devised a surefire way of making them aggressive. This was to light a candle under the tin and watch as the heat did the trick! They would attack each other with gusto, each blaming the other for their discomfort and a fight to the death would ensue.

Guns were always present: I can't remember when my juvenile love affair with them began, but David, at the grand old age of nine, was a crack shot with a .22 rifle. I, by the age of six, had accompanied him on many expeditions into our beloved valley with shotgun and rifle. I can remember skinning many deer in his garden.

David then decided that the time had come for me to get my 'eye in' and to learn all about guns and to treat them with respect. He spent hours trying to get me to hit a target with a gun that I was barely able to lift. Eventually I could hit any stationary object, usually tin cans. I was thrilled by the way they would twist and spiral away into the air as the bullet made contact, but the day came when David thought I was ready to shoot at moving objects.

The first thing I saw was one of our beloved doves, whose soft calls woke me every morning at dawn. I pointed the rifle, never for an instant thinking I would hit the bird, pulled the trigger and then watched in horror as it tumbled to the ground, stone dead. For the first time in my life I realised the true meaning and finality of death. I was heartbroken and I have never enjoyed hunting since. But, however utterly pointless and wasteful killing any living creature seemed, I also had to keep up appearances and swing with the tide of my peers, so all during my youth in Africa I spent many hours hunting.

The only pleasure involved in those expeditions was the company of my friends and the roaming of the wide open spaces. Underneath I loathed the 'sport' but, as I grew older, I came to understand why the professional culling of many species is necessary for the preservation of all the different animals in the wild. As civilisation upsets the balance of nature, this regulated killing is scientifically and humanely carried out by experts for the mutual good of both fauna and flora.

By the time I was six, David had become my constant companion and ally and I managed to keep up my air of fearless bravado at all times. By day, nothing did frighten me, but the nights were another matter. I hated the dark and especially on the many occasions when we were left alone in the house whilst my parents were out. The Africans slept in their own quarters, and because of the fear of burglary, every door in the main house was kept locked.

Betty and I were shut in our separate rooms, where the expanded metal shutters provided the only light, giving stripes of moonlight across the room. Although I knew that Betty was only just down the corridor I felt terribly alone and the night sounds seemed to become louder and louder, closer and closer. Each night the barking of the jackals, the whooping of the hyenas, took on monstrous physical solidarity, and to my terrified young mind they all seemed to be gathered beneath my window. Feverishly I tried to block out the images of those hideous slavering muzzles. I squeezed my eyes as tight as I could to shut out the images, but one night it all became too much for me.

Quite innocently, one of the Africans decided to check on us and, hearing nothing, tried to see if I was all right by pressing his face to the shutter. At that precise moment, I opened my eyes and saw this face, squashed out of all recognition by the shutters, staring at me through the moonlight.

I started to scream. I was totally hysterical and completely out of control. My petrified screams were so loud that even the neighbours heard. David himself came rushing over from his house a couple of hundred yards away, pleading with me through the window to calm down, unable to get to me because of the locked door. He talked to me for ages, trying everything to allay my fears. He explained that it had been one of the guards who was worried about us, but his words fell on deaf ears. I was out of my mind with fear.

Betty, equally unable to get to me, was terrified not knowing what had happened and added to the hubbub by shouting hysterically herself until David told her I was all right. She was quite convinced that I had been bitten by a snake. After something like two hours of panic and hysterics David managed to calm me down. Then, rushing back to his house he returned with some records which he pushed through the metal shutters.

'Here you are,' he said, 'these will cheer you up. Tomorrow morning you can play them.'

It did the trick!

Records were my only real toys. I loved them. To most six-year-olds a soft toy would have been a comfort, but for me he couldn't have chosen a better gift. Playing records had become my favourite pastime, my father having bought a wind-up recordplayer for me. I wanted nothing else for Christmas and birthdays than the latest Carter Family, Jimmy Rogers, Wilf Carter and George Formby records. I played them incessantly and everybody, relatives, friends and my parents alike, knew that all they needed to get the Whittaker kid was a record.

One of my fondest memories is of creeping downstairs in the middle of the night, having kidded my parents that I was asleep, finding my new records, stuffing some socks into the horn of the gramophone player, and listening so hard at the muffled sounds that I never noticed my mother and father standing in the doorway until I heard Dad in his 'kali' voice say,

'Get to bed!'

Now, when I visit Nashville to record with my friend Chet Atkins and all those wonderful musicians, it impresses upon me how much of an influence those early artists had both on me and the record industry as a whole.

Whenever David or our friends weren't with us, Betty and I played alone. With no one in the house we managed a great deal of mischief, I can tell you. Both overly endowed with imagination, our wild behaviour often brought down the wrath of our mother on the heads of our poor ayahs and they took most of the blame.

Betty and I had devised two imaginary personalities for ourselves and spent hours being 'Mrs. Goulkin' and 'Mr. Kelling'. From what I remember, these two characters were decidedly undesirable and degenerate, smoking and drinking with impunity. Just like the adults we met! Mrs. Goulkin and Mr. Kelling discovered that dried daisy stems or the dried

24

silken tops of corn cobs made excellent cigarettes and tobacco, and that crème de menthe was definitely 'à la mode' for tippling. We would sit with legs elegantly crossed beneath dirty old shorts, toasting each other and offering drinks to invisible friends until we were quite dizzy!

My parents, who only drank on rare occasions, discovered this misdemeanour when entertaining a very important guest who was 'à la mode' and wanted crème de menthe. Our faces told the tale when she saw the level in the bottle and we hightailed it out of reach of mother's slipper as fast as our legs would take us. Actually, that slipper hardly ever managed to make contact as we were far too quick. Mother would lay in wait behind doors to try to catch us, but we sprinted up the avocado tree and refused to come down, often sitting there in the dark wondering if the coast was clear.

We were never at a loss for escapades and our poor ayahs, who loved us dearly, were always loath to give us away. But sometimes our pranks were beyond laughter. The final straw came when we persuaded the gardener at a shilling a time to pour warm water across the verandah whilst we, stark naked, slipped up and down on our stomachs. The water slooshed from one side of the verandah to the other. Bucket after bucket was poured and the game carried on most of the afternoon amid squeals of delight and fun, the poor gardener unable to get on with any other job.

It was only when I went inside to collect a towel that I discovered where most of the water had gone – under the doors of the drawing room French windows! The room was awash, the carpets actually floating. I yelled to my sister and as fast as we could we hightailed it on our bicycles down the road, passing my parents coming the other way. My mother was surprised to see us pedalling by so fast and remarked on it to my father. The reason for our rapid exit was soon discovered. The mess was unbelievable with much of the furniture soaked and stained. But, as my mother later admitted, one of the carpets which previously had been very dark in colour was now washed clean and that was the only saving grace of the whole episode.

Fortunately, not everything we did caused consternation and damage. Both Betty and I loved entertaining. She would dance and I would sing. We would give performances for our friends and forbearing neighbours who would follow the signs 'to the theatre' which was our drawing room. The curtains which fell from floor to ceiling and which were, I am sure, my mother's pride and joy were punctured and string tied through in order to provide tabs for the performance.

Of the artistic contents of those epic performances, I remember very little, but some of the introductions come to mind. In particular, when announcing my sister I finished with the phrase 'bloody awful' which was greeted with stony glares by our already bored adult audience. Since those days I have heard many appalling introductions but one that still makes me smile came from France, in which the compère, introducing a famous artiste of the day, announced her name and was greeted from the balcony with a shout of,

'*C'est une putaine!*' ('She's a whore!')

To which the compère replied after a very pregnant pause,

'That may be so – but, nevertheless, here is Mademoiselle . . .!'

I suppose those childhood attempts at theatrical production could be considered the start of my apprenticeship, but I never had a thought that one day I might become a professional performer.

One of our other burning passions was bicycles. My father gave me a bicycle with the words,

'Look after it – it's the last one you're getting.'

I suspect he gave me this bicycle to keep me out of his car, since shortly before that particular birthday I had removed the keys from the ignition, put them in an empty record needle box and hidden them in the upholstery of the driver's seat. After frantic searching, my father had to hot-wire the car in order to start it and his temper as a result was not of the best!

We rode our bicycles everywhere, public transport in the form of buses being the barest minimum. Riding bicycles on those badly made roads was a test of stamina and your ability to repair punctures, but the worst hazards were the dogs. Each household had at least one dog and many a pack, the fiercer the better. These animals hated bicycles and chased us with a fury and a passion equalled only by a hungry lion chasing a zebra. To this day I treat strange dogs with great suspicion, particularly if they follow close behind my ankles.

Many of the dangerous incidents I experienced during my childhood years could well have been avoided had I not been so high-spirited. However, there was one precarious aspect of living in the tropics that could not have been – disease. Tropical diseases were a common and terrible scourge in those years, particularly malaria. Sometimes I wonder that we survived.

In truth, I almost did not. Cases of malaria in Kenya – as elsewhere in Africa – although more serious, were considered no more unusual than a cold would be in northern climates. I don't think any of us ever took malaria pills then and in fact it was many years before malaria was finally eliminated around the city of Nairobi. It's still a hazard out in the bush. It seemed to hit almost everybody, and it hit me one day as I was sitting quietly on the lawn with my ayah. Suddenly I felt awfully dizzy. The next thing I knew I was in bed with a raging fever. Within hours I was delirious and was rushed to the hospital where the doctors diagnosed a severe case of cerebral malaria.

As I recall, I was unconscious for about ten days. The doctors and my parents feared for my life. But somehow children have a remarkable way of successfully fighting an illness that would kill or cripple an adult and I came out of the coma. Perhaps it was because my rugged upbringing had given me a healthy body with which to fight. In any case, I recall emerging from my coma to find myself in a high hospital bed with a mosquito net tucked tightly under the mattress – talk about closing the stable door after the horse has bolted! The next thing I knew I was sitting on the floor looking up at a great rent in the netting. How it happened I had no idea. My only thought was, 'Holy hell! Someone's going to be cross!' I remembered all too well my mother's wrath when I tore mosquito netting at home; apparently they were quite expensive. Fortunately the only reaction at the hospital and of course from my parents was one of joy that I had emerged from my coma – albeit rather violently.

As I've said, I was a scrappy little kid, filled with a sense of adventure and exploration, anxious to experience each and every aspect of life that came my way. As a result I got into more than one scrape that required medical attention and I daresay at times I drove my parents to distraction. In desperation, I guess, hoping somehow to instil a bit of discipline into their little savage, they decided to send me to boarding school. And Betty with me.

In fairness it needs to be said that it was not just our mischievous behaviour that led us to being sent to boarding school, but also the onset of the Second World War in Europe. Although thousands of miles away from the front line, Kenya was put on a war alert footing and all British subjects were required to register for service. Due to his ill health, my father was unable to take any active part and therefore was not called up. However, like so many others he enrolled as an A.R.P. (Air Raid Precaution) warden and was in charge of the sand bags, sand buckets, stirrup pumps, etc., in case of aerial attacks.

My mother had managed to avoid the usual forms of war work such as being a land girl, 'digging for Victory', growing vegetables to send to the front to the troops, or nursing. She convinced the authorities that the secretarial work she was doing on the entertainment side was sufficiently important for both the welfare of civilian and army personnel alike.

As soon as the military personnel moved into Nairobi the schools were reserved for their offspring, so my schooling had to be quite a distance away at a town called Eldoret. The school was called the Hill School. I was first taken to see it by my mother and a family friend, George Burrell, my father at the time being too busy to leave his business.

My impression of that school in 1943 was that it was akin to a prison camp. It was a mass of wooden nissen huts with tar roofs and open drains running between the buildings. The stench was terrible. Around the whole complex was a barbed wire fence, ostensibly to keep the animals out, but to us it appeared to be there to keep children in.

When the day finally dawned for the start of term and the packing done, Betty and I were taken to the station by our mother. My brief visit to the school before enrolment had left me with a very frightening impression and the nights before we were due to leave I had hardly slept. The sight of the train was just too much for me; I clung to a bench on the platform and cried my eyes out, saying I would never go and hoping that my mother would relent and take me home with her.

But they prised my fingers off and with torn fingernails I was shoved on board the train and shut in the compartment with Betty. She sat in the corner, as far away from me as possible, sulking, disgusted at my cowardly behaviour. As the train pulled out we looked through the window and, passing my father's office, we saw him get up and wave briefly to us, then return to his work.

We had not gone two miles when the door of our compartment opened and a large boy whose name I will never forget, Henning, put his head through the gap and exclaimed,

'Oh ho! You're the new boy. Aren't you a small fellow! Wait till we get you to the school. I'll give you a good bashing.'

At this point I must explain that we were English children and most of the children going up to the Eldoret School in those days were of Boer extraction and disliked the British intensely. The antagonism between the two nationalities goes back into history. The Boer children, mainly from farming families and extremely tough in their upbringing, were more than a match for us British kids, however wild we had been up until then.

My sister, who had been sitting there quite quietly until this point, still seething over my behaviour, suddenly lifted her foot and, placing it against the edge of the sliding compartment door, said,

'Oh no you won't!'

And with that she kicked the door shut with all the force she could muster, crashing it onto his fingers. He screamed the place down, but as a result of my sister's courageous attack, he left me alone all the time I was at school. He and others regarded me with a wary eye – the word having got around that my sister was somebody to be reckoned with. In fact, the girls' department was totally separate from ours, but I think he and the others always feared that somehow she would pop up from behind a bush and give them what they deserved!

Memories of those early days at school tend to blur, the images merging, fading in and out; it's difficult to get them in order. They have a dreamlike quality; the sharpest images, understandably, are of the best and the worst of experiences.

At Eldoret I discovered very quickly indeed just what discipline was all about. For a little boy of just seven and a half,

29

used to having servants running around picking up after him all those years, it was a very difficult transition.

The British private school system encourages self reliance from a very early age, combined with team spirit and care and consideration for others. This starts with the basics. On the very first day I found that I had to make my own bed, and having never done this before made a terrible job of the task. I was swiftly marched to the housemaster and given nine strokes of the cane across my backside. At every turn I seemed to get another hiding.

Beaten for this, beaten for that, with no explanation and frequently with no justification, beaten for the most minor of offences and no excuses allowed, you soon learn that you might as well get thrashed for a really bad 'crime'. Consequently I became bolder and bolshier!

I very quickly became inured to the beatings. But the nastiest and most vicious punishment I ever encountered was dealt out by our housemistress. At breakfast one morning, she decided that I had been overly indulgent with my helping of marmalade. Her cure for my wicked sin of greed was to force-feed me spoon after spoon of marmalade until I was physically sick. To this day I cannot abide the sight or smell of the stuff.

If you were to ask me what I'd learnt in my first-and-only year at Hill School, Eldoret, I would have to search my mind to find anything of value on the academic side. On the other hand I can recall vividly catching moles, making kites, and lying on the ground underneath the school bell, surrounded by senior boys wielding cricket bats, whacking me on every part of my anatomy. These things took precedence over spelling and all the rest.

Within the first year I developed a nervous skin complaint, causing my body to erupt in weals like raised maps of the continents and the skin on my hands peeled off leaving angry red blisters.

You know how sometimes just the sight of something will trigger off a sense of remembered smell – for example, passing a hospital will give you a whiff of antiseptic although you don't really smell it? Well with me, to this day the sight of an open drain makes my nose twitch with the memory of the stink of the Hill School, Eldoret. At the end of the school year my parents were convinced that they had to move me and Betty back to primary school in Nairobi.

The war seemed a million miles away and if it hadn't been for the presence of the military personnel, we would have been totally unaware of the horrors in Europe. As with thousands of households throughout Europe, army personnel were billeted at our house. Young as I was, a few names stand out.

One was Ted Legg, who rode a motorbike (to my delight!). Ted shot a civet cat that had found its way into our pigeon loft and had decided to make a meal of the one hundred and thirty or so pigeons we had. Another was a US airforce pilot called 'Red' – Uncle Red to me. I remember the time in my very early days at the Primary School when he came up with my mother for a visit and while we were watching a movie in the evening he gave me some chewing gum. It was the first I had ever tasted – liquorice flavoured 'Black Jack'. I loved it! I remember sitting through the movie shoving stick after stick in my mouth till my jaws could hardly move. I confess – I've been addicted to liquorice ever since.

The ever-changing pattern of the theatre of war meant that most of the men who stayed at our house were moved on fairly quickly. I still remember the sadness I felt when I heard that 'Red', who had been my particular favourite, had been killed while flying in the Pacific.

From North Africa came a steady stream of Italian prisoners of war. Very few showed any enthusiasm for repatriation while there was still fighting in Italy. Harmless and friendly, they mingled with the population and in the event were of enormous benefit to our community. Most of them were artisans of the highest calibre, and their talents were put to good use in the building of roads and houses, in fine metal work and expert woodwork.

Our first encounter with these extremely cheerful and contented ex-soldiers came during the holidays when Betty and I discovered them building a house near to ours at Groganville. Italians adore children and very soon we were all great friends. We spent a good part of our holidays in their company, because we soon found that in spite of the language barriers, we had one important thing in common – music. Before we knew it they had made a guitar for me and a mandolin for Betty

31

and during their work breaks they gave me my first guitar lessons. At the age of seven, I was to be found clutching this precious instrument rather than my teddy bear, although it had been made full size and therefore was difficult for my arms and fingers to grasp efficiently.

Nobody worried about the presence of these P.O.W.s; in fact they melted more harmoniously into the community with every day that passed. My mother still proudly shows off the beautiful set of fire irons crafted for her by one of our ex-soldier friends.

The only scare the war in North Africa ever gave the Kenya population was when a solitary bomber flew low over Nairobi. Chaos ensued. Everybody dived for shelter, and I clearly remember that for some strange reason we stood under a huge fig tree that would have afforded little protection had it been a real bombing raid.

However, the leviathan rumbled its way into the distant sky towards Mombasa some four hundred miles away. We heard later that it had dropped its bombs out at sea where they could endanger neither persons nor property, then returned with an escort of two Hurricanes, the crew cheerfully surrendering at Eastleigh Aerodrome. I rather suspect that the crew along with many other Italians were amongst those who stayed on long after the war and made Kenya their home.

With our parents being so busy, this was the time that Betty and I wandered further and further afield and began to make friendships that were to last all our lives. One such couple were Patsy and Eddie Davis. It was Eddie Davis' father who took us to the Nairobi races on one occasion where I bumped into a small ferocious boy called Howie Clark. He immediately challenged me to a fight and upon finding out that I was about to go to the Nairobi Primary school, promised to repeat the episode when I enrolled, he being an 'old boy' of the school already. As so often happens with small boys, he kept his word but we became friends for life.

His aggressive attitude continued for a good few years, but he is now one of the most mild mannered, courteous and thoughtful people you could wish to meet. At Christmas recently, when our two families got together, he laughed remembering the day when he rushed up to one of my sister's friends and gave her a hearty kick, whereupon my sister turned around and sent him flying with a slap across the ear! Times seem to have changed little, or rather small boys, as I watch my youngest son, Alexander, fighting incessantly with his *very best friend* like a couple of terriers, enjoying every moment of the fisticuffs!

Maybe it was the atmosphere of the war that influenced us, but our small boys' traditional gang wars became more than a trifle dangerous, particularly with the acquisition of air-rifles by all and sundry. I had begged and cajoled my parents into giving me one for Christmas and finally I wore them down. I was so anxious to have this gun that Mom actually gave into my pleadings on Christmas Eve. I loaded it and went out into the dusk to find a bird to shoot. But before I could fire the gun, darkness fell and I was called in for supper. Remembering, or so I thought, all that I had been taught, I released the spring by breaking the gun, pressed the trigger and shut it again, which left one pellet in the barrel.

After supper, the dogs made a noise in the garden, and full of bravado I grabbed my gun and ran outside. Momentarily I broke the gun and thereby charged the spring. Forgetting about the pellet and thinking the gun was ready to fire, I put my thumb over the end and pulled the trigger to test the power and velocity. I remember thinking to myself 'by jove, this gun's got some power' and it was only then that I noticed a very sharp pain in my thumb and a trail of blood behind me. The pellet was lodged between my thumb bone and nail. Needless to say, Christmas Day that year did not find me the most popular of small boys. Under general anaesthetic, the offending piece of lead was removed while the ham and turkey were burnt to cinders by my anxious mother.

With sore, bandaged thumb, I was nevertheless now a fully-fledged member of the gang. Eddie Davis, Ginger Griffin and myself were in opposition to a rival gang lead by Ginger Griffin's elder brother, Donald, and his friends. Apart from pellets we fired rotten pigeon eggs and rocks with unabashed hatred from thoroughly lethal catapults made from wattle branches.

We would creep home and dig out the pellets that had found their mark and cover the other scars and wounds as best we could with excuses to our parents of having fallen off bikes or run into trees – the usual white lies that hide from parents the mischief their offspring are really getting up to. Most of us carry scars to this day.

Unlike children today who are exposed to explicit violence and death on the television or cinema screen, we had no such influences, so I can only assume that those scientists are right who claim this aggressive, destructive violence is inbred. As with children of all generations who have never experienced death at first hand, to us it was merely something we read or heard about. We did get hurt and on many occasions suffered quite considerably from our wounds, but the finality of death had not struck within our circle of friends. That is, until the day we were finally sobered sufficiently to end our extremely violent games by a tragedy that, thank God, had nothing to do with any of our immediate group. Nevertheless the event left its mark.

On the banks of the Athi River, not far from Stan Morgan's farm, was a disposal dump for damaged aircraft and other military equipment. Tanks and vehicles of all kinds were left lying around. There was little or no guarding of the dump and some of the boys used to climb in, over and around the wrecked aircraft and vehicles, pretending they were Spitfire pilots, Lancaster gunners or whatever, and re-enacting the exploits of their war heroes.

There was an understanding that none of us would pick up or handle any of the live hand grenades or shells to be found there. But on the day in question a couple of boys from our school visited the dump and during their scavenging one of them discovered a .45 Colt revolver. The temptation was too great and he hid it in his shirt. Soon afterwards, as their 'war game' hotted up, the lad drew the revolver from his shirt and, not imagining for one moment it might be loaded, pointed it at his friend and cried, 'Put up your hands, or I'll fire!'

The other boy of course tried to joke his way out of it, saying, 'Don't play about with guns. Don't be so stupid!'

But in an awful, unthinking act of bravado, the boy with the gun squeezed the trigger. His friend fell to the ground, a .45 calibre bullet in his stomach – mortally wounded.

The tragedy shocked us all, shocked the fun and excitement

right out of our violent games. We realised, for the first time, that we all had been flirting dangerously with death in our wild, irresponsible 'gang wars'. From then on, we went hunting for frogs and fished from our river barge, and treated life and each other with a great deal more respect.

I must make the point that not all my time out of school was spent fighting or seeking Tarzan-like adventures out in the bush. I was also fascinated by the theatre work in which my mother was involved and where I spent a fair amount of time hanging about. She was part of the New Theatre group, responsible for bringing films and live entertainment to Kenya. She not only booked performers and groups but organised their trips to Nairobi and took care of them when they arrived. During the war years, with all the troops to entertain, her work took on particular significance, which was why, as I mentioned earlier, she felt no compulsion to get into 'war work'.

There were many internationally famous names who took the time and trouble to voyage all the way to Nairobi to entertain the troops. I remember in particular Alicia Markova, and my hero of the time – George Formby.

Every time George Formby was on the radio I made sure that the entire family listened and my record collection, though quite varied, was predominantly the self-penned renditions of Mr. Formby. One day, as I was walking across the playing fields towards the main road, I saw a big black car by the crossing. I crossed the road, someone beeped the horn of the car and I heard my name called. As I approached, the back door opened and my mother's voice said, 'Hello darling. Do you know who this is?'

I looked into the back of the car and there was my idol!

'It's Mr. Formby!' I cried.

But that was it. I was totally tongue-tied and at a complete loss for words. George Formby looked at me for a moment and with his famous toothy grin remarked, 'Eee! Isn't he a chubby little lad?'

I stood silent, in awe, as my mother told me that she had to dash off with Mr. Formby for his performance that night. When the car drew away I ran, my heart thumping with joy, to join my school mates and regale them with my tale of meeting such a wondrous performer. Not all of them shared my enthusiasm for the works of Mr. Formby, but to me it was the greatest thing that could ever have happened.

Sometimes, when I was idling about aimlessly and my mother could find nobody to guard me (and I needed guarding!) she would take me along with her, either to a performance or to a film screening with Colonel Brown, with whom she worked on the censorship board. Colonel Brown was to play an important part in my life and be a great influence on my thinking. He was quite happy to have me sitting in on the screenings and used me as a gauge in deciding what film was, or was not, suitable for children to watch.

In those days violence was never permitted in close up on the screen and therefore fatal moments in murder mysteries were left very much to the imagination. There was one particular old Ronald Colman movie in which he strangled the heroine and her last moments on this earth took place behind a sofa. All you could see were her kicking legs – the movements becoming more feeble by the second. Occasionally a hand would grab at the sofa back and flop down again, accompanied by strange gurgling sounds. When the film ended and the lights went up, Colonel Brown turned to me to see if I had been disturbed or distressed by this particular act. But according to my mother my only comment was, 'Well, at least he could have done it in front of the sofa, or they could have moved the sofa so that we could actually see her dying!'

I particularly loved being backstage at the theatre, where I spent many evenings. The electrics fascinated me. The crashing and banging, the testing of the lights, the general hubbub and bustle that goes on backstage before the curtain rises – this was Theatre! I used to sit, quiet as a mouse, tucked out of the way in the wings, and listen to the sounds of the audience as they filtered down the aisles and into their seats. Then – the silence; and the curtain would slowly rise. When the performer stepped on stage my heart was as much in my mouth for them then as it is today for me at the start of one of my shows.

There were special times, much to my delight, when a performer would actually mention me by name to the audience. Laurence Tibbett once burst out into a rendition of 'Mammy's Little Baby Loves Short'ning Bread' especially for me and my little chest fairly burst with pride. And there were others too. No question about it – the 'theatre bug' had bitten. Of course I didn't realise then that I'd been bitten, unlike some others in showbusiness who were actually out there performing while still in knee pants. But, as many a performer can tell you, when you're bitten, know it or not, you stay bitten. The bite is incurable; with me it just took a little longer for the serum to work its way into my bloodstream. At the time all I thought about was how wonderful it was to be entertained and to be part of the backstage scenery.

My interest in the theatre seemed to have little effect on my mischievous behaviour. I was fine when I was busy backstage somewhere, or watching films for censorship or even out playing with friends. But the moment I had nothing to do I became bored, and the moment boredom got hold of me it was like the devil at work – I got into mischief. I wasn't unique, I guess, but maybe just a bit more irresponsible than the other kids.

I recall one particular incident, during a school holiday period, when my carelessness went over the top. For some stupid reason, I'll never understand why, I disobeyed a standing order from my father and took his precious violin out of the cupboard to play it. I hadn't a clue how to play the violin, but that wasn't going to prevent me from trying. Betty tried to stop me; she had her orders about the violin, too, including orders to keep me away from it. Finally, disgusted with her nagging and tugging at me, I put the violin back in its case, which lay on the bed, and began wrestling with her. You guessed it – I gave her a mighty shove and sent her flying backwards onto the bed, right onto the violin lying there in the open case. Her weight and the violence of my push crushed the precious instrument. Both of us were instantly paralysed with fear.

Well aware of what the discovery of the smashed instrument would mean, I persuaded our servant and my friend, Masini, to say nothing until we had gone back to boarding school. He kept his word and showed my father the broken instrument the day after we were safely out of the way.

My father's rage must have been terrible to behold. Nothing my mother could say or do could calm him. He decided that he did not wish to see me again for quite some time.

'Either he goes, or I do!' were his last words on the subject. For all her usual influence on him my mother was unable to alter his decision.

For several holidays thereafter I was banished from the family home and was sent to stay with poor Stan Morgan on his farm. How on earth they persuaded Stan to take me on in view of my reputation I will never know, but he was kindness itself and seemed to have an inbuilt understanding of just what my restless spirit required.

I say he was kindness itself, but it was not immediately apparent. Stan was a taciturn man, hard of hearing and hard of character. His farm was called Masai Wheatlands and ran to about a hundred thousand acres. The land was black clay soil locally known as 'black cotton' which grew superb wheat, provided you could keep the animals out of it. In the past I had spent some time with him and had helped to chase off the game that wandered onto the farm.

As with diseases in Africa, so bugs and all forms of pests are rife, not least the revolting ticks that lurk in the long grass. Wearing only shorts and shoes meant that our legs were constantly under attack and the evenings would find us with our legs black from knee to ankle with those revolting creatures that burrow into your skin. Stan would run a hot bath full of Dettol into which we would plunge, one after the other, and scrape the ticks off our legs. The Dettol did little for the rest of our anatomy and frequently caused great sore spots in the most delicate areas.

Stan was right in his opinion that the only way to keep small boys out of trouble was to make them work and be active from dawn to dusk. When I think of what we packed into a day, I am not surprised how well we slept. But it never seemed like work, it was always fun.

We would hunt with the Africans who had been sent to shoot the grazing animals who were ruining the crops. Marauding herds would destroy thousands of acres of wheat if not controlled. In those days the plains were black with animals as far as the eye could see: wildebeest, kongoni, zebra, endless herds of gazelle – all followed by the relentless predators: lions, cheetahs, hyenas. Today they have nearly all gone, with most of the herds confined to game parks.

To try to run a farm of a hundred thousand acres, on a soil itself volcanic and subject to great cracks in the dry season, was an almost impossible task and protection from the grazing herds was of the utmost importance. Stan Morgan had many of the Italian P.O.W.s helping him out and frequently they would be hunting with us.

None of the animals that we shot was ever wasted; we quickly got used to eating zebra or the meat of other animals that had to be shot and what we didn't eat was distributed to the Africans.

By the time Stan reported back to my father that he considered I was under control and my values had changed, I had learnt to drive tractors, shoot guns and had quite a substantial knowledge of the running of a farm in Kenya. My banishment at an end, I was finally allowed home to see my parents again. I confess it was a much subdued small boy who returned to Nairobi.

A few years ago, I brought the violin whose destruction had been the cause of my banishment back to England for repair and, now fully restored, it belongs to my lovely daughter, Lauren. Since the label inside is dated Cremona, 1504, I can understand my father's anger.

Trying my best to be of little trouble as possible at home, I transferred my thoughtless exuberance to my school behaviour. Within weeks of arriving at Nairobi Primary School, I soon came up against our headmaster, Jimmy Gillette, a huge man with a forbidding demeanour.

One day, hot and tired from playing football, I ran into the washrooms to get a drink of water from the filter. Filtered and boiled water are essential in Africa as cholera and typhoid are rife. What I didn't notice was that the glass cylinder on the filter was cracked and that a paper slip had been glued across the crack. In red ink someone had written 'Do not use this filter'. The problem was that the ink had run and you couldn't read what it said.

The African in charge of the washroom saw me take my drink and immediately grabbed me by the collar and frog marched me straight to the headmaster's study. Without enquiring further into the incident and with the remark, 'I would have thought better of you, Roger,' he gave me four of the best with a cane.

I only dwell on the details of this incident because as far as I was concerned it was the proverbial straw that broke this camel's back. I remember thinking, 'Well, if this is the way they want it, I might as well be hung for a sheep as a lamb.'

From then on I probably justified most of the beatings I received and my lack of concentration on my studies meant that my grades fell from 'A' to 'D'.

Nearly everybody on the staff in those days relied on the use of the cane or the tennis shoe as a punishment, but we boys quickly got used to it and developed backsides like rhino hide!

They weren't all bad times. I soon enough devised ways of getting out of school for my own amusement. Visits to the dentist and the oculist were great routine breakers. I hate to think how many teeth I had 'pulled' and how many pairs of glasses I went through at that time. Mind you, I did seem to have had far too many teeth in my jaw, necessitating the pulling of some of them, and my eyesight had always been appalling.

Rugby, if you were good enough at playing it, meant that team practice took you out of other classes and that was another escape. My love of music and the fact that I could sing allowed me even more leeway as I joined both the school and the cathedral choirs, giving me two evenings a week off for practice.

Recently I watched my older son Guy singing a solo at St. John's College, Cambridge, in the role of the Angel in the choral version of Lazarus. It made me smile. Behind that angelic voice and saintly visage lurks a small character who reminds me of myself. To me choir practice meant two things: beautiful music and equally satisfying scraps behind the cathedral with Howie Clark. He and I had the most magnificent fights and I wonder to this day how the choirmaster ever put up with us. Even today, whenever I hear Handel's Messiah or the St. Matthew's Passion, my emotions combine the beauty of the music with memories of the enormous fun Howie and I had as we engaged in our world featherweight championship bouts.

Stan Morgan's theory about keeping small boys busy was

paying off, however, for with all my extra curricula activities my behaviour pattern gradually improved and subsequently so did my studies.

But it was a slow and painful transition. By the age of eleven I had not really noticed girls. My sister and her friends I considered nothing but pests. But suddenly one day, there I was in love. Erica Preston was older then me by about three years and a beautiful, well developed and friendly girl. She went to my sister's school and I must have driven her crazy mooning around on the edge of the hockey field as she wielded her stick and did her best to ignore me. Eventually I got the message. My first case of 'puppy love' came to an end with considerable heartache and anguished feelings of rejection. But I guess it was all part of growing up and shortly afterwards another incident, far more serious, gave me a further educational lesson in the harsh realities of life.

Writing this, I can remember the day with such clarity that it might have happened yesterday. I was at home, enjoying the school holidays, and was surprised to hear my father returning home early from work. For him to break his normal routine of working till all hours of the night was totally unheard of. I went out to greet him but he rushed straight past me and into the bathroom. I followed, sensing something was radically wrong, and found him vomiting violently into the basin. To my horror I saw that what he was regurgitating was not food, but blood.

I burst into tears, almost hysterical with fear. I knew my father was not in the best of health and despite my mother's entreaties had been refusing to see a doctor or slow down. Now he had no choice. My mother rushed him to the hospital where he was found to be suffering from perforated ulcers. This was sufficiently serious that the doctors told him he should retire from work at once. It was a case of 'stop or die'.

He was only forty three but, unyielding a man as he was in many ways, he knew he had to accept his situation. It nearly broke his heart, I know, because he had worked so hard to build up his business. Still, he wisely decided to live a little longer to enjoy some of the fruits of his labours. Astutely – for he was a good businessman – he did not sell the buildings or the land, just the business itself and immediately proceeded to build another house at Kikuyu.

The planning and supervision of the construction occupied him sufficiently to ease the trauma of his early retirement. He immersed himself for months in working out every detail. He placed the house in the middle of twenty acres of beautiful land in the heart of the Kikuyu Reserve, where the Kikuyu traditionally had their farms and, conveniently for my mother, right next to the golf course. Groves of wattle trees grew all over the estate, the bark of which is used for the tanning of leather and hides. The sale of this bark eventually paid for his retirement home, but the house rapidly took on the name of 'Whittaker's Folly'! Being way out in the bush, it was a paradise in good weather, but whenever it rained the 'folly' of its location became apparent.

It still makes me smile to this day when I remember my mother driving into Nairobi from Kikuyu with sausages falling into her lap from the dinner we had interrupted because it had started to rain.

Now, for any of you who have not experienced monsoon type rain, I must tell you that it literally comes down like a waterfall, and within a very short space of time, possibly as little as ten minutes, the rough dusty dirt roads are just liquid mud with glutinous cascading water rushing down slopes and making the roads impassable until the rain stops. In fact, it can get so bad that the road disappears completely and gulleys many feet deep appear. Until repair crews fill them in, they are dangerous traps.

My mother, in her usual efficient, organised and determined way, had made provision for such eventualities, caching bedding and foodstuffs in a room above her office in Nairobi in case of emergency.

The heaviest rains always seemed to start at night and usually in the middle of dinner. We would leap from the table, grabbing the food as we fled, jump into the car and head for Nairobi. However, on many occasions, the rain was too fast for us and in no time at all the old Teraplane Hudson would get stuck in mud right up to its axles. Out we would pile, all except my father, who because of his bad legs was always very careful not to damage himself. He would rev the engine, letting the clutch in and out, while mother, Betty and I pushed on either side of the car, quickly covered in thick mud from head to toe from the spinning wheels. Mother would yell at me, 'Get in the car, you little fool! You'll get your legs broken!'

So I'd get in the car and then my father would say as I climbed back into the seat, 'Get out! Push, you idle little swine!'

This sketch was repeated during many a torrential rainstorm and I never knew whether I was coming or going as I was kicked out by Dad and kicked back in by Mother! And this would go on until somebody came to our aid. It always ended in laughter and a hot shower when we finally made it into town.

Living in such isolation meant it was important for us to have guard dogs. Our family was never without at least two dogs and they came in all shapes and sizes. One black and white mongrel called Dinky seemed to resent his lack of genetic purity and at every opportunity took his revenge on the human race for this apparent slight, sinking his teeth into any part of your anatomy he could find. He was regarded locally with a wary eye and visitors studiously avoided him.

On one occasion, poor old Sam, my very favourite Sealyham, was bitten through and through by one of the larger cats. There were holes in his little body into which you could put your finger. His intestines were punctured, and as it had taken him several days to drag himself home, dozens of flies had laid their eggs in the open wounds. We rushed him to the vet and begged him to put our poor suffering pet to sleep, particularly in view of all the revolting maggots that had hatched out and were eating away at him. We were quite convinced that he would die anyway, and this seemed to be the kindest option.

The vet, however, refused to destroy Sam saying that since he had managed to survive the first few days, the maggots were actually aiding the healing process by eating away the putrid flesh. He gave us pain killers for Sam and we loaded him back into the car and took him home, totally convinced that the vet was wrong. But to our delight, within a very short period little Sam recovered and lived for many more years.

With such an abundance and variety of animal life around us, it was not only dogs that were kept as household pets. Many orphaned animals were adopted and raised in the house.

People kept young Thomson gazelles, antelopes, and even baby zebras. Many kids kept mongooses, spiders, or deadly snakes and other reptiles, but for me the people who really epitomised the difference between growing up in Kenya and more 'civilised' countries was a delightful family by the name of Lennox Brown, whose son Barry was at school with me.

My first invitation to tea with the family was an experience I never got close to repeating – fortunately. Barry had neglected to tell me that the Lennox Browns had their own small zoo, comprising ten dogs, eighteen horses, four cheetahs, an extremely aggressive and dangerous monkey and a fully grown lion! My father dropped me at the gate and as I got out of the car I was immediately surrounded by a pack of growling, snarling dogs. I stood stock still, quaking in my shoes, until a voice from the house yelled, 'Don't worry! Walk straight through and shout at them not to be so silly!'

That was easier said than done! But I finally plucked up my courage and marched on, head held high. After a few aggressive passes at my ankles the dogs assumed that I had a right to be there and finally let me alone.

Somewhat shaken I went to meet the owner of the voice who turned out to be the animal handler. She was a gorgeous young lady by the name of June Watkins. And I mean gorgeous – she was in fact the Miss Kenya of that year. As Barry was nowhere to be found, she decided to take me on a guided tour of the grounds and house. The first of the large animal occupants of the house she took me to meet was the lion, who sat looking very bored in his cage. To my horror, she let him out! He bounded towards me and rolled on the ground at my feet. Then, wrapping his enormous forepaws round my shorts-clad legs (and by now quaking knees) he very gently tugged me towards him. My face must have been a picture. June howled with laughter.

'Don't worry,' she said, 'he plays with Barry like this all the time.'

Trying to keep my balance and holding my precious Box Brownie above my head, I yelled, 'Get him off me, June. I'm scared stiff!'

She laughed and touched him lightly with a leather thong, whereupon with a look of disgust in his bright gold eyes and a sigh of relief from me, he went off to play with the dogs. Apparently this was his favourite way of letting off steam. June would let the dogs out into a field with him, and he would run off at full speed with the dogs in hot pursuit, yelping and baying as if to tear him to pieces. Suddenly he would screech to a halt and the dogs would shoot past him, desperately trying to put on their brakes, and the last unfortunate would receive a hearty cuff on the backside in passing. For all his size and strength, never once was he known to hurt any of the dogs.

Barry appeared then and joined us to watch the fun, and when June considered the dogs were tired out, we all repaired to the house for tea, the lion following in our footsteps like any other domestic pet. As we sat in the beautiful dining room, the table laid with white cloth and fine bone china, the huge animal sat quietly in the corner. Mrs. Lennox Brown momentarily stood up from her chair at the end of the table to hand one of us boys a plate of cakes. At that moment the lion decided that he wanted to take his place at the table and, pushing his nose through the back of the chair, tried to squeeze his way onto the piece of furniture. He managed to get halfway when his massive body overtaxed the strength of the joints and the chair splintered in all directions. Mrs. Lennox Brown rounded on him yelling, 'Get out, you stupid creature! That's the last time you break up the chairs. Go back to your cage!'

With June in pursuit, he slunk back to his cage and through the window we could see him sitting there despondently.

I still had not met the cheetahs; it wasn't until after we had finished tea and I went into the drawing room that I came face to face with what is now my favourite animal in the whole of Africa. The first cheetah I ever saw close up was sitting in the window seat gazing serenely through the window at some object far in the distance. Slowly he turned and his amber eyes looked me up and down. With the grace that only the cheetah shows to such perfection, he slid to the floor and padded over to me. He began to purr so loudly I thought he was growling, then, for all the world like an overgrown tabby cat, he licked my leg from knee to hip with a rasping dry tongue while I fondled his head and scratched behind his ears. The monkey I never got to know. The Lennox Browns were too softhearted to destroy him, but he was in fact extremely dangerous and would have savaged anybody that tried to handle him.

With growing maturity I began to take considerably more interest in my surroundings and the animal life. It was then that Colonel Brown came back into my life. When he saw that I had begun to appreciate wildlife, he decided to encourage me in every way possible. He decided that I was the ideal pupil for photography – his own special and treasured hobby and at his instigation I spent one of my holidays trying my hand at it. Before he allowed me to go out on this photographic expedition, he showed me many of the photographs and movies he had taken over the years. In his youth he had spent a great deal of time in India and he showed me a picture of a tiger he had shot. To my consternation, tears coursed down his face as he said, 'How bitterly I regret ever hurting such a beautiful animal.' As with so many of us, one incident and one particular animal had changed his whole viewpoint. From that moment on, he had never lifted a gun again. His deep love of animals transmitted itself to me totally. He took great pains to teach me about the environment, habits and needs of the animals that surrounded us, which until then I had just taken for granted. He spent hours patiently teaching me what to look for and how to capture on film the creatures in their most natural state, drilling into me, time and time again, that patience was of the essence.

Until that particular holiday, I'd crashed my way through the countryside on tractors and other farm vehicles. But now, under his instruction, it was a joy to drive slowly along the quiet Nairobi National Park roads while he filmed his animals from the passenger seat. Once, my enthusiasm got the better of me and I pushed the car towards a spot over which vultures circled indicating a lion kill or a natural death in the bush. I hurried to get to the place and, not seeing any lions about, leapt out of the car. I had only gone a few paces when an entire pride emerged from the undergrowth and I retreated to the vehicle like greased lightning, saying, 'Perhaps that's not such a good idea.'

Colonel Brown just smiled.

Suddenly, though born in Africa, I was for the first time really learning to live with my environment.

My first attempts at printing my own photographs were

disasters. Without any textbooks on the subject and being young, stubborn and impatient, refusing to listen to the advice of those in the know, I attempted to develop the negative by logic! I thought you had to leave the negative on top of the photographic paper in the sun for a few hours. Finally, agonisingly, I learned by my own mistakes, and eventually became so immersed in my new hobby that I was allowed to turn a large cupboard in our Kikuyu house into a darkroom. There I eventually printed some quite respectable photographs. My enthusiasm pleased Colonel Brown but before our relationship as pupil and instructor could develop any further, his inordinate love of the natural life around him became his epitaph. One day he drove into Nairobi National Park alone, and it wasn't until the park wardens realised, after dark, that he had not returned that they sent in search parties to find him. After much searching they found him, camera in hand, gazing sightlessly at the herds of animals he loved so much. The lessons he taught me have stayed with me all my life and my memories of that wonderful man are very warm indeed.

I've been living in Britain for many years but my love for African wildlife has never left me; I carry memories of Kenya always in my heart, wherever I go.

At the age of fourteen, however, I was smitten by another love that I carry with me around the world – golf. I picked up four golf clubs somewhere and within two years, using just those four inadequate clubs, I achieved a respectable handicap of twenty-four.

One of my golf partners at the time, Martin Matthias, used to amaze me by spending his entire round – when not actually swinging a club – sniffing around the course picking up 'clues', explaining to me that one day he would be a policeman. How right he was! Later he was to become head of the Kenya Fraud Squad. Martin was one of my dear friends who knew exactly where he was going in life, unlike me, who had an indifferent academic record and not a clue in which direction to go.

When the senior school leaving exams loomed on the horizon, my parents were called in for a chat with the headmaster. He told me that he was totally convinced I had no future whatsoever in any academic field and advised them that the best course was for me to enter the army; no other service, he said, would accept me and apparently I wasn't good for much else than plain soldiering.

That statement I regarded as a challenge. Maybe it was just what I needed – a direct challenge to my intelligence. In any case, during that final year at school I put more energy and concentration into my studies than I had during all my previous years at school put together.

To the astonishment of my parents – and I may add to myself – I sailed through ninety per cent of all my exams. Consequently the decision was taken to keep me on for a further two years of higher education with a view to entering university. My parents, from the day I was born, had decided that I was destined for the medical world.

I was not so sure about that, but having let them down so badly in the past, I applied myself now with total dedication to my studies.

But, 'the best laid schemes o' mice and men' etc. to quote that great Scots poet Robert Burns, whatever plans my parents had for me, or plans I and my friends had for ourselves, were soon to be altered drastically by dramatic events in Kenya.

Chapter 3

Now   if you load your rifle right and if you fix your bayonet   so

I HAVE ALWAYS approached a stage performance from the point of view that the audience has paid to be amused and taken out of themselves without too much effort on their part. To me that is the essence of entertainment. With that in mind I try to perform material that doesn't tax the mind too much or create feelings of antipathy or sadness, but at the same time tells a story.

As one of my dearest friends, Jeanne Mathews, once said to me, 'Roger, always remember that what you were has made you into what you are. You cannot change the past, you can only live today and let tomorrow take care of itself.'

How right she was.

I am leading into the reason why this chapter is one of the most important to me and yet very difficult to write. It concerns my transition from carefree schoolboy into responsible manhood, a change that was to be swift and dramatic.

Kenya, having avoided the actual fighting in World War Two, was suddenly faced with its own bloody internal battles. The organisation known as Mau Mau appeared, gradually gained momentum, and finally achieved its aims.

The stark facts about this struggle and this guerilla organisation can be gleaned from a number of books, and it would serve no purpose to burden you with too many details.

In a nutshell, however, the Kenya African, along with members of other Commonwealth countries, had been called up to serve in Her Majesty's armed forces throughout the war. The Kenya African soldiers, making up the King's African Rifles, distinguished themselves as jungle fighters and became renowned as some of the finest and bravest troops. But in spite of their record in the field, no African soldier could ever attain a rank above that of Warrant Officer.

After the war, these valiant men returned home to find that their heroism was forgotten and that their place in society was the same, or less, than it had been before they left to fight for the British Empire. Understandably, this led to a great deal of frustration and anger and, having seen how the rest of the world lived, a desire for self expression.

The end of World War Two brought phenomenal changes throughout the world, not least the wish of the peoples who had been colonised by the Europeans to obtain their autonomy. Indo-China, Malaya, Cyprus, India and many of the African nations decided they wanted to have the controlling hand in their own destinies. Within Kenya a concerted nationalist campaign by the Kenya African Union, created to unite the many tribes, attempted to sway the British authorities. Many of the leaders were the soldiers that the British Government had trained so efficiently. The training had included thinking for oneself and taking responsibility, but suddenly these men were told that back in civilian life they were to have no further say in conducting their country's affairs.

When the talking came to nothing, Mau Mau gradually emerged, bringing with it a wave of violence. For six years, from 1950 to 1956, many black Kenyans displayed both active and passive resistance to British rule. The active resistance was frequently horrendous and violent in the extreme. All Kenyans, both white and black, were affected and those years were filled with stress, tension and fear.

The friendships we had formed, the love we had for and the trust we placed in our black brothers disappeared. This, to many of us, was hardest to bear for almost overnight those who had been our friends became potential enemies. Familiar faces in the street returned a greeting with a glare. Sometimes this was out of fear for themselves as they, too, were under threat if they did not fully support the cause of Mau Mau. Any association with the White Man could be treated as collaboration.

After the first few attacks on civilian homes, precautions were taken that turned the average household into a fortress. High wire fences were erected and more dogs brought in.

Above all, no African, even if he had been a member of the household since childhood, was allowed in or near the house after dark. The loyal servants, too, had their living compounds surrounded by high wire fences, but this did not prevent a great many of them suffering at the hands of the terrorists.

My last two years at school were punctuated with extra curricula instruction in weaponry. All of us were trained in the use of both handguns and heavier weapons. At home, the ordinary housewife carried a handgun strapped to her belt at all times. It rapidly became known that many of the house servants were in fact Mau Mau recruits, and you never turned your back for one moment, as in the opening of this book when our gardener was sent to kill me.

The older boys, once they had mastered the accurate firing of their weapons, patrolled the school compounds to protect the younger children in the event of a full scale attack; schools, hospitals and police stations were regular Mau Mau targets.

We had a combined cadet force at the Prince of Wales School, where I spent my last boarding years, and the senior boys were familiar with heavy calibre rifles: .303s. Carrying these over our shoulders and smoking through the nights on patrol (an offence that in earlier years would have brought six strokes of the cane!), we wandered inside the barbed wire perimeters and had our first taste of what life would be like when we were finally called up into the army.

Boys came from all over East Africa to the Prince of Wales. Sons of civil servants, missionaries, doctors, in fact all the walks of life so badly needed in Africa at that time.

Two of my special friends, an American called Larry Renier, the son of a Seventh Day Adventist medical Missionary, and Arthur Sparrow, the son of a Civil Servant based in Tanganyika (now Tanzania) invited me to spend the long summer holidays at their home in Kasulu, southern Tanganyika. With the onset of the 'emergency' in Kenya there could be no more wandering and camping in the Kenya bush. The possibility of becoming just another war statistic was all too evident.

I jumped at the opportunity and joined Larry and Arthur for weeks of adventure that most boys can only dream of. Knowing it was our last taste of freedom added spice and daring to the time we had available.

The railway being incomplete between Kenya and Tanganyika, the only way to navigate Lake Victoria was by the paddle steamer, a wonderful colourful relic of old Africa. By the nature of African life, the trip was a leisurely one. The boat was packed. Every deck was covered with people, parcels and goats all crowded together. The noise, the bustle, the clanging of the bell, the rhythmic thump of the huge engines, and as we left the dock, the rolling swell of the flat bottomed boat heralded 'mal-de-mer' for any who did not have the strongest of stomachs.

As with everything African, the length of the trip was unpredictable, and on extended stops at various ports of call, Larry, Arthur and I alleviated any boredom that threatened by taking in the ever changing surroundings. If we were not meandering around the markets, haggling with local traders, we swam in the lake itself. However, as the hippopotamus accounts for the largest number of human deaths in Africa, we made sure that we only entered the water at designated spots where the hippo were kept at bay by massive submarine nets.

Mwanza was finally reached and from there the rest of the journey would be by rail. However, again Africa took over and we had a further two days to wait for our train. Timetables were haphazard and frequently the train would double back to Dar es Salaam before collecting the boat passengers to go further inland. We felt no sense of urgency and many happy hours were spent with our air rifles pinging away at the unfortunate reptiles who infest the baobab and mango trees. When the errant train finally returned we rattled off to Kigoma where the families met us. The journey still wasn't over. A further hundred miles of heavy bush country had to be negotiated before we finally arrived at Kasulu. The entire travelling time amounted to nearly six days, a journey which nowadays only takes three hours by air. It was infinitely more amusing and colourful in the 1950s!

The first difference between Kenya and Tanganyika that struck me was the flies; they had the most appalling bite that made life extremely uncomfortable and refused to die even when rubbed between finger and thumb. They were tsetse flies, carriers of the dreaded sleeping sickness. Larry's father and the other doctors at the Mission were involved in the task of taking blood samples from the many thousands of people who inhabited the area. The samples had to be stained onto slides, and examined under the microscope there and then, to detect the trypanosomes that heralded the disease.

I found myself following the doctors around and realised my growing fascination with their research. On a visit to a bush clinic I noticed that many of the patients were afflicted with a condition that led to the loss of toes.

It was not, as I first thought, due to the leprosy rife throughout Africa. The cause of the missing toes lay with tiny burrowing insects found in the dust and, as we all walked barefoot, I found myself daily inspecting my toes and feet most carefully for weeks after visiting the area!

The medical teams were far too busy to worry about us and, providing we didn't hinder their work, we were allowed to watch more or less anything they undertook. The hospitals and clinics were just rough shacks, or in some cases open tents. Nevertheless surgery was carried out with results that would lend pride to the most modern European hospitals.

There was one particular operation, however, that still stands out in my mind. A young African girl, I would guess no more than nineteen, was wheeled into the operating theatre. She was suffering from goitre, which is very prevalent in Africa. Her goitre was so large that if she put her head back too far, she was unable to breathe. Anaesthetic in the form of ether was administered drop by drop onto a face mask and in no time she was asleep.

Hours passed with Larry, Arthur and I green about the gills. In my case it was the first time that I had felt the slightest bit queasy at the sight of blood and knives, but I was so intrigued that I couldn't take my eyes from the table and every move the surgeon made. Finally there was one cotton thin nerve still attached to the now fully exposed goitre. The atmosphere suddenly changed and the surgeons exchanged looks. Then one picked up the scissors and snipped. Instantly the girl stopped breathing and nothing they could do could bring her back to life. They explained later that there was no choice and the risk had to be taken.

All the following operations passed without event but the

surgeons were depressed for many weeks afterwards at having lost one patient. Considering the conditions in which they had to work, I think they achieved miracles. The simple people who benefitted from their ministerings might have had their faith temporarily shaken by 'white man's medicine' but it would have been impossible to explain the intricacies of the surgery to them.

Far from showing any resentment for mistakes or mishaps, everywhere we went the Tanganyikans showed their appreciation in their own inimitable way, showering us with warmth and hospitality. After many long days in those hot, dry, dusty, conditions the doctors and us boys were rewarded with lively evenings as guests of the local chiefs. They would ply us with pombe, and with our stomachs sloshing with this local brew we would dance the night away in the light of the flickering fire in the centre of the huts.

The musical accompaniment for the dancing was provided by African musicians who were replaced, when exhausted, by an incongruous wind-up gramophone wheezing out Fats Domino's Blueberry Hill. We danced barefoot, whilst most of the population danced completely naked. Our versions of the loose limbed gyrations of the African brought giggles from all and sundry. To this day Natalie is loath to get up on the dance floor with me in case I suddenly launch into what I call my 'African Stomp' entailing much wiggling of the backside, with lots of rhythm but very little else!

Those holidays served to feed my avid interest in tribal customs which, within any one country in Africa, can differ so vastly. Even today I never cease to be fascinated by the varying beliefs and traditions. On one of our village visits the local chief decided that the time had come to appease the spirits. This was done in the form of teams of drummers placed on the tops of seven hills surrounding the village. At a given signal they began to beat the drums in the most marvellous series of echoing rhythms that seemed to reverberate from hill to hill, an effect obviously achieved through generations of experience. Days came and went and each time we returned yet another team of drummers was up on the hills. Each relay of men, with sweatbands of animal skin around their heads, beat seven drums in each team. They started with a high treble drum and finished on a huge bass which was beaten with a knobkerry.

They never missed a beat while hundreds of villagers danced around in the dust below, carrying palm fronds. Years before the people had carried spears and in their frenzy so many got stabbed that the Government decided that palm fronds made a better and less lethal token spear.

After many days, the festivities finally came to an end when the priests dug a huge hole in the ground into which they put the carcass of a cow. The theory was that in the night the spirits would arise and accept the cow's flesh as an offering.

When not spending all our waking hours with the doctors on their rounds, Arthur and I would take off on hunting expeditions armed with a shotgun and a .22 rifle. Maps would have been of little use as the terrain was completely wild, but somehow we always managed to find our way back, often after night had fallen. We encountered very little danger, or rather we were oblivious to any threats from the lurking wildlife.

These were certainly high days but as we started out on our week-long trip back to Kenya, the reality of what we could expect to meet came home to us, and we grasped at every last moment of freedom on that journey.

The last term of school was now in front of us. There could be little socialising as Mau Mau gangs would attack without warning and evening activities were curtailed by curfew. Nevertheless, this did not prevent me from falling in love at every opportunity. Since my first encounter with Erica, I had met few girls I really liked, but now the slightest glance heralded another heartbeating episode. My poor sister Betty was embarrassed on many an occasion when she brought friends home and I proceeded to pursue them.

Until that time, I would never have imagined for one moment wanting to watch a girls' hockey match, but suddenly Betty found that I was her constant companion. I am sure she read my motives clearly, but I was to embarrass myself almost as much as her. I had spotted one special girl in a red sweater which she filled to perfection. I was silly enough to tell my sister, so she organised a meeting on my next visit to her school. Although I was pretty cocky, when suddenly faced with this apparition of loveliness I became unusually shy, and as her prow sailed over the horizon I turned and ran, much to the disgust of my sister and to the amusement of her entire school.

A couple of times a term school dances were organised, leading to many an encounter and romance. These romances, however, were of the most innocent kind with a lot of daydreaming and not much action. For all our years of freedom, surrounded by the wildlife and dangers of Africa, nothing was as frightening as actually socialising with the opposite sex. We had been cocooned and kept in ignorance of the facts of life.

Distracted by the Mau Mau emergency and the discoveries of the charms of the opposite sex, our final examination results in our last senior year must have disappointed both headmaster and parents alike. But, knowing that the moment we left school we would be in the army, we were faced with the possibility that there might be no future for us, that injury or death could greet us on the morrow. Consequently, none of us talked, planned or even imagined the future after the army years. All discussions of university and careers were dropped.

It was a very quiet Christmas at home that year before I left for the training centre at Nakuru. I was issued with my kit at Regimental Headquarters and with mixed emotions came home and tried it on. It was only when Mother wept as I came downstairs clad in my uniform that I realised just how deep her fear was of losing me. She had lost her brother during the First World War.

As soon as she had heard that I was to be called up on leaving school, she had done her best to persuade the Tribunal that I and my two best friends, Neville Jones and Mike Leete, were essential university material and therefore should not serve our time doing National Service. However, unbeknown to her, I had already been to see our headmaster, who was in fact in charge of detailing our army careers in co-operation with Regimental Headquarters. I told him he was not to interfere or lend his weight in any decision that the Tribunal might have made in favour of our university studies. For the first time I saw him smile with approval and treat me with considerably more respect than he had done when I had been a mere schoolboy.

The bright January day that heralded my admission into the army felt somewhat like the day when my parents had first taken me to school. But as I entered the gates of the training centre at Nakuru the similarity ended. I was thrown into immediate contact with British Army permanent staff instuctors or PSIs. The first man we bumped into was a Regimental Sergeant Major with the Argyles, a very tough outfit indeed, who smilingly through his teeth promised my parents that he would treat me and the others with thoughtful kindness and careful consideration. Ha! Anybody who has done army training will know that the Regimental Sergeant Majors say that to *all* parents.

What was in store was to be a shock to the system. The introductory lecture started with instructions to ignore the four-letter foul words that would be thrown at us at every given opportunity. These, we were told, were merely a way of drilling our brains and shocking us into quick reactions. As bad language was a rarity in those days, our education into the usages of English was widely broadened in a very short space of time!

There were four platoons of new conscripts (twenty-eight men to each platoon) and each platoon was under a PSI from the Black Watch or the Rifle Brigade. Our platoon, Number Four, was under the auspices of a PSI by the name of Robertson from the Black Watch. Over the next few weeks Robertson was to turn us from boys into men; not necessarily in the kindest way. Our training was in fact shattering, but very soon we became aware of our responsibilities to each other and that any lack of teamwork could prove fatal.

One person who came back into my life, called up at the same time, was a fellow called Neils Hvass. At school we had been anything but friends, but suddenly here he was in my platoon along with another old school colleague called Ken Oulton. Ken, older than us, had already spent a considerable time at Edinburgh University and owned a car, in which he generously ran us about. Neils Hvass was one of the most complicated people I had ever come across. Whilst we were still at school in Nairobi as very small boys, I had known him as a pathetic little character who had been escorted into class without shoes or socks and just wearing a pair of shorts – in other words, a complete little African.

Neils' mother had died at his birth, and his father had gone into such a period of mourning that he had placed the new baby in the sole care of the Africans. As a result it wasn't until Neils reached school age that his father suddenly realised that his son spoke hardly a word of English, only Swahili, and was in need of European education. Neils suffered miserably during his emergence into our white boys' world, enduring many hours of ragging from us. It was no surprise, therefore, that when we met again at the training centre, he bore many grudges. My initial impression of him was one of a very tough, volatile and antagonistic fellow. His antagonism was physical, and he took every opportunity to start a fight.

One of the PSIs borrowed Ken Oulton's car. Ken, a very friendly and generous chap, was always willing to help anybody, no matter what his rank. This particular PSI, however, had a drink problem and whilst drunk drove Ken's car into one of the six foot deep storm ditches. The result was that he wrecked the car beyond repair, but strangely it was Neils, not Ken, who was the more angered. The PSI's final mistake was to come into our sleeping quarters later on the night of the accident. Still the worse for drink he shouted at Neils, shaking him awake, for what reason we will never know. Neils, who had been deeply asleep, awoke with a start and without a second thought leapt up and caught the PSI with a perfect right hook, breaking his jaw.

This meant trouble, in capital letters! As with any army in the world, to strike one's superior is a Court Martial offence. Neils was hauled up in front of the CO and given fifteen days confined to barracks. That was the minimum he could have expected for such a crime and clearly those in authority realised there were mitigating circumstances.

Robertson, our PSI, and I expect all the other PSIs, decided that we all had to learn a lesson in discipline resulting from this episode. Neils' punishment had not been sufficient in their eyes.

The Rift Valley, where our training camp was situated, is one of the driest, most difficult areas on earth in which to carry out military exercises. The terrain is rocky with little vegetation and, what there is, is tough, brittle and thorny. The rocks are quartz and crumbly and the sun burns like fire.

The day following Neils' sentence, Robbie paraded us all at

about two p.m. with shirts off, bayonets fixed to heavy old Lee Enfield rifles and asked us, 'Do ye know what "straff" means lads?'

We hadn't a clue.

'Straff,' he explained, 'means "punish" and today it's Robbie's straff Four Platoon! Do you see that white hut there?' he asked, pointing to a building that appeared as a shimmering dot in the haze some five miles away, 'well, today we're going to do a platoon attack on that building. You'll run with your rifles above your heads 'til I blow the whistle once. Then you'll stand and fire five rounds. When I blow the whistle again, you'll run again, until I blow it twice. Then you'll kneel and fire five rounds. Then you'll run again 'til I blow it three times. Then you'll lie and fire five rounds. Then you'll run again until you reach that building!'

Off we went. The first couple of miles presented no problems to us younger conscripts, but the older members of our platoon (there were one or two over thirty) began to feel the strain. After a while we were lugging not only our own weapons and kit, but helping with theirs. Finally, exhausted, we reached the building, whereupon Robbie, who had gone there by Land Rover, greeted us with a wolf-like grin saying, 'Now we go back the same way!'

Everyone groaned, but we did it. And survived!

I suspect the purpose of the whole exercise was to turn us against Neils Hvass, who was considered by his superiors to be a 'troublemaker', but in fact it had just the opposite effect. We had all understood his reaction, and had we been woken as he had, we could easily have done the same thing. Whatever the psychology, this and other similar incidents formed us into a tightly-knit team. Neils became one of my greatest lifelong friends and in fact is now godfather to my youngest son.

The ten weeks over and our initial training at an end, we were considered able – rightly or wrongly – to launch off into the bush in pursuit of the guerillas. The first area of Kenya we were sent to was an area called the Masai Reserve, the centre of which is a small town called Narok. This town lies about ninety-eight miles from Nairobi in the heart of some of the most beautiful, untouched territory in the world. The Masai themselves were not affiliated with Mau Mau. Their tribe migrated centuries ago from the Sudan and they are a fiercely proud and elegant people. By tradition they are nomadic warriors, whose only source of income is their cattle. They were constantly at loggerheads with the Kikuyu who made up the mainstream of the Mau Mau guerillas. Kikuyu are by nature farmers, and were and are still greatly antagonised by the wandering habits of the Masai and their herds of cattle.

Temporary Masai villages are called manyattas and their social structure is highly complicated. The women and men live totally separately, in particular the 'Moran'. The Moran are the young men, come of age and circumcised, and in the process of being trained as warriors. Part of their training is the tracking and killing of lion single handed, armed only with a spear. Until this is done they cannot be considered true warriors. And warlike they are!

Their homes are made from wattle and cow dung which dries to a bricklike hardness, and are surrounded with a high thorn fence to protect their precious cattle from lions who over the years have discovered that they are the perfect trapped prey. The Masai had been at odds with the Kikuyu for centuries, but when the British settled in Kenya, they put a stop to the inter-tribal warfare.

The Moran, being pure warriors, saw us young British conscripts as being akin to themselves, and their help proved to be invaluable.

When we arrived at Narok a Masai chief's daughter had just been abducted and the Masai were convinced she was with a group of guerillas we were tracking. So we worked hand in glove helping each other in the search for twenty-three terrorists.

The Masai never eat any meat but live on the blood, urine and milk from their herds. Their area, the Mara as it is called, is teeming to this day with wildlife. Our patrols were punctuated not only with the thought of running into enemy gangs, but with the possibility of disturbing the elephant, rhino, buffalo and lion that were hidden in the lush undergrowth. We were more frightened of nocturnal encounters with the wildlife than with our unseen enemy, and every crack of a twig seemed to herald stampedes!

The presence of these imperturbable and friendly African

Ted and Vi Whittaker, my parents.
Very formal picture of what had been a most unusual wedding. Mombasa 1929 (Note the new design in wedding dresses – permanently creased!)

Was I rubbing my hands in glee at the prospect of mobility?
Below: Mother holding me at my christening in 1936 — still blissfully unaware of future mischief.

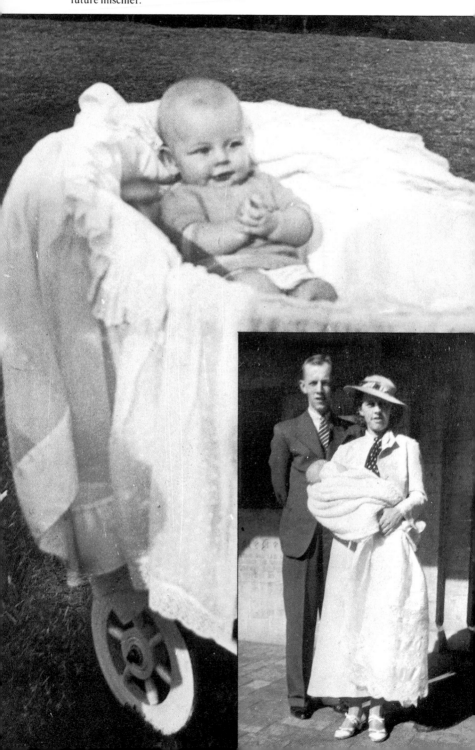

Back in Kenya. What had I been up to?
That look is too innocent.

Left: My poor long-suffering Nanny — Wantjerv — she was to alibi so many of my pranks.

Right: Minus beard again, for a short while — and trying my act on British audiences for the first time in 1961.

Far Right: Nearest the camera — I was well pleased to meet Lord Baden Powell.

Below Right: Betty displays her future dancing skills during rehearsal for one of our 'plays'. Seconds later I tripped her.

Below: Toting a gun — aged 17 a few months before entering the army.

University Graduate 1962, B.Sc. Zoology and Biochemistry — and no serious thoughts of showbusiness.

Ted and Vi Whittaker left — nervous groom and bride centre — Leo and Toby O'Brien right. The innocent pageboy is Natalie's brother Lucius, who made a mini-fortune that day!
Below: Two of our first friends made when we moved to the country — Mike Duffy (publican) and Mike Bayer at the Red Cow, Chrish'all.

Above: Brett — we never knew who dug up the garden more — him or Barney and Bunty, the bulldogs pictured with him.
Below: My image was still 'folksy' for Ulster Television's 1966 series — the third — "Thirsty Boots".

allies, combined with the outstanding beauty of our campsite, sometimes made us forget the real reason for our being there. After the dust, heat, noise and physical and emotional shock of training camp, it seeked like a paradise to awake to the sounds of birds as dawn crept over the horizon. The camp itself was sited beside a winding river and afforded a view of Africa that tourists pay thousands of pounds to see.

Reality soon returned when we were paraded in order of stature. Ken Oulton, myself and one other poor soul, being over six foot, were designated Bren gun carriers. This entailed carrying an extra twenty-three pounds of gun, plus a further twelve pounds of ammunition, together with the eighty pound pack that we all had to carry. Suddenly the reason for those weeks of endless seemingly pointless running around in training became apparent. The muscles and all-round fitness we had developed were now a blessing.

Our pre-patrol briefing had concerned not only the tracking and fieldcraft reminders needed for the twenty to thirty days we would be away from camp, but also strict rules and regulations on avoiding contact with dangerous game. We Kenyans needed little telling, but I remember the odd twitches of smiles from the overseas soldiers who had joined us. Those grins were to be wiped off their faces on many occasions as they learnt that out there in the lush undergrowth the animals were far from the docile creatures they had seen in their zoos at home.

As we shouldered our packs and cradled our weapons, we all set out feeling confident that no problems would present themselves, but after the first ten miles I began to feel my legs start to wobble. Suddenly a voice said, 'I'll take that!' and my Bren gun was whipped out of my grasp and replaced by a much lighter rifle. It was Neils Hvass. Shorter than I, but considerably stronger, he proceeded to stride ahead as if carrying a feather.

Intelligence had told us that the gang for whom we were searching had eleven automatic weapons among them, so we were alert. The Masai Moran, armed with just spears, strode at a regulated steady pace. Loath to appear weak, we tried to keep up with them but it was impossible. Soon they were out of sight and disappeared like ghosts into the bush to scout ahead, no doubt more silently and efficiently than our crashing around.

They never seemed to stop to drink or eat until we camped at night. We were forever pausing to swig from our water bottles as although like the Moran we soon learned to live on one meal a day, thirst was impossible to control. After a couple of days we persuaded them to let us into their secret. It was an extremely simple solution: smooth pebbles placed under the tongue. From that moment on, we talked little but rolled the pebbles around encouraging saliva to flow.

Camping at night was a very make-do affair. Every evening we built a bivouac. This was made out of two forked sticks, with a cross member stuck in the forks, over which a waterproof poncho was placed to form a rough tent, with a groundsheet underneath. The poncho was the only protection against the heavy rains and was big enough to cover you and all your vital equipment. Two men slept in each bivouac and to say it was cramped would be a severe understatement. However, by the time we had lit a fire and eaten our meal as the sun set, we were ready to crawl into our makeshift tents and sleep like the dead.

My particular assignment on night patrols usually entailed driving a truck to drop off a section of men who would then work a specific area. Our section leader was a chap named Ben Christie, who very quickly displayed a talent for leading us into action – not with the enemy, but with dangerous wildlife. On my first night patrol he gave me directions into the bush; at the offload point he indicated, I stopped the truck and the patrol began to jump out. At once we all heard the same sounds – a growling and crunching that were the unmistakable noises of a lion kill. As silently as possible the patrol formed up and moved out, carefully skirting the lion pride. As for me, I backed the truck away gingerly, careful not to grind the gears, and returned to base.

I got the rest of the story the next morning, when the patrol staggered back in, very late. Having safely skirted the lions, the patrol, still led by Christie, crawled through a hedge and found itself smack in the middle of a herd of Cape buffalo. Now without doubt buffalo are the most irascible and unpredictable of African animals and extremely dangerous. The patrol could do absolutely nothing all night but sit still in the middle of the herd, hoping the buffalo wouldn't get the wind up and turn nasty.

Then there was the incident with the elephants. These massive, noble, gentle creatures like to mind their own business – but when crossed or threatened they will charge – and at great speed. At that time elephants were everywhere in the Mara, relishing the lushness of the foliage and the cool rivers. Hardly a day passed without some contact with them but we were careful to keep our distance.

Then one day Ben Christie led us to a beautiful spot to rest. No sooner had we set down our packs and rifles than the undergrowth around us was teeming with an enormous herd. The order was whispered down the line to sit still and keep quiet until the elephants moved off. However, one tiny Dumbo character decided that Ben Christie was his mother and, showing no signs of fear, proceeded to amble through our midst and nuzzle up to him. The herd was of course well aware of our presence but as long as we stayed put, the elephants were perfectly content to settle down to their meal of lush undergrowth and leaves.

After a couple of hours of this we decided that the wrath of our superiors was an even greater threat than a herd of angry elephants and we decided to move out. Slowly, silently, we slipped away. We had made about two hundred yards when a desperate 'Psssst!' from the back of the line halted us. There, trailing behind us, was our little elephant friend. We pushed and shoved and argued with the little devil but couldn't get him to return to his family. It sounds amusing in the telling, and I suppose it was even funny then, except the herd was beginning to show signs of restlessness and we knew the truant's mother would be missing him by now. And that could mean real trouble.

There was nothing for it but to return young Dumbo to the herd. A brave chap named Harry Shellow volunteered and, bold as brass, he marched right into the centre of the herd, holding the little truant by the trunk, seeking his mother. We watched, hardly daring to breathe, certain Harry would be attacked. But, to our astonishment, aside from a bit of side stepping and foot shuffling, the herd took little notice of the intruder. Suddenly our little friend gave a squeak of delight, quickened his step and rushed up to a large female. After the usual trunk twining of greeting he shoved his little head between her front legs and began to suckle. We all got out of there then – on the double! Harry had the good grace and honesty to tell us he'd never been so terrified in his life and that he was still shaking from the experience.

I suppose we were all a bit jumpy at night. The boldness of the game gave us more sleepless nights than worry about the enemy in the bush. Despite all the campfires, we had a fair share of nocturnal visitors and all around us there was a constant thrashing and growling and thumping in the undergrowth. The Masai, too, would make us jump as they suddenly appeared at the campfire from nowhere, spear points and shields glinting in the firelight. These warriors had long since given up patrolling with us. Our regulated, systematic patrolling of section by section over a given area was beyond their comprehension and they would disappear for days on end. Then, just when you'd think they'd abandoned you entirely, they'd drift back into camp at night, join you in a meal and exchange intelligence about the Mau Mau's whereabouts. They weren't having too much success either, finding only the ashes of recent campfires and signs that the enemy had been – and gone.

On their visits the Masai would bring gifts of fresh milk. However, one evening, as we made camp beside a water hole, the Moran warriors decided to show their respect for us – soldier to soldier – by presenting us with a goat, which they slew on the spot. After collecting the blood, which they mixed with milk for themselves, they hung the carcass in a tree – right above my bivouac. I thought nothing of it that night as, exhausted, I crawled in to sleep alongside my tentmate, a guy named Butt de Brain.

We hadn't been asleep more than an hour, when a grunting and snarling heralded the presence of an entire pride of lions hell bent on making a meal of the goat hanging above our heads. In the past, Butt had regaled us with stories of his family of hunters who had experienced lions walking in and around their tents on many an occasion without mishap. Those stories did little to allay our terror as we lay rigid, our hearts pounding in our chests. The flimsy covering around us bulged and swayed as the lions jostled to find a way of getting at the tasty morsel above their heads. They seemed totally unaware that there was a more satisfying meal right beneath their feet! I was convinced that at any moment a large paw would land right on my face in a desperate move to get up the tree!

Fortunately, as often happens with lion, they quickly became bored and left in search of an easier food supply.

It was not only lion that visited our camp; as I said, the campfires did little to keep game at bay. In fact on one occasion the fire actually incited an attack. Sitting dozily drinking cups of tea before retiring, our peace was shattered by a thundering of animal hooves that shook the ground, coming our way. Not knowing what was approaching at such speed, we all shot for the cover of the nearest tree – and only just in time as an enormous rhino charged into the centre of camp straight at the fire. With bellows and snorts, it proceeded to demolish the fire, scattering the burning logs in every direction with its massive feet. Finally satisfied that its foe was destroyed, it shambled off into the dark. Unsure of how far off it had moved and much shaken, we went to bed without relighting the offending fire.

You might well ask at this point, 'Did you do any actual fighting, or was it all one big safari?' The truth is that our particular group hardly saw any action at all. In the thousands of square miles of very heavy undergrowth it was almost impossible to flush out the enemy. We were aware that on many occasions we were probably only a matter of yards from death, but for some reason we were never attacked. Often those we were searching for had doubled back behind us, content merely to avoid a battle.

It was terribly frustrating knowing how close we came, without making contact, but it wasn't until our return to base camp, after three or four futile patrols, that we discovered one of the prime reasons for our lack of success. Another patrol had had more luck and taken several prisoners. During interrogation one prisoner had been directly asked just how they managed to evade the troops.

'Simple,' the man replied, 'we can smell you.' Our clean clothes, soap and even toothpaste had given us away.

From that moment on all normal hygiene, as we knew it, was forbidden. From the day we started a patrol until our thirty days were up, we cleaned our teeth with twigs as the Africans did, never washed except in clear water, with the result that by the time we returned to base camp our clothes were nearly walking off us. The first time I returned to Nairobi straight from patrol, my mother nearly wept and, after a bath heavily laced with Dettol, I collapsed into bed, whilst my mother used every item in the laundry in an attempt to return my uniform to some semblance of its former self.

History records that there were plenty of bloody and futile battles and civilians continued to be constant targets, but my own days in the field were short. Cut short in fact when Major Seed sought me out with the words, 'Whittaker! I hear you are hoping to be a doctor. How would you like to run the M.I. room?'

I leapt at the opportunity little realising that the doctor in charge was about to be reassigned. He dropped the bombshell quite casually one morning.

'I'm off in three weeks, so you've got that long to learn the ropes. I don't know when my replacement will arrive, but you've got no worries as nothing much happens around here.'

For those three weeks I worked alongside him, desperately trying to absorb as much knowledge as possible. Having spent those holidays in Tanganyika with the medical missions I had a basic knowledge of dosages and hypodermics, but I pitied the poor devils who were to be my first needle victims! Under the doctor's supervision, I readily grasped most of the first aid and emergency essentials, but all too soon those weeks flew past and I found myself alone.

'Don't worry. Nothing much happens around here.' I was to hear those words echoing again and again in my brain, as almost as soon as he waved goodbye, all hell seemed to let loose.

Every morning's sick parade saw another queue of African soldiers suffering from gonorrhoea, the results of visiting the local brothels. Batches of penicillin came and went, until finally, as the replacement doctor was still nowhere in sight, I decided to tackle the source of the problem, and with a couple of orderlies set up a mobile medical centre in the middle of the town. The prostitutes were delighted and appeared in droves to get their shots. After two repeat visits the incidence of VD dropped dramatically. The only case of syphillis I had occasion to diagnose was done so from a goodly distance and with the aid of a stick! Never has one camp been more grateful for the discoveries of Alexander Fleming!

Stitching wounds was another matter. My many accidents as a child, resulting in stitches without anaesthetic, had left me with very strong memories of the resultant pain. I was very relieved when my first patient in this category had a relatively simple wound to stitch, having split his finger to the bone whilst starting an electric motor. My next patient arrived with half his cheek missing, having been bitten by his opponent during a dreadful brawl amongst the soldiers. It was like trying to do a jigsaw puzzle with half the bits missing. What he really needed was a plastic surgeon but he grinned from ear to ear at the jagged wound, regarding it like a duelling scar.

Fortunately cases requiring surgery were rare because appendicitis sufferers and other serious cases had to undergo the appalling journey on almost unmade roads to another camp, or even back to Nairobi.

The most interesting case I had to deal with came not from the ranks of our soldiers but from one of the prisoners being held. There were many women amongst the gangs we had to catch. Brothers George and Joe Newby (Captain in the Intelligence Section and Regimental Sergeant Major respectively) presented me with one such female terrorist. She had been shot through the lower part of her arm which required minimal treatment, but her real discomfort came from her engorged breasts. When captured, she had still been feeding her toddler child but during interrogation the child had been placed in the care of someone else. Never having been faced with anything but natural weaning, she did not know how to stop the milk production and she was in agony.

As a grubby little schoolboy I had thumbed through a family health book in an attempt to learn the facts of life. Fortunately for this poor woman, I remembered the section on the manual expression of milk, and set about trying to explain how she could relieve her swollen breasts. In no time she was happier and more comfortable, but my greatest achievement was her smile when I explained that the milk could be sent to her child who no doubt would be upset by the sudden change in diet. She smiled from that day on, unlike her fellow captives, who steadfastly remained uncommunicative and, not unexpectedly, sullen.

When not practising my amateur medicine, I relaxed with my constant companion, my guitar. I literally had a 'captive audience'. Those returning from night patrol had their hard-earned sleep continually interrupted as I burst into early morning song. I could have started a shop with all the boots chucked angrily in my direction by disgusted colleagues. But in the evenings my repertoire, consisting mainly of rock and roll interspersed with self-composed ballads, was welcomed as unpaid cabaret and light relief.

Finally we were moved to Narok which meant not only a sad farewell to our Masai friends, but also to many of the guys we had trained with. We were to leave the paradise of the Mara to go back to the fighting which had now been centralised on the mountains and in the bamboo jungles. Although driven off the plains, the guerilla fighters were now in their element. Their superb field craft and jungle skills precluded any real chance of success for the British troops. We Kenyans were therefore seconded to British regiments in an effort to impart a smattering of inbred African instinct to the confused Tommies.

No doctor had been found during all that time in the Mara, so I found I was still attached to the medical room at my new location. Finally a doctor from a nearby Irish regiment came to see me.

'Who's in charge here? Where's the doctor?' he barked.

'I am – sort of, Sir,' I replied.

'Good God! Killed anybody yet?'

'No.'

'Good, but you'd better send all your patients to me from now on,' he ordered.

The last few days before rejoining our units were idled away. The doctor had taken over and, after packing my kit, I spent my hours strumming my guitar and composing. One title, 'Aberdare Blues', put into song some of a soldier's thoughts. Wandering through the main building one afternoon, I saw that one end had been set for a concert with piano, microphones and amplifiers. I couldn't resist, and whilst the stage hands continued their tasks, I jumped on the stage and let rip with my own songs, and as the noise floated outside I found myself with a large audience of fellow soldiers.

Before I knew it, I was belting out 'Jezebel', 'Sixteen Tons', 'High Noon' and several of the current popular songs. Inspired by the enthusiasm and applause, the whole place started rocking. Guy Campbell, our C.O., was trying to make himself heard on the telephone (no mean feat at the best of times) and came rushing in.

'Shut up!' he bellowed and rushed back to finish the call. Five minutes later as we were drifting away, he rushed back in with a huge smile and ordered, 'Carry on!'

And so my career as an entertainer was born!

At first I only entertained fellow troops. Later, I started singing in civilian clubs and bars.

At the time my entertaining was always purely for fun. I never regarded it as anything but an escape from army routine.

Those last few months of army life were not all spent in singing – there was a fair share of silent cursing involved, too, as I chased through the mountains after our elusive foe. With some of my old friends, such as Howie Clark, Ben Christie and Martin Foster, I discovered the delights of a certain 'Delilah'. This wondrous lady was not, as one might expect from the name, endowed with a sylph-like figure, although indeed a Samson on the scene would have been made welcome. This lady had legs like tree trunks. In fact they were tree trunks; 'Delilah' was the name given to a fort we had to build eleven thousand feet up in the mountains, made of wood and bamboo.

This may well have been the worst job of my life (not counting some club engagements I experienced later on!). Each piece of material for the fort's construction had to be passed hand to hand up a steep gradient that measured nine thousand feet. To add to all the obvious problems was the fact that the road, such as it was, had been largely washed away by the rains and what was left churned into thick mud by passing elephants. With an eighty-pound pack on your back plus a Bren gun, it was two steps forward, one step back, slipping and sliding into the mud. It was a nightmare. When we finally got to the summit of this mountain after a day's toil we were so bushed I dread to think of the outcome had we come under attack. It was all we could do to focus our attention on the water bubbling for tea.

Day after wretched day we made that trip up the mountain hauling logs and bamboo. On one descent I lost my footing and fell arse over tip some three hundred feet down the slope, finishing face down in the mud at Ben Christie's feet. He gazed at me and murmured laconically, 'No need to rush, Rog. No need to rush!'

Finally the fort was finished and so were we – fingers torn and bleeding, filthy from head to toe.

Of course this being the army, no sooner had we finished the fort when another outfit took it over, enjoying the fruits of our labours as we were sent off again to look for Mau Mau.

It was about this time that a new friend came into my life. Henry (Hal) Oliver was superbly fit and a man of enormous humour. Like the rest of us, he carried a full pack and weapons, but in addition he burdened himself with all sorts of bits and pieces nobody else could be bothered to carry. Included in this extra pack of goodies were items such as puddings, sweets and liqueurs. As a result, when our C.O. visited camp Hal was able – in the middle of nowhere – to concoct a three-course meal complete with after dinner liqueurs. Hal was an inventive man; little did we know then how our lives were later to become inextricably woven together.

The future was little in our minds as we roamed the mountains chasing Mau Mau ghosts. All we thought about was staying alive. As native Kenyans we were expected to impart our knowledge of the bush to the British troops, but it was no easy task even for us to match the wiles of the Mau Mau. They had more cunning than we, lived closer to Nature and knew this country better than we did. As we moved as silently as we could through the dense undergrowth we knew that it was possible for a Kikuyu to be barely two feet away, unseen, poised to slice our necks open with his machete.

In fact we never came face to face with any Mau Mau. Once again it was the wildlife that gave us the harder time. Our camp – an abandoned logging camp – was in an area teeming with elephant and rhino. They resented our presence and to make matters worse the RAF had been bombing suspected terrorist hideouts, making the animals nervous and angry. We never knew when or from where the next animal attack would come. Once an enraged rhino charged right into the centre of our patrol, scattering us in all directions. Then the rhino fixed on one particular guy and went for him. In sheer terror he scrambled up a tree like a monkey, but in doing so he dropped a full magazine of machine gun ammunition. To abandon it was a court martial offence.

Meantime the rhino had disappeared into the bush. Fortunately rhino have poor eyesight and, failing to see any of us after his charge, he returned to the undergrowth. But we couldn't guarantee that he wouldn't suddenly reappear and charge again. So we waited for a few minutes, listening for telltale signs that he was still nearby. Finally, satisfied that the angry beast had gone, the guy climbed down from his perch and retrieved his ammunition and we resumed the patrol, nerves tingling.

It was the elephants, the most prolific breed in the area, that really gave us our worst moments. Our camp was across a small ravine, spanned by a cedar-wood bridge. The first night we made camp and got our fires going the elephant residents saw red and spent the hours of darkness roaring their disapproval, thrashing about, stomping the ground as they bellowed. Nobody slept, convinced that a full charge by the entire herd was imminent. But they kept their distance and the next morning we discovered just how they had vented their frustration. The bridge was no more. It had been stomped into matchwood, which we promptly used for our fires. We didn't bother to rebuild it. The ravine wasn't flooded and we could scramble up and down the banks.

Elephant encounters became as routine as our patrols. We always tried to give them a wide berth but often they would wander closer and closer to where you knew another group was patrolling, unaware of the elephants. Shouting a warning would set off a charge so we would discreetly withdraw or stand still as statues whilst sending a runner over to our neighbouring patrol to give warning.

One day, walking either side of a rough track, we came across a set of enormous footprints. From their size this was definitely a large bull. Water was still oozing from the tracks, meaning he had only just passed that way. Silently and slowly we followed the tracks until they veered off into the bush. We quickened our pace, anxious to put distance between us and him before he came out of the bush again.

Suddenly we all froze. From behind us came an ominous rapid rhythmic thumping . . . ta-da-DUM . . . ta-da-DUM . . . ta-da-DUM . . . the bull elephant! The damned animal had doubled back behind us and was charging! You've never seen a group of men scatter so fast. I shot behind a rotten tree stump, from which vantage point I could see the road, but would get little protection should the beast pick on me. I saw two other men dive into a ditch and another climbed a tree – although the idiot remained at elephant eye level.

Hearts in our mouths we waited . . . ta-da-DUM . . . ta-da-DUM the thudding sounds came ever closer. And then, around the bend in the road came a Land Rover, its tyres vibrating on the tree roots growing across the road . . . ta-da-DUM . . . ta-da-DUM . . .

Red-faced and as nonchalantly as we could we scrambled back to the road in patrol formation, snapping to attention and saluting the officer who was a passenger in the vehicle. He returned the salute, albeit with a somewhat quizzical look in his eye, and as the Land Rover rounded the next bend we all collapsed in a fit of nervous giggles. But the incident showed what a state our nerves were in.

That particular patrol took place during my last few days of service in the armed forces. Thank God I had seen little active fighting, a fact I do not regret. Still they had been useful, formative days, filled with rich experiences and a sense of camaraderie, forging friendships that were to last to this very day.

Our university places had been held open for us and our demob date timed to coincide with the beginning of the academic year. And so, with promises of reunions to come and everlasting friendship, we shook hands and went our separate ways to seek our fortunes.

Chapter 4

Seems to me that being young is some kind of being free

WITH RELIEF AND delight I discovered that three of my old school friends, John Bradish, Neville Jones and Mike Leete, were also enrolled at the University of Cape Town, South Africa. The presence of these old school chums was to prove a mixed blessing; they were soon to enhance my reputation as a singer and all round 'fool' entertainer – a reputation, however, that would distract me from my serious studies.

I had chosen medicine as my career. There were two good reasons for this choice; for one thing, this was what my parents saw as my proper future; for another, my army experiences in medicine had actually aroused my interests in such a career. Unfortunately, my frame of mind was not quite ready for the serious pursuit of an academic course – much less the intense concentration medicine needed. I suppose too many years spent within the disciplines of school and army had left me with an urge to kick up my heels for a time, to break out, relax, enjoy myself and responsibility be damned.

I say all this with introspective hindsight. As I boarded the Lloyd Triestino luxury liner bound for Cape Town out of Mombasa, I was not analysing my feeling or my motives. I was still under the influence of the 'living day-by-day' attitude that was a relic of our service days. My old school friends were in the same frame of mind and we regarded the boat trip as the launching of our new found freedom. My own 'break-out' began auspiciously with a promising shipboard romance. As we were boarding I'd helped a young lady struggling to get a pram up the gangplank and we soon struck up a rather close friendship. She was a recent divorcée and, like me, was in the perfect mood to have a good time.

Unfortunately our ardour was swiftly cooled with a literal

dousing of cold water. The romance had hardly got going when, shortly after leaving the (then) Tanganyikan port of Dar es Salaam we hit a terrific storm. Wave after wave engulfed the boat, leaving most passengers in a state of collapse. Although both the young lady and myself weathered the battering better than most, it did make romance difficult and, as the storm lasted practically till we docked at Cape Town, our new-found love died as quickly as it was born. As we disembarked the lady and I waved goodbye forever.

That first sight of Cape Town took my breath away, as no doubt it had and has done to many thousands before and after me. There before me was Table Mountain, storied and magnificent, dominating the landscape, majestic, powerful and yet serene. It was bathed in glorious sunshine with just the occasional wisp of a cloud passing below its summit. The university itself lay in the shadow of the mountain and as time passed I was to spend hours, far too many hours, gazing out of the window in awe and admiration at the ever-changing display of light and colour playing on its crest.

Quickly I settled in, made new friends and began to enjoy myself. But when it came to my studies I was completely unable to apply myself. I just couldn't scrape up enough enthusiasm. The only part of the curriculum that appealed to me was rugby, which I played at every given opportunity.

The realisation that a medical career was not for me dawned during a practical anatomy lesson. This first visit to a pathology laboratory, the sight of the dissecting tables exhibiting cold, dead parts of what had only recently been warm living human beings, triggered a trauma I could not sustain. I knew then that even if I managed to qualify as a doctor, even if I never had to visit a pathology laboratory again, I would not be able to face the reality and the hopelessness of terminal illness.

Almost immediately after that anatomy lecture I built a wall around myself and withdrew inside it; I went through the motions of studying but my heart wasn't in it.

Whether or not I would have fared better had my academic interests taken me into more lighthearted studies is moot. Possibly I was too frivolous in any case. I can honestly admit that most of my time at Cape Town was spent in irresponsible idling, drinking vast quantities of beer and romancing. I fell in love at every turn. It was fabulous! Somehow, despite all the carousing, I managed to scrape through my first exams and lighthearted with relief set off for home and summer vacation, neglecting in my euphoria to notify my parents I was on my way.

It was quite a voyage home – the highlight of my year. As it happened, a friend of mine named Reg was desperately in love with a girl from Kenya and, as he was driving home to see her, I offered to go with him in his Mini Minor. It was a journey of approximately 2700 miles as the crow flies – but unfortunately Mini Minors do not fly as crows. Outside Lusaka, in what is now Zambia, we left the main road to look for petrol on what appeared on the map to be a respectable track. However, like so many African roads, especially then, that's exactly what it was – a track. But Reg continued to bat along as though we were on a tarmac motorway and sure enough we hit a five-foot ditch with a resounding crunch that completely demolished the gearbox and just about everything else underneath the car. We limped back to the main road and managed to stop a vehicle able to tow us to the nearest garage. Actually, it wasn't a real garage but a small hotel with a petrol pump. Fortunately Reg was a mechanical genius and, notwithstanding an audience of goats that butted us in the rear end every time we bent down, he was able to remove the gearbox and patch up all the other injuries to the car's undercarriage.

There was no way this so-called garage could repair the gearbox, so Reg decided to thumb his way to Lusaka while I remained behind to guard the car. Who got the better end of the deal I'm not sure because although I was able to laze around in the sun, the only food I got from the hotel's proprietor was curry – and hot curry at that!

Eventually Reg returned with the gearbox and re-installed it. From there on he drove a bit more prudently. Twelve days later we finally arrived in Nairobi; my relief at arriving safely was mirrored by my parents, but ten times over. Since I hadn't bothered to tell them I was coming, they'd telephoned the university to ask for me and had been told I'd left for some unknown destination with a chap named Reg in his car. Knowing me and knowing Africa and its roads, as the days passed with no word they had begun to fear I'd been killed or at the least seriously injured in a road accident. What an unthinking lout I was!

During those initial terms at university, encouraged by my close friends, I had gained a certain popularity amongst fellow students with my singing and guitar playing. Now, at home during the summer holidays, I approached the manager of a Nairobi club called the Equator to see if I could earn a few extra pennies. They took me on, and there I was, singing in a nightclub professionally, much to the delight of my friends, who appeared in droves to heckle me, and to the disgust of my parents. It was one thing to sing at home or at school for friends, but quite another to appear in public and make a damn fool of myself in front of their friends and neighbours. They heaved a mutual sigh of relief when the summer holidays ended and I returned to Cape Town. There, they hoped, my attention would once more focus on my medical studies. It was not to be. Back at university I did little more than enjoy myself and propagate my reputation as a singing Lothario. Girls, guitar and the good life, that was me. Perhaps needless to say, at the end of the university year I had to tell my parents I'd failed my exams. Understandably they were furious. Their anger was further swelled by my announcement that I didn't want to continue studying, that I felt my future lay in entertainment. My father exploded. He made it quite clear I had blown the one shot at university he had been prepared to pay for and that as far as he was concerned I'd better go out and find myself a job and pay my way at home or else . . . He didn't actually kick me out of the house in so many words but I knew he meant it; if I wanted to live there I'd have to make my own living. From my father's point of view, whilst he was working all hours under the strain of an awful physical handicap, all I'd been doing was frittering away two years of my time and his money. I suppose at the time I resented that attitude a bit but in actual fact it was a most salubrious ticking off.

Well, I wasn't one bit interested in following in his footsteps and becoming a storekeeper, but I was vaguely interested in my mother's educationalist background. I recalled that all the teachers who had held my attention during my school days had been exhibitionists. And my limited experience in showbusiness had taught me that sometimes, to hold an audience, particularly an inebriated club audience, you had to treat it like a classroom of naughty children.

I joined the Civil Service, became a trainee schoolmaster and actually loved every minute of it. Some of the kids I taught were not much younger than myself. At first they couldn't figure out how I caught them at their tricks so easily; then they understood that it was because I had been up to the same mischief myself only a few years before. My teaching was a bit unorthodox; I brought my guitar into the classroom and combined music with academics, a combination that paid off winningly, as the exam results of my classes proved.

I packed in a full life. When not teaching, I played rugby, composed songs, entertained at the Equator Club – and fell in love again. I survived on three or four hours' sleep a night – but I was young then! With the extra money I earned at the club and a little help from my grandparents I scraped together enough for my first sports car – an MG TF. Black paintwork with green upholstery and, best of all, wire wheels. I was the King of the Road!

Hal Oliver had come back into my life about this time and had re-introduced me to photography. We would spend every free hour, at no matter what hour, pottering around in his darkroom developing and mounting our latest masterpieces. Around two o'clock one morning, leaving the Equator Club with him motoring to his darkroom, I was discussing the problems with my act when to our horror oncoming lights veered across the road straight into our path and hit us head-on. Hal ducked down under the dashboard just before we hit and to this day carries a dent in his temple made by one of the knobs. I was thrown right over the bonnet and landed in the road some yards from my car.

I picked myself up, racked with pain and dripping blood. I didn't know the extent of my injuries, of course, but I knew I was alive and I could walk. Feeling about my head, from where all the blood was oozing, I realised that my nose was smashed, my head and cheeks were ripped open and one eye seemed to have popped a bit out of its socket. I was a mess. But any anguish or pain I felt at that moment was diminished by the pain and anguish I felt when I looked back at my beloved MG. It was totally wrecked.

I saw the other driver lying in the road. Now any pain I felt was numbed by my anger. I went across to him, picked him up by his shirt collar and I'm not sure what I would have done to him had a voice at my elbow not said sharply, 'Have you heard of assault, sir?' The tone of authority made me turn and in the gloom I saw that the man was a policeman.

'I was just picking him up to get him off the road,' I said, confused for the moment by the sudden appearance of the uniform but not so confused I hadn't caught the whiff of booze on the driver's breath.

'The man's drunk as a skunk,' I said. 'He should be given a breath test.'

'I know my job. Don't you tell me what to do,' the policeman replied sharply.

In the shock, excitement and confusion of the moment, it wasn't until Hal and I were being whisked away in the ambulance that I understood the sudden appearance of the uniformed policeman. He'd been a passenger in the other car!

The reaction of my parents was predictable and understandable. My mother cried when she saw my smashed face. My father's relief at learning I'd suffered no serious injury turned to anger – at me as well as at the other driver; I hadn't exactly the best reputation behind the wheel. My students offered me their condolences, as though I'd lost a dear friend – which I had indeed for the car was a write-off.

To these injuries the insurance company added theirs. In all honesty, I had been involved in more than my fair share of scrapes in cars and, in a small community where everybody knew everybody else, most of the insurance company people were friends of my parents. So the company announced that with reluctance they would have to refuse me further coverage. My parents were delighted, of course.

There is an interesting epilogue to this unfortunate incident. When the case finally came to court, I sensed there was something a bit fishy about the proceedings; it was too low profile for my liking. Soon enough I understood why. When the charges were read against the driver of the offending vehicle, it turned out he was a police inspector.

'Inspector, you are charged with driving without due care and attention. How do you plead?'

'Not Guilty.'

I was determined he wasn't going to get away with it that easily, so when the magistrate called me as a witness I said I thought the driver was drunk.

'You cannot say that,' the magistrate said 'It's a conclusion, an opinion, hearsay evidence and could prejudice the case. Please stick to the facts and tell the court what the defendant said immediately after the accident.'

Somewhere in my brain a bell rang and, with utter relish and to the delight of the public gallery I went into a complete drunk routine, slurring my words and swaying in the witness box until even the Judge permitted himself a smile.

'All right! All right! I think that we've got the message,' he said. He banged his gavel once and announced, 'Guilty of driving without due care and attention. Fined £10.00.'

No mention of driving whilst under the influence, no compensation for my ruined car. My lawyers advised me to drop the case in view of the profession of the driver. It was a hard and bitter pill to swallow.

Somehow I managed to persuade another insurance company to provide cover, but at a very high premium. I replaced my MG with a Ford Zephyr, a blow to my ego and a comedown for my image. However, I tinkered with the engine and could get quite a respectable turn of speed out of her. At the same time I fell in love again, this time with a girl by the name of Joy Macfarlane. She and all her family were successful and talented.

As with many young men, love drove me to introspection and fantasy; for the moment at least, it made me wish I had more to offer, that I had been more resolute in the pursuit of a medical career. As a 'Dr. Kildare' I would appear a more dashing, more promising suitor. As it was, an impecunious primary schoolteacher with a sideline singing in clubs was not a prospect calculated to endear himself to Joy's family.

Anyway, she was in love with a superintendent of police.

Undaunted, and by fair means or foul, I began to win her away. But then a third contender entered the fray – Don Spencer, an Australian entertainer. I'm sure Joy enjoyed some of the tricks we got up to, trying to win her away. Unfortunately the rather juvenile competition got out of hand and ended in near tragedy; I confess I was the culprit who instigated the act but no-one could have foreseen the consequences.

One night, after we'd all been to an outdoor cinema, I challenged the superintendent to a race. Of course it was stupid – stupid of both of us; me to challenge, to prove some sort of 'macho' superiority, stupid of him to accept and compound it by letting Joy ride with him. And so, with both of us driving at outrageous speed, he overtook me on a sharp bend and lost control. The car flipped over and cartwheeled off the road turning over and over. I screeched to a halt and raced to the nearest telephone for an ambulance.

It was a miracle that both were alive, although their injuries were serious. It was then left to me to tell Joy's parents. It was, I can relate, a harrowing experience and not without justification the Macfarlane's laid a fair share of the blame on my head. I was not a popular name in that household for a long time, long after the wounds healed.

My broken heart at losing Joy mended, as broken hearts will, with my falling head over heels in love with a ballet dancer named Lynette. We shared a love of photography and for many months our romance took us on trips all over Kenya, in particular to the coast. With her help and encouragement, before long I had enough pictures to qualify for a degree from the Royal Photographic Society, but I never entered the portfolio, having missed the entry date. I still have that entire, treasured collection today.

Lynette and I actually got engaged. We thought we knew each other well enough and had so many interests to share that marriage was inevitable. But somehow, after a time, and I'm not sure why, we began to drift apart and though still engaged we talked less of marriage. Perhaps each of us, without wanting to tell the other, began to realise that we were still young, with much to see and do, and were not yet ready for the ties of marriage.

Fickle chap that I was, as I sensed this cooling of our romance, my eyes began to wander. It wasn't difficult to meet gorgeous girls; my evenings at the Equator Club offered me contact with many and soon I met a fabulous beauty named Jasmine, later to become Miss Kenya.

She already had a boy friend but that had never discouraged me before and it didn't stop me then. We began to see more and more of each other until I finally regarded her as my girl. The only trouble was, I was still seeing Lynette – for the first time in my romantic life I was more or less playing both ends against the middle. The situation began to take on the elements of a French farce with me concocting the most elaborate schemes to keep both ladies on the hook and unaware of the other's existence.

One fatal Wednesday morning it all came to a head at the Thorn Tree Coffee Bar, a favourite meeting place at the New Stanley Hotel in Nairobi. Jasmine then worked in a shop in the hotel and, as she had many times before, that morning took a coffee break to meet me. As we sat there, eyes locked in romantic embrace over a cup of cappuccino, I spied Lynette making her way through the crowded pavement, heading without a doubt toward the terrace where we were seated.

Reacting quickly, I said to Jasmine, 'It's getting hot out here. How about you trying to find a table at one of the cafés indoors while I hold this one down just in case?'

With Jasmine safely out of the way for a moment or two, I greeted Lynette warmly and sat her down for a coffee. I then made an excuse and dashed inside to head off Jasmine's return. I found her and we ordered another cappuccino at the coffee shop indoors. A minute later I excuse myself to go to the men's room and fled outdoors to resume my coffee and conversation with Lynette. For the better part of an hour I raced back and forth between the two coffee shops, making one sort of excuse or another to disappear for a few moments – and believe me with all the coffee I was drinking at both tables, sometimes the excuses were genuine!

Inevitably, on one of my visits to Lynette's table, Jasmine came looking for me. She walked over to the table, said not a word, looked at me, at Lynette, at me again. Lynette, also without a word, looked at Jasmine, at me, at Jasmine again. Discretion being the better part of valour, I abandoned ship and sailed full speed ahead to the Stanley Long Bar for a drink and to await the storm.

There was no storm. Instead I was becalmed. Both girls just dropped me cold, leaving me a sorrier and a wiser man.

I was also becalmed as far as my future was concerned. Although to a large extent I was preoccupied with singing, photography, rugby and girls – not necessarily in that order – I appreciated that my career as a teacher was going nowhere. I was good and I enjoyed it, but with no real qualifications there were severe limitations on promotion.

I suppose I had realised this when I was desperately trying to win the affections of Joy. I still hankered after a future in entertainment, but parental opposition was solid on that score. So much so that when my father asked me what I wanted for Christmas, and I told him I would like some cigars, my parents' faces lit up. A family friend joined us for Christmas that year, and as I unwrapped a huge box of Hoffner cigars of every size, he remarked to my father in horror, 'Teddy, you'll ruin his voice!' To which my father replied with relish, 'The sooner the better!'

Need I say more? It was a losing battle and the only answer was to try seriously for a university degree in the sciences; then at least I could return to a career in teaching with prospects of climbing the ladder in that profession. There were, however, two stumbling blocks in my way. The first was that I would have to try to enter a British university, having blown my chances at Cape Town. The other was my father, who decided he had little faith in my sincerity. As far as he was concerned, his hard earned money had already been squandered during my time in South Africa.

The stubborn streak I had inherited from my mother drove me on, and when finally I was accepted for a place at Bangor University in Wales, my father weakened slightly. He agreed to give me my fare to England, and a very tidy allowance for my first year. After the first year exams he would review the situation.

The allowance was obviously going to be enough to provide for my basic survival, but costs being enormous in England compared with Kenya, I was not going to ask for more. I threw myself into as much cabaret work as I could get and saved every penny. The ladies whose company I relished so much had a pretty lean time of it where dates were concerned;

sandwiches with a half pint of beer were offered in place of a candlelit dinner with good wine!

My friends had seen me go through moods of immense enthusiasm before, and I think that, like my father, they were all laying bets that I would return to my old ways within the year.

I sold my car, my guitar and my amplifiers to swell my funds and in September, 1959, bade my friends a fond farewell, kissed my parents goodbye and boarded a plane for England.

As I landed at London's Heathrow, my aunt and uncle were there to greet me and introduce me to the city which to this day remains my favourite place in the world. London . . . in autumn and spring there is not a city like it. I am sure my relatives and the people sunning themselves in Hyde Park thought I was quite mad when I asked the taxi driver to stop whilst I danced amongst the flowers with sheer joy.

Uncle George and Aunt Enid Camacho were kindness itself, and went out of their way to show me around as much as possible before I had to leave. I explored every tourist spot I could, and delighted in taking boat trips up and down the River Thames. My uncle was Head of the BBC Light Programme and took time off to show me round Broadcasting House. Neither of us, of course, realised that in years to come I would spend a great deal of time in that bastion of radio broadcasting.

All too soon those glorious days in London came to an end and I was on a train to Bangor. I found myself assigned a room with a fellow Kenyan named Purchace, then went to register my studies. I had chosen botany, zoology, physics and chemistry. As I filled out my form, the zoology professor leant over my shoulder and said, 'I do hope you will take this course seriously, because so far you Kenya boys have a pretty bad record here.' With Purchace he was right and in that first year, I, too, was tempted to give up and crawl home, tail between my legs.

After a couple of years messing around I had lost the technique of actually studying and it needed all my strength of character to apply myself. Another factor that made that first year so difficult for me was the cold Welsh winter. From the bright colours, the warmth and the sounds of Africa, my surroundings had given way to dull skies, biting cold and comparative silence as students scurried from building to building. Everything, including the faces, seemed to take on the grey of the slate, and as the sleet, snow and ice bit into my bones, I wept inwardly. Had I not been so determined to reach my goal and prove to my parents that I could do something worthwhile, I am sure I would have given up that first freezing February.

At first I found the English students aloof and introverted, but the more I got to know them, the better I liked them. It dawned on me that their apparent lack of warmth was in fact a protection against distraction. They were dedicated to achieving the best qualifications; and even in the 1960s really good jobs were at a premium, the competition fierce.

I soon found myself influenced by their serious approach and applied my nose to the grindstone. I set my music to one side – except at weekends when I could earn a few pounds singing for the customers in local hotels.

When the first summer vacation arrived and I had successfully passed my exams I returned to Kenya with a real sense of achievement for the first time. I had proved to myself and to anybody else who doubted me that I could do it if I tried. Still, money was very much on my mind. I was not going to ask my father to subsidise me entirely, so after a few days of visiting friends and family I took up my old job at the Equator Club at night and spent my days composing radio commercials. Ron Partridge, who owned the Equator Club, took it on himself to act as my agent, finding me extra work in Uganda, Tanganyika (now Tanzania) and along the Kenya coast.

Without realising it then of course, that summer of 1960 saw the true beginning of my professional career as an entertainer. Until then all the singing I'd done had been on a handshake basis between friends. Now, suddenly, I found myself making deals and signing contracts – and, I may add, earning really solid cash. In fact I earned enough money that summer for me to return to Bangor in the autumn with no financial worries for the next year.

My success as a performer did not escape the attention of the university authorities and in my second year I was invited to join its charity shows. As at most British universities, at Bangor the students got together in Rag Week to put on shows for charity and I became heavily involved. But this time my singing did not interfere with my studies; I now knew how to organise my time and energies. What I did not know was that one of my suggestions for raising charity funds was to completely change my life.

Chapter 5

My son you make your footsteps don't follow in my own

THE BRIGHT IDEA I presented to the rag committee was that we should record some original songs and persuade a London company who manufactured the slim plastic discs to sponsor us. We hoped they would press a few thousand that we could sell to the unsuspecting public.

All the musical talents in the university got together and eventually a finished record was made. The idea worked so well that plans were made that in my third year we would repeat the process but we would be more professional and record in a proper London studio.

Despite my involvement in the entertainments side of university life, I managed to keep my mind on my studies and once again my end of year exam results showed good academic achievement. For the first time my parents began to believe that I was serious and might eventually follow a career reflecting my upbringing.

Inwardly, however, I still was intent on having fun. Although I knew those summer holidays would involve a great deal of work singing, once again to raise funds for the following university year, I also intended chasing as many girls as I possibly could!

The expression 'if you can't be careful, be good – but if you can't be good, be careful!' really meant something in Kenya. To purchase contraceptives at a store where the owners and staff knew our parents was extremely tricky. So shortly before I returned to Kenya that summer I purchased a stock of the finest contraceptives from a fellow in our residence who ordered them by post. Optimistically, I ordered a large quantity and jammed them into my metal box file containing zoology notes and forgot all about them. The few days before I flew to Nairobi I stayed with my beloved Aunt Enid and Uncle George, and my cousin Nick decided to escort me to Heathrow.

As was my wont I arrived at Heathrow with only minutes to spare but when my case was weighed I found I was twelve pounds overweight. With no extra cash with which to pay the extra charges, I frantically opened my suitcase and grabbed the nearest heavy article I could find. My zoology file! I thrust it into Nick's hands, slammed my suitcase shut and ran for the plane.

Halfway to Nairobi I realised what I had done. My heart skipped a beat and my brain lurched into top gear as it created the most horrific image of my genteel and delicate Aunt Enid opening my file and saying in her innocent way,

'I wonder what these are?' and moments later fainting away, never to speak to me again!

I didn't sleep a wink on that flight. The first thing I did when I got home was write to Nick explaining why I appeared to be a travelling salesman in the contraceptives business. His reply arrived by return post.

It began, 'Dear Roger, the Devil looks after his own . . .'

Apparently Nick had responded to a call of nature and had visited the gents at Heathrow and with my zoology file tucked under his arm took his place along the row of urinals along with the rest of the gentlemen. The mind boggles at the picture of Nick trying to perform a juggling act with the box file without having an unfortunate accident. In fact, when it came to the crunch he let go of the file which dropped to the concrete floor with a crash, the lock sprang open and 'The World's Finest' cascaded all over the place!

Amid hoots of laughter, Nick beat a hasty retreat. As he put it,

'I hope you don't mind, Roger, but I walked out and left them there!'

I'm sure I would have done the same thing in his place and indeed the Devil does look after his own. Nevertheless, Nick's failed juggling act made life back in Kenya just that much more difficult for our particular circle of friends who had relied on my famed initiative for their holiday antics!

Back home, I spent the first few days with my parents, catching up on the news and much-needed sleep. Then I went back to work, singing at the Equator Club. Ron Partridge decided, however, that since my previous expeditions to Uganda and Tanganyika had been successful, he'd send me off again. This was cabaret work of the most fascinating kind, working on the same bill with all sorts of performers, many of whom had nothing whatsoever to do with music.

I worked very hard that summer and once again earned enough money to see me through the next year. At the same time I made plans to return over Christmas and put in four more weeks of cabaret work. This was Christmas, 1961, and I knew I couldn't return for the following summer holiday since I'd be studying right through to September, when I'd be sitting my finals. Time flies when you're having fun, and before I knew it Christmas had come and gone. I felt a pang of regret when I left in January, knowing I'd not be home again the following summer.

Little did I know that it would be twenty years before I'd set foot in my home country again.

Back in Bangor I worked out my budget for the year carefully. I discovered that after allowing for all expenses, I had just sixty pounds spare with which to buy a car, an item I desperately wanted.

After searching for a few days, I found a BSA sports car within my price range. The fact that the car was as old as I was probably had some bearing on the price. Papers signed, the keys were handed to me and I set off over the hills and dales back to Bangor. Feeling mighty proud of my new wheels, I swept up the main drive and into the courtyard. My grand entrance, however, was ruined as the engine coughed, choked and finally died in full view of my fellow students. One look under the bonnet told me that minor patching would not be the answer and a complete mechanical overhaul was needed. Carefully the entire engine was removed and ceremoniously carried to the basement of our residence.

The chilly wet winter and spring days were occupied with tinkering with the engine which I and my friend Brian Cook stripped bare in the snug hideaway below ground. The car sat just where it had stopped, but with typical student humour was now draped with a huge wreath across the bonnet.

Finally, the repairs were complete and the engine rehoused under the bonnet. As Brian had done most of the work, the honour of the maiden drive fell to him. With the entire student body hanging out of every window, the ignition key was turned and with a mighty push from myself and a couple of others, the car exploded into life. The power we had put back into the engine took Brian totally by surprise and he only just managed to control the vehicle as he careered towards the polytechnic college five hundred yards away.

I really fancied myself driving that car and would hurtle through the Welsh mountains, my passenger usually hanging onto his door with white knuckles. That poor BSA was finally put to rest after a cabaret date I had just completed in Conway. Conway is a very hilly town, and as I crested the top of one particularly vicious piece of road, the brake cable snapped. I just had time to think 'Thank goodness it didn't go on the mountain curves' when before me loomed the back of a stationary bus. With oncoming traffic, there was nowhere else to go. With my passenger and myself braced for the inevitable impact, my precious car smashed into the back of the bus.

The bus was virtually undamaged, but my car literally fell apart. The hood flopped down around my passenger's head like a monk's cowl. The mud guards fell off. The horn wouldn't stop and the battery leads sparked against the bodywork in a most spectacular fashion.

Solemnly the passengers, conductor and driver of the bus got out and stood around and, gazing at the unprepossessing sight passed comments ranging from,

'What do you want to drive that thing for, man?' 'Get it off the road!' to 'Look at that, what's he want to kill himself in that for?' Having established that the bus was intact, they all piled back on board and drove away, leaving me considering my pile of junk. Eventually I had to pay a garage to remove it.

From then on I had to rely on the kindness of others or public transport to get me to and from the singing engagements I undertook at weekends. As it was the final year of my studies, the weekdays found me restricting myself to the grounds of the university itself. One of my professors, Charles Evans, had found the elusive key for imparting knowledge to my brain, and under his tutelage the mysteries of bio-chemistry took pride of place. Fascinated by the subject I immersed myself in learning. It was a year that I thoroughly enjoyed, despite all the hard work.

Rag Week came round again, and we found a professional studio in which to record our plastic charity records. A copy of the disc found its way into the hands of a publisher, Fred Jackson by name. He took it to Fontana Records in London. They contacted me and invited me to come to London for an audition. So with Gwyneth, my current girl friend, I went to London and sang a few songs with my guitar as accompaniment.

It was a pleasant weekend outing but I never expected to hear anything more. On the Monday morning I was back at my desk as usual, peering through a microscope. Imagine my surprise at receiving a letter a few days later offering me a recording contract! After the initial shock I sobered up and thought, well, it all sounds fine but it probably won't amount to much more than a diversion from academic life and a bit of extra cash. Anyway, I signed the contract they sent me and forgot all about it for I was hip deep in cramming for my final exams.

In the middle of it all came a call to come to London to record – my first professional record! I must admit I was a bit excited over the prospect. The song was 'The Charge of the Light Brigade'. Most singers remember with fondness their first record. Not me. I wanted to forget that one almost as soon as I'd made it. Even my best friends, upon hearing it, could not fake any enthusiasm for it. They greeted it with stony silence. It was, let's face it, a dog. I was terribly embarrassed about the whole business. To this day, DJs and interviewers take maniacal delight in springing it on me during the course of a live radio show.

My second attempt was better. Fred Jackson found a song called 'Steelmen' which told the story of the collapse of the bridge at Second Narrows, Vancouver. Many men had died. Although the subject of the song was tragic, it was quite up-tempo and folksy, and with the aid of the record producer and good musicians it turned into a record I am still proud of. It also caught the imagination of the radio DJs and was heard more and more during my last weeks at university in 1962.

My friends kept me updated on how many times it was being played, but I can honestly say that I ignored it, preferring to study for my exams.

I had kept in constant touch with Hal Oliver, who was now married with a baby son called Brett. He and his wife had a small apartment in Kingston-on-Thames, forty minutes from the centre of London. They offered me the spare bedroom at a very small rental. So, as soon as the final exams were finished, I moved down there. At the time 'Steelmen' was climbing the charts and was in the Top Thirty, and before I knew it I had a manager, Philip Solomon.

On the strength of the record, Philip put me into summer season in Port Rush, Northern Ireland. I was delighted and welcomed the chance at working alongside established professional entertainers. Not so my parents! There was very little doubt that I had passed my exams, and with whatever grade would be awarded a degree. At last their son and heir had answered their prayers and they could be proud of him. In anticipation of my degree they chose that summer to come to England to visit their families. My sister, Betty, had delighted them with a highly desirable marriage to a successful professional soldier and they had already produced two beautiful sons. But up until now their layabout son had hardly been the subject of illuminating conversation. Now at last they could boast of my accomplishments.

I had told them about the record.

'Very nice, dear,' was Mother's comment, not realising its significance. I suppose they thought it would keep me occupied until I could start searching for a job to go with my degree. Halfway through the summer season, my exam results came through and I was invited back to Bangor for the Degree ceremonies. My parents joined me and proudly saw me mount the dais, dressed in full gown and mortar board, to receive my Bachelor of Science award. Not the medical doctorate they had really wanted, but a highly respectable science degree.

Flushed with their new-found faith in me, my parents agreed to take a break from duty calls to relatives and accompany me to Northern Ireland to see me perform. It was not one of my brighter ideas.

Very soon their happy bubble burst. My own spot wasn't bad, where I sang a few songs and played the guitar, but most of my time on stage was spent playing straightman stooge to the comic, Frank Carson. And I was having a ball! Frank taught me how to change my performing as though I was a solo act in an empty room and play to the audience. Quickly we established a great ad-libbing routine, the act changing from night to night as we milked every last laugh out of the audience. But one sketch that remained constant involved me having water poured down the front of my trousers.

My parents were not amused. The sight of their scientist son behaving like an irresponsible undergraduate again sent chills through them, especially as it was obvious that I was enjoying every moment of it.

Just before they left we sat down quietly and began to discuss my future. My parents wanted to know when 'this nonsense' would come to an end and where I was going to find employment. Then I dropped my bombshell. I had already discussed my future with Charles Evans, my professor. I still wanted to see if I could make it as an entertainer, in spite of my degree. He advised me to take a year off and either succeed in entertainment or at least get the 'bug' out of my system. If I found show business was not for me, then he advised that I should return to Bangor and get a Ph.D. My place would remain open until my decision.

To say that my parents were furious would be an understatement. But I was adamant. I would take one year off to give entertainment a chance. So we parted company under a very black cloud, my parents' disgust showing in their frosty farewell.

Within that first year I began to think they were right. My big 'hit record' disappeared into obscurity and nothing I recorded seemed to raise any further interest. What money I had soon ran out. Philip Solomon lost interest in me and passed me back to Fred Jackson. I then found myself struggling to catch the attention of inebriated servicemen at American bases a couple of weekends a month for a few meagre pounds. Fred managed to get me on a tour of Scottish dance halls in the midst of the coldest winter on record, and miserably I shivered and shook from place to place with my dreams at night haunted by visions of the sneering rock fans that frequented the halls.

At the end of that tour I returned to Hal's flat and slept for twenty-four hours, but woke to find that my depression had only deepened. Hal's wife had left him; so, as my days of work were few and far between, I spent my days caring for Brett, a lively two-year-old, whilst Hal finished his studies for an engineering degree.

The three of us muddled through that atrocious winter. We slept in tracksuits under piles of blankets, but nothing kept out the cold and I would wake in the morning to frost on the inside of the windows and ice formed on my beard from my own breath. We pooled every penny, but in the end I was so broke that I was forced to sell my last valuable and sentimental possession – my Linhoff camera with which Lynette and I had recorded golden days in Kenya. Those days now seemed a million miles away, in another world.

Eventually my stubborn pride surrendered and I plucked up the courage to write to my parents for assistance. A letter appeared by return, containing a hundred pounds and a few short lines to the effect of,

'Your mother has asked me to write. I really feel I am doing the wrong thing, and until you take up an occupation more worthy of your background and education, I will assist you no more.' It was signed, 'Your father'.

Dear Dad, years later I was to tell him that it was his letter that spurred me on and induced me to break my promise of taking only one year away from science. I set my jaw and determined I would prove I could make them proud of me again, but as a singer.

In an effort to further my career, I naively formed an association with some Liverpool businessmen. I had yet to learn the hard side of showbusiness, but my experience in that relationship started my education. I worked, but wherever they wanted. They could see my potential, which was more than I could, but the direction they were taking was obviously wrong, even to me. However, the rewards were not quick enough for them, and painful disagreement after disagreement led to a parting of the ways.

Fred Jackson was still in the background, but I was only earning enough to keep him in matches. My recording contract with Fontana was still valid but Jack Beaverstock, the Fontana recording manager, became more and more despondent as each attempt at finding a successful song turned sour.

Only one person in Fontana had faith in me. Barbara Hayes (Jack's secretary) and I would spend hours in her office going through ideas. It was nearly impossible to present Jack with original songs. He had made up his mind that my contract and all my records were merely a legal formality. He was completely uninterested in the material. As long as he released a set amount of records he was honouring Fontana's side of the deal.

The previous summer I had made friends with quite a few people in Ireland and although they could not help my career, I still went across from time to time to see them. One night at a party I got up and sang. It was a spontaneous, fun performance, and afterwards a gentleman approached me and introduced himself.

'I'm John Schultz Conway and I have a programme on Ulster Television called 'This and That'. It's forty-five minutes long. I wondered if you would like to do the whole show one week?'.

I jumped at the opportunity, and after a few weeks returned, having designed the entire show.

I was elated when we finished the taping. I knew it had worked. When I saw the finished product I broke into exuberant laughter as the credits rolled at the end. I was right, too, and before I could catch my breath I was signed for a series of forty-eight shows. It turned out to be the first series made by a small independent station to be networked all over Britain, and although shown late at night, it caused a small stirring of interest. That late showing proved to be the break I needed. Most of the public might well have already retired to their beds, but in the massive network of clubs throughout Britain, managements would be putting their feet up on their desks for some late night viewing whilst waiting for the punters to finish their night out downstairs.

Gradually offers of club appearances trickled in. I found myself an agent by the name of Emlyn Griffiths. He was the absolute opposite of every other agent I had ever met. He looked more like an ex-army officer than a flash showbusiness hustler. He even had a bristling little moustache and affected a monocle. Maybe it was just that impression of a typical English gentleman that enabled him to infiltrate the most pompous clubs and restaurants in Britain. One such venue was the famous Quaglino's in London's posh Mayfair.

After the relaxed, loud, brash atmosphere of the northern clubs, the snooty, staid feel of this London nightspot was quite intimidating. I was greeted at the door for my first audition by a beribboned and highly superior young doorman, who just managed to glance down his nose at me before imperiously informing me,

'The tradesmen's entrance is round the back.'

I was nervous anyway and badly needed the work and his attitude made me see red. With one finger in the middle of his chest and with a not so gentle shove, I hissed, 'Bugger off!' and strode past him into the flashy interior. I was still seething during the audition and it was probably my temper that added some spice to my performance because the nervousness never showed and I was booked for several seasons.

The audiences in most clubs could be difficult, enthusiastic or downright rude, but never quiet, and you could always gauge what was needed to entertain them. These London audiences, however, were a totally different kettle of fish – cold fish! Maybe it was the plush surroundings that inhibited them, or maybe they felt it was 'just not done' to let their hair down and become involved. Whatever the reason, I and all the other entertainers would sweat blood trying to get some positive reaction out of them. I remember Dave Allan, sitting with his head in hands after struggling through two performances, saying,

'What the hell do you have to do to entertain these people?' On rare occasions polite applause would tell you that they had noticed you for a brief moment before returning to their champagne and caviar.

It was all experience, however, and gradually I began to enjoy the challenge. Working in London also meant I was in the centre of things and as my association with the Liverpool businessmen was reaching a dead end and becoming acrimonious, I needed a lawyer – and a sympathetic bank manager. I found both – and somebody else. Natalie.

Barbara Hayes was moving to another record company, and

on one of my visits to her office to try to inveigle a meeting with Jack, there was this young lady learning the ropes. Strangely, the first feature I noticed was her forehead. She reminded me of a deer, the way she moved. Above all she was such fun. She bubbled with life and her eyes twinkled with laughter. I knew that if I allowed myself I would fall in love, hopelessly and forever! So I kept my distance and restricted our relationship to business only. Mind you, I was in and out of Jack's office almost daily on some pretext or other!

Uppermost in my mind was the fact that I still had cardboard in my shoes, and as my survival was in the hands of the bank had nothing to offer a girl. I left Natalie alone socially, and continued seeing the divorcée I had been dating for a year.

I had found myself yet another manager. This time the gentleman was an ex-bass player I had met while playing one of the American bases. Because of the Ulster TV series he was able to find me a considerable amount of work. Three shows a night for fifty pounds a week didn't bring him a lot of commission, but to me it was a fortune.

His most important achievement, however, was playing Cupid between Natalie and me. He knew how I felt about her, and decided that devious methods were needed to break down the barrier I had imposed.

Quite simply, he approached Natalie one day and told her that I wanted her to go down to Quaglino's to see if there was a song in my stage act that might be recorded. To me, he announced that Jack Beaverstock wanted Natalie to be at the show to pick out material. You can understand Natalie's confusion when I said,

'I understand you want to come down to Quaglino's?'

However, neither of us thought about it too deeply and one Saturday night I arranged to collect her from her parents' house. She was still changing when I arrived, and her father asked me if I would like a drink. While we were waiting he asked how I would get home to Kingston that night, with no trains running that late. I told him I would hitch-hike, as usual.

'Nonsense!' he exclaimed. 'You'll stay here, and have lunch with the family tomorrow'. You didn't argue with Toby O'Brien. He and I liked each other instantly. By the time Natalie joined us, I was enthralled with his conversation and

96

Natalie had to remind me fairly forcefully that I had a show to do.

Whether it was the mood of the club that night, the wine, or the dancing after the show, something changed between us, and when I left her house the next day, I knew my fate was sealed.

Later Natalie told me that she hadn't been so sure about me and when, following my departure, her father told her that I was the man she would marry, she had protested vigorously.

'Never! I'll never marry an artist!'

Despite her opposition to her father's prediction she and I started to see each other every day after work. I immediately broke up with my other girl friend, and after only three weeks decided that I had better propose to Natalie without further delay. I kept dropping rather obvious hints as we wandered around window shopping one day.

'What kind of crockery do you like?' or 'What would you call your first child?' She must have been laughing inside at my inept and supposedly innocent questions.

Finally, after a particularly romantic dinner, I plucked up the courage. As we strolled along the banks of the River Thames that beautiful May evening, I stopped and gazed into her eyes.

'Varicose veins run in my family, but would you marry me?' I blurted out. Hardly what I had meant to say.

She laughed outright and replied,

'What do you think? You fool!' Equally unromantic reply.

'Well?' I asked.

'Well . . . of course I will!' Hugging and laughing we decided I had better ask her father's permission. I was quite terrified of that interview as I would have to lie through my teeth if he asked if I could support her. The fateful conversation had to be delayed a day as her parents were away.

The following day as I was working in the studio, Natalie put her head round the control room door and told me a taxi was waiting to take me to his office.

Oh Heavens!

I don't know how I got through the last few moments of the session as half my mind was composing a speech with which I hoped to impress him.

We arrived at his office to be greeted by his secretary who showed us in. He was dictating to two secretaries at the same time, surrounded by ancestral portraits dating back to the fifteenth century. He looked up.

'I'll be with you in a moment,' he said curtly, looking at me over his half glasses.

Finally he finished, dismissed his secretaries, positioned himself in front of the fireplace, put his hands behind his back and said,

'WELL?'

Natalie sat demurely to one side while I breathed deeply, forgot every word I had rehearsed and mumbled,

'Natalie and I want to get married!'

He removed his half glasses and placed them in the top pocket of his immaculate city suit. I thought, 'My God, he's going to hit me!' but he didn't. Instead he said,

'I'm delighted, my boy! Delighted! Let's ring Leo (Natalie's stepmother) and tell her Natalie is engaged.'

The worst moment came later when Natalie told Jack that she and I were engaged. He flippantly and sarcastically said, 'Well, I suppose it could have been one of the Rolling Stones.' No congratulations. He had absolutely no faith in my future, and proceeded to make Natalie's life hell, trying to keep us from seeing each other. If there was a late night recording session, Natalie was assigned the job. Funnily enough Natalie understood him a lot better than I did and was actually quite fond of him. She played along with his game, not letting it phase her for one moment.

I was still basically a folk singer, and my heavy beard and the loose sail-cloth shirts I wore did little to belie the image. I was starting to do more and more musical TV shows alongside such equally unknowns as The Beatles and others now internationally famous. I used to shrivel inside when I managed to catch sight of myself later, in the privacy of my own sitting room, as I attempted to work to the cameras. Overall, my appearance did nothing to enhance my career.

Fortunately Natalie has always been one of the people who believed in what I was doing and the slow but steady development of my own individual brand of entertaining.

During our engagement we both developed a philosophy

that we still retain – total fatalism! We could both laugh at life and agree that this has been the saving of our sanity in the rough-and-tumble of my profession. Toby's (Natalie's father) name and popularity with the press immediately sparked coverage of our engagement that my career to date did not merit. Delightful as the attention was, it also brought all the worms out of the woodwork and our happiness was to be temporarily marred by a musician I had worked with in the past.

Seeing the press reports, he must have got the impression that my career was really taking off, and leapt at the opportunity to further his own poor endeavours in showbusiness. He did this through a puerile, sordid attempt at blackmail. His demands were that I should continue to work with him, his family and friends, and would sign a contract. If I did not do as he demanded, he would expose to the public and to Natalie that until the time of our engagement, I had been consorting with a divorcée!

Twenty years ago I think that kind of exposure wouldn't have done my image as a family entertainer any good, but fortunately my relationship with Natalie has always been one of total honesty, and of course she knew all about this affair. She was wild! In fact she was so furious that it provided the first indication of her 'claws out fighting' spirit.

She carefully arranged to get everybody into my agent's office and persuaded me to inveigle the man into 'phoning on the office number. A solicitor and two independent witnesses were listening in on the other extensions. I led him on sufficiently for him to find enough rope with which to 'hang' himself, and when he repeated the threat, Natalie butted in, quietly and firmly,

'I think we have enough for an extortion charge, don't you?'

The poor man was terror stricken and begged for the incident to go no further. Financially he was on his last legs. He pleaded for help. I have always been amused since then that I haven't seen his career flourish, because as an actor, he was so convincing that if I had had any money to spare, I would have been persuaded to lend it to him, and no doubt never have seen it or him again! Fortunately, I was so broke that it was just out of the question.

After that hiccup we settled down to organise our wedding. I was still living in Thames Ditton with Hal and my godson Brett. Hal agreed to be my best man and we invited my parents over for the wedding.

For a month or so before the wedding I went to live in London where I found a tiny flat for us – all I could afford. It was with great trepidation that we met my parents at the airport. My mother seemed happy enough but my father had his 'stony' face on. I think he believed I was marrying a typical tarty showbusiness type.

When he met Natalie his face softened, he nodded hello, and when he saw our little flat he said,

'Huh! This is much better than your mother and I had when we were married. Can I use your telephone?'

From then on we got on like a house on fire and the two families had dinner together many times in the days before the wedding.

August 15 dawned bright and clear – which is more than I can say for my head. My bachelor party had been a beauty; I didn't remember much of it but by the size of my hangover I reckoned it must have been pretty good. By noon I'd recovered from the traditional ordeal and by two o'clock, when the curtain was to go up, I was ready for the ceremony, all decked out in top hat and tails. The wedding was scheduled to take place at a tiny Catholic church in the heart of London so that there would be no break in the merriment that followed and the guests could continue their enjoyment by going out to dinner nearby. Donough, Natalie's older brother, had put his Lotus sports car at my disposal for a quick getaway.

In the vestry, awaiting Natalie's arrival, I was offered a large Scotch to steady my nerves by Father Barrett, a family friend. But a booming voice heralding the arrival of the Archbishop told me most firmly that tea was all I was allowed to imbibe.

Natalie arrived right on the dot of two; in fact, she told me, she and Toby had arrived too early and had to drive around for a few minutes before entering the church. I still tell her she was early because she was so desperate to catch me! (A clout around the ear usually follows.)

When the formal ceremony was over, ring on finger, the bride kissed and the introductions of the reception line done with, the affair rapidly turned into an Irish hooley. Our Jewish showbusiness friends pinned money on Natalie's veil, as was their tradition, while her boss kissed her warmly and said his present was a piece of advice,

'Tell Roger to get out of showbusiness and do something he's been trained for. He'll never make it as an entertainer!'

Natalie has had the pleasure since to remind him of his remark.

During the shenanigans Natalie's young brother Lucius, aged six, came up to my mother and asked her to look after the handfuls of silver money he kept collecting. Puzzled, my mother asked him where it was all coming from, to which he jauntily replied,

'Oh, I just go up to lots of grown-ups and say – if you give me some money, I'll go away!'

He obviously looked sufficiently devilish to be worth paying off!

But it was 'Uncle George' who gave us the biggest laugh. The height of elegance in his morning suit and top hat, everybody kept remarking to either myself, Natalie or one of the family,

'What a pleasant man, and what a pity it is that he hasn't been to many more of the family gatherings.'

He smiled and chatted and drank his way through at least two bottles of champagne before I remarked to Natalie that her Uncle George appeared to be getting a trifle merry.

'What do you mean, my Uncle George? He's *your* Uncle George!'

Dead silence! Then shouts of laughter from all and sundry. He was nobody's 'Uncle George' – just a professional gate-crasher! One of our most treasured possessions is a photograph of this gentleman, who had the unmitigated audacity to stand in the reception line, warmly greeting our guests as if he had been a member of the family all his life!

At about seven that evening Natalie's parents tactfully suggested that we might think about getting ready to leave as the champagne was about to run out. Somehow I had been conned into taking Natalie to Ireland for our honeymoon. The main reason seemed to be that all her elderly relatives, who had been unable to get over for the wedding, wanted to meet and either approve or disapprove of me. I've often heard that the Irish are butts for jokes, but we experienced our own true 'Irish-ism' on our first day.

We had travelled through southern Ireland on our way to County Clare and had stopped for lunch at a tiny market town. The only hotel had one dining-room which was extremely busy and we therefore had to share a table with another couple. Typical of Sunday lunch in southern Ireland, the fare was boiled mutton. Most of the people, having come straight from Mass, were dressed in black and read the newspapers with hardly a glance in our direction. When we had ordered our meal, the other couple at our table downed their papers briefly to say,

'Good morning!'

Then they lifted them again; through the rustling of the papers we heard the following whisper,

'It's certainly him – but it's never her!'

Our wedding photograph, very badly reproduced, had given rise to the very first gossip of a mere twenty-four hours of marriage!

To add insult to injury, during our five days at the hotel in the heart of O'Brien countryside, I was either referred to as 'Miss O'Brien's husband' or asked,

'Mr. Whittaker, will Miss O'Brien be joining you for lunch?'

I never once heard her referred to as 'Mrs.' Whittaker! Natalie found this highly amusing. One night, sitting in the lounge Natalie laughingly said, as she thought sotto voce, she had never lived in sin before and how it was quite a new experience. The red-faced matron sitting behind us growled, 'Disgusting! Disgraceful!' and rushed away.

Six days were all we could afford for our honeymoon – and six days of fun and bliss they were, too. We were not quite ready to return to the real world so on the spur of the moment I decided to round off our trip with a visit to my old university at Bangor. It was more or less on the way back to London and wouldn't delay our return.

Since it was unplanned, my wonderful old teacher, Professor Evans, was not readily available to meet Natalie and I was terribly disappointed, but at least I was able to show her the laboratories where I'd worked, my old rooms, and walk with her along the shores where I'd spent so many exciting hours collecting marine specimens.

Just as we were leaving, a student rushed out to say that Professor Evans was free. We went back to have tea with him and after a delightful period of reminiscence, he dragged us to another laboratory and pointing to a table littered with microscopes and equipment, announced,

'That place is always available for you to return and do your PhD, Roger, if your musical career comes to nothing.'

As we drove away, I remarked to Natalie that I would give it one more year – the same promise I had once given my parents, and then I would take up his offer. She smiled and said,

'It's nice to know the door isn't closed, but I don't think you'll ever need it!'

So on 21 August, 1964, we returned to our diminutive flat with a positive determination to overcome any hurdles that got in our way.

Chapter 6

A   *man without love*   *is a*   *man*   *without dreams*

SNATCHING MOMENTS TOGETHER was to become the pattern of
our married life.

As temporary bread winner, Natalie had to return to her
office routine, and I was signed for several weeks of cabaret
through the auspices of my new manager. Some of the cabaret
was in the London area, but the majority of clubs were in the
provinces and, in particular, in the north of England. During
the weeks when I was performing in London, I could join
Natalie for lunch between studio sessions, or collect her in the
evenings for a quick meal, having already done most of the
domestic chores. Natalie in turn would stay up doing the
ironing and other household chores until I got home at some
ungodly hour in the morning.

My parents stayed on in England for a few weeks, but the
atmosphere had become decidedly frosty. In their hearts they
hoped that the responsibilities of marriage would alter my
plans, but the discovery that Natalie was a willing ally to my
ambitions, coupled with the fact that all the O'Briens seemed
to be bordering on the eccentric, did little to endear her to
them.

I am eternally grateful that they never offered, or wanted, to
come to my cabaret appearances, other than the London dates.
At this point, I am going to indulge myself in a trip down
memory lane as I recall some of the funnier experiences that
went to make up my true apprenticeship in my
profession – that is during the ten years I spent on the cabaret
circuit before I concentrated on concert tours.

Cabaret, ladies and gentlemen, in London as in any other
major city in the world, is a sophisticated and genteel additive
to a pleasant evening of gourmet dining and good wines. At

least so I thought, due to the fact that my initiation into the London scene had been in some of the best restaurants and nightspots such as Quaglino's and the Mayfair Hotel. However, money being in very short supply after our marriage, I agreed to do what is commonly known in the business as 'doubling'.

That meant I dashed from one of the smart restaurants, having performed to an audience of 'Hooray Henries, Debutantes and Duchesses' who applauded politely between mouthfuls of caviar washed down with champagne, to many of the sleazier, rowdy, noisy East End clubs. Thoughts of the experiences in those East End clubs make my hair stand on end to this day. Liberally dotted amongst the ordinary London folk was a hefty percentage of gangland and other shady characters, whose presence was balanced by an equally heavy percentage of undercover policemen.

It took me many weeks to discover what was going on, and it was a kindly CID officer who advised me who and who not to associate with, or rather who it was safe to know. Many of the tales that the police told me I took with an enormous pinch of salt. However, having spent one very amusing evening with a group of people after a Saturday night engagement, I picked up the Sunday newspapers to read that they had been involved in a shooting incident only moments after I had left the club. This had a very salutary effect on me. I soon came to realise how dangerous it was to associate with certain elements of my audience. It is impossible to know who, or what, the many charming fans are and I have therefore made it a rule ever since not to get involved unless personal introductions have been made.

Natalie, who had had an extremely sheltered upbringing socially, was terrified of my association with these particular clubs, and begged me to discontinue as quickly as possible. However, we also discovered problems with members of the public from the 'upper crust' establishments, not least Toby, who would appear in the middle of my cabaret act and stand and heckle me throughout my entire performance.

After the first couple of times, I learnt how to outmanoeuvre him, announcing to the audience that the hooligan element in the audience was my father-in-law. I followed with some crack about him still regretting my marriage to his daughter. What did make all of us laugh was that he would put his drinks on my bill, and in one week actually succeeded in drinking more than I was earning! To add insult to injury, he then proceeded to tip the head waiter an equal amount, thanking him for an enjoyable evening.

Natalie's stepmother, Leo, had long since given up hope of keeping track of her effervescent husband, and far from discouraging his nocturnal sorties on my place of employment, actually welcomed the fact that her new son-in-law was successfully deterring him from more disreputable wanderings.

London work was only available for a few weeks of the year, so most of my cabaret time was spent in the fantastic working men's clubs in the Midlands and north of England. Nowadays, with the advent of heavy gambling and very blue comics, these have unfortunately ceased to be the places of family entertainment they were in those days. At that time, they were already gambling clubs, but the clientèle and the behavioural requirements were such that you could take your old granny or your teenage children to one of the shows without offence.

Before I regale you with club stories, I have to endeavour to create for you the atmosphere of those clubs and the life-style. For me they were some of the happiest years – the growing years and Natalie and I talk about them with great affection. Engagements usually ran six nights from a Sunday through to the Saturday night, and I and other artists were like a band of gypsies or travelling circus wandering from place to place and living in 'digs' – hotels being far too expensive.

There were hundreds of these clubs. Only a few could afford the really big names and as most of the time there would be a stripper, a comic, a band singer and then a top 'star' act, all but the stars earned little. Before I discuss the clubs themselves, I must tell you about the digs we lived in. Showbusiness landladies are an institution all their own; wonderful, gruff substitute mothers who look after you in their homes. These are the paragons of the circuit. They take care of you and feed you, but their rules are strict and must be obeyed.

Innumerable times I have arrived and found that there were only two days when bathing was allowed – and half an hour was the limit. Behind the doors was pinned the statutory Rules and Regulations: 'No women in the rooms' 'No slamming doors' 'No loud music'! Often these ladies would appear abrupt, particularly in the north of England where strangers are not made welcome until they have proved their worth, but behind those stern masks beat hearts of gold.

I cannot ever remember getting to my lodgings, even at four o'clock in the morning, without my landlady having stayed up to greet me with a cup of tea and a huge cold snack laid out on the table. Many are the times that I have forced myself to eat a mound of sardine sandwiches and fruit cake with the guilty knowledge that the dear soul had been waiting up for me all that time, whilst I was having a beer with the boys.

There was one hilarious incident that I will never forget. It just so happened that Natalie had got time off work to join me for that particular week. My manager had advised me that there was an excellent boarding house in this large town, far and above the usual quality of such lodgings, although it would cost me a couple of pounds more than usual.

I collected Natalie from the station, and we drove through the suburbs of the city, eventually finding the street, tracing the address to a rather magnificent house. On ringing the doorbell, we were greeted by a rather portly, highly made up and very enthusiastic landlady who proceeded to rush us to what she called 'The Bridal Suite'. Natalie's face was a picture when we entered the room, which was completely decked out in lavender coloured satin with gold trimmings as far as the eye could see, with a huge canopied bed!

'This,' our landlady announced, 'is where I keep all my best people! No rubbish and all the stars have stayed here, and I think you're going to be a star, lad! We have the usual rules and regulations and one of them is that it is best if you use the front staircase on all occasions. You will be given a key, as I will not be waiting up for you late at night.'

And with this, she left us to unpack.

Shortly afterwards I left for my band call at the club, leaving Natalie to rest in her elegant lilac boudoir.

The week opened well; the audiences were good and during the day I played golf, or we drove out into the countryside. By the Thursday, Natalie decided that she didn't want to run around too much and spent the day resting back at the lodgings. Our landlady's son had asked me if I would care to accompany him on his rounds collecting rents. As I hadn't seen much of the town I thought this was a good idea and off I went. It seemed curious to me that at all the places we stopped at to collect the rent, some very glamorous ladies greeted the landlord with a big smile instead of the usual grumbles I had expected. But it wasn't until I returned to our lodgings to find Natalie doubled up with laughter and bursting to tell me her story that the questions were answered.

She had spent the afternoon reading and had suddenly been taken with an urgent desire for a cup of coffee. Unable to find our landlady and lost in the maze of the great house, she had decided to explore. She had gone down the forbidden corridor and back staircase to be met by some glamorous and delightful young ladies, who had taken her to the kitchen and plied her with the coffee she so craved. From their state of dress and from the conversation, it took Natalie but a few short moments to realise that that side of the house was in fact a high class brothel, and what I had been doing out on the road was collecting the rents from the girls who didn't live in!

But not all lodgings were as glamorous or interesting. In fact, our very first Christmas was spent in Manchester in such circumstances that, had we not been newlyweds with an enormous sense of humour, it would have been a catastrophe. Natalie drove up, and we moved into lodgings on Christmas Eve. This particular landlady was one of the few who was not a warmhearted old soul, but a mean, very rude, mealy-mouthed harpy. There were two very hard beds on top of a cold linoleum floor with one gas fire and a television set; thin curtains and hardly any bedding; no easy chairs to sit in and watch the television – you had to curl up on the bed. We could only get the room warm by pumping coins into the gas meter and, as it was a particularly cold winter, I seemed to spend my entire time going around the croupiers at the club, gathering two shilling pieces from their change boxes.

The club itself was enormous fun, but for Natalie it was a revelation. She had never seen striptease before and was a bit embarrassed. However, she was quickly put at her ease, helped mainly by liberal whiskies handed to her at every possible opportunity. As for me – I had a most enjoyable performance, more like a party! The ladies wept into their whisky and the men into their beers every time I sang a Christmas song. We staggered out of the club at four in the morning, laden with bottles of champagne, oranges and cheddar cheese that the club owners had thrust upon us. We returned to our freezing lodgings, clambered into bed, wrapped ourselves in blankets, toasted each other out of tooth mugs with the champagne, and giggled like a couple of teenagers, all the time feeding the gulping monster of the gas meter in our efforts to keep warm.

The following morning we scoured the town for somewhere to have a traditional Christmas lunch, but to no avail. So we returned to our room, once again to huddle around the little fire whilst eating the oranges, some nuts and cheese and downed another bottle of champagne. Finally that night we found somewhere to have a meal – a Chinese 'take away' in one of the suburban streets of the city – and sat in the car ravenously eating out of cardboard boxes, vowing that the following year we would have a proper Christmas somewhere.

I could tell dozens of stories about the different kinds of accommodation Natalie and I had to share whilst I was on the club circuit; instead I'll get onto the clubs themselves. As I've noted, one got to the clubs on a Sunday afternoon to be greeted by traditional tatty, stained carpets, endless mountains of empty beer mugs and the stale smells of beer and cigarette ends. The dressing rooms, (except for the 'star turn') were usually next to the kitchen and the staff lavatories, so, added to the unsavoury garbage smell, the all-pervading stench of the urinals managed to reach into every corner. But come show time the lights, the bustle of waitresses, the air of excitement, the babble and the sight of people just out for a good evening successfully masked all the ugliness.

Throughout the cabaret entertainment, which as I said earlier consisted usually of four acts, the slot machines and gambling tables were forever in motion, providing a cacophony of background noise. The serving of drinks never ceased, and I quickly found that I was extremely grateful that the good Lord had endowed me with a strong loud voice, as even the best of sound equipment could never overcome the noise of battle below the footlights. And I do mean battle! On some occasions, although the clubs had strict rules and regulations on behaviour, there were outbreaks of drunken brawls. On my very first appearance, second after the stripper, I found myself singing louder and louder as two gentlemen proceeded to hit each other over the head with beer bottles as hard as they could; the rest of the audience paid little or no attention to them until the blood started to flow somewhat liberally. At which point, I stood at the very front of the stage and yelled at the audience,

'Watch me! Not them!' and took them straight into an audience participation rendering of 'Michael Rowed The Boat Ashore'. Somewhat incongruously, everybody joined in, whilst between them ran bouncers and bloody combatants. Such incidents usually resulted in the people involved being 'black balled' from the clubs. All clubs were on a membership basis and designed for family entertainment. Fortunately, not too many incidents of this kind occurred for discipline was strict.

Northern humour is dry and to the point. If they don't like a particular act, the cat-calls and boos make it quite obvious. When Shirley Bassey was just starting out, she appeared at one of these clubs during an especially rowdy evening. Apparently she was nervous and not at her best that night. After two numbers the cat-calls and boos were so bad the master of ceremonies marched out on stage in front of her, grabbed the microphone and with a deep northern accent bellowed,

'Settle down! Settle down! Be quiet! Give the poor cow a chance or I'll put the bloody comic back on!'

Raucous laughter followed but Shirley managed to finish her performance that evening with true professionalism.

My performances seemed to attract single individuals hell bent on 'testing' me. One night in Leeds, the club had a most peculiar layout, a huge stage with only six tables directly in front and with a huge mirror so positioned that you could see yourself all the time you were performing. Forty tables were placed on either side of the stage, so you had to keep turning from side to side to entertain the entire audience.

During my very first night at that club, everything appeared to be going well until a gentleman rose, and climbed onto the stage. He calmly walked across, hitting the microphone as he passed, creating a boom and screech throughout the sound system. I carried on, pretending that nothing had happened.

Five minutes later, he walked back on, doing the same thing. This he did four more times, until I was beginning to lose my temper. There were odd titters of amusement from the audience and I was now extremely hot under the collar. Fortunately my act then came to an end. I stalked off backstage, fuming.

'Who was that?' I growled to the club manager.

'No idea, son!' he said, grinning.

I walked back to my dressing room, muttering under my breath about drunks and damned fools. Natalie was waiting for me there and since in those days an artist was allowed to go into the main club after the show to have a bite to eat, we worked our way towards a table for two. I was still seething with anger and Natalie was doing her best to calm me down when an enormous figure loomed behind my chair and a huge hand gripped my shoulder.

'O God!' I thought as I looked up into the face of my stage opponent, 'there's going to be a punch-up!' Suddenly the face above me split into a grin from ear to ear and the big hulk said to me,

'Eee lad! You're fine! You'll do great!'

I was thoroughly but pleasantly surprised and asked him why on earth he had tried to ruin my show.

'Eee, I'm on t'Entertainment Committee at this club,' he said, 'and I was waiting to see if you were the kind of turn we'd ask back again. If you could stand up to my nonsense, then you could stand up to the folks hereabouts. So I was just testing you! Got that! Just testing you!'

He then decided to join us while we ate and bought us a bottle of champagne. I experienced many examples of this kind of barracking and testing; at certain clubs the same faces appeared every time, usually with big grins, with comments to the effect that I hadn't been beaten by the system yet!

My experiences were not uncommon. Any entertainer who appeared on that circuit will get a misty look in his eyes and the inevitable smile will flit across his face with the memories of those times. It did not matter what your status was – star or support act – we all mixed in together and, as in the army, friendships were forged which remain firm to this day. The difficulty with keeping such relationships is our gypsy way of life; flitting about over countries and continents, it is often years before you find yourself returning to the same city and seeing the old familiar faces.

My generation did not become involved in the kind of drug taking unfortunately so common among young performers today. True enough, we had our share of vices – notably drinking and 'playing around'. But even then it was never as serious or as frantic as these activities appear to be today and a lot of it was more or less light-hearted in spirit. Certainly there were plenty of young ladies about willing to 'oblige' a lonely fellow, homesick and heartsick from weeks on end staring at the four walls of his hotel or lodging room. But amongst all my friends of that era, I don't remember any serious hurt inflicted or any outrageous scandals. I'm sure it was largely due to the fact that we never stayed in one place long enough to become deeply involved.

The pace was frantic. If you were appearing at a club in one part of the country, and booked for television in another, you simply drove from club to theatre through the night, grabbing a greasy bacon and egg breakfast at a motorway café, did the television show and drove back again in time for the evening's performance. You just didn't let yourself feel tired until, after weeks on the road, you finally returned home and to the disgust of wife or husband, collapsed for days on end, sleeping as and when it was necessary. (Sometimes I find that my pattern is the same today, but with a slightly more elegant way of running.)

Saturday nights, after the last show, a party inevitably 'happened' and many a Sunday's journey to the next town was undertaken by decidedly fragile individuals who then had to struggle with the inevitable band calls and rehearsals.

On arriving at a new club, you were never quite sure what was in store for you; not least of which could be a group of musicians ready and eager to distort or destroy the accompaniment for your act.

My greatest luxury today is travelling with my own band of musicians, who are used to my every mood and music change. But in those days I was totally at the mercy of the resident musicians. My travelling essentials were, of course, my clothes, my guitar and an old holdall filled with my precious

112

orchestrated band parts. The clothes and guitar could be replaced, but those tattered pieces of paper were gold dust.

The worst of the travelling around was done in winter with nightmare drives through ice, fog and snow. An audience will accept no excuses for your non-appearance. Even when you are ill you must appear, and with gritted teeth next day read the critics announcing that you have lost your voice and that you can no longer sing without the benefit of pleading violent influenza! There was one occasion when I thought that neither I nor the audience would show up and that was at Redcar on the northeast coast of England.

It was mid-winter and, as fate would have it, Natalie had chosen yet another week of terrible weather to join me. After some twenty minutes of trying to find the sea-front, we finally found the road that led to the club, but the sea seemed to be between us and the entrance. Gales had lashed it into twenty foot high waves that threatened to wash away the road itself. We managed to get through without the car seizing up, found an alleyway behind the club away from the flood waters, and parked the car.

The next joke was to try to get in through the front door as no amount of hammering on the back entrance received a response. Knee high in rushing water, we thumped and banged on the front door, waiting for somebody to answer, soaked to the skin with every wave that broke over the sea wall. Finally a man appeared, unbolted the door and let us – plus several gallons of water – in at the same time, then slammed the door behind us, trying to shut out the tide. We were shown into a darkened cabaret area where another man sat swinging his legs over the edge of the table – this was the owner, who greeted us with a cheery grin. I asked him whether the show would be going on that night. He told me not to worry as they would sandbag the doors once the audience arrived. But would the audience come?

'Oh yes, lad! They'll all turn out to see you – we've got bookings paid up to the ceilings.'

And he was right! That evening as I waited in my dressing room, I watched the audience arrive clutching dripping umbrellas and encased in wellington boots and macintoshes. Carrying plastic bags they hurried to the nearest toilets to change out of their soaking clothes and into their finery. True grit!

The drummer in the band had offered us rooms in his house, and a cup of tea and a warm bed were all we were looking forward to as we left the club that night. But to our horror it was to be yet another of the 'lodging nightmares' as we had begun to call them. His house was totally unheated and there wasn't so much as a gas fire, metered or not, in our room. As we fell into bed, shivering and shaking, we realised that there was hardly any bedding either. With the temperature way below freezing, there were only two sheets and a thin blanket! We gathered all the towels we could find, all our warm clothing and our coats and sandwiched them between the sheets and the blanket. We then huddled together in one of the single beds, hoping bodily warmth would keep us from freezing to death!

But, back to the clubs. Considering my 'family entertainment' image today, I'm sure a lot of people will be shocked at my revelation that for ten years of my life I shared my 'show time' with strippers. But that, as they say, is showbusiness. Most of the strippers were in fact delightful ladies who you could meet at a tea party without questioning their occupation. Some of them, however, were a bit more raunchy. Raw would be a more apt description.

Later in this book I will tell you of my very last engagement involving a stripper, but that is a story on its own. Anyway after years of having bare boobs and bums flashed in front of my face, coupled with the realisation that the mood of club audiences was changing along with new comics, who were becoming decidedly filthy, I put a 'No Strippers' clause in my contracts. This limited the number of clubs willing to engage me and it did take quite a time before I was in a financial position to dictate my own terms.

During those years Natalie enjoyed a couple of entertaining moments of her own backstage. For many years one of my regular London engagements was the American Forces Club in London. Some of these shows were in the afternoon but that did not deter GIs from putting away enormous quantities of alcohol. One particular Sunday afternoon Natalie came down to join me as we were off on the road that night after the show. Fortunately for her, Joan Rhodes was my support act that day.

Joan was billed as 'The World's Strongest Woman' and her biceps would frighten a Suomi wrestler! It was traditional for Natalie to walk down to the wings to see me successfully onto the stage, at which point she'd return to the dressing room to tidy up. On this particular day, half a dozen drunken GIs decided that she was going to join them for a drink whether she liked it or not. As she tells it, from nowhere Joan appeared and literally lifted two of these over-enthusiastic lotharios off their feet, at which point three more grappled with her. She quickly floored the lot of them, then both she and Natalie barricaded themselves in the dressing room. Ignorant of all this I returned after my show, walked through the door, and was jumped on from behind in a wrestler's neck-hold and nearly strangled until Joan realised it was me.

On another occasion in one of the northern clubs, the support act was an 'exotic dance' team, consisting of brother and sister. We all had to share the same dressing room and when Natalie returned there as I went on stage, the brother and sister offered her a drink. Very pleasant, Natalie thought. The sister then proceeded to question Natalie about our sex life. Somewhat taken aback, Natalie assured her that everything was absolutely all right between us. This lady then proceeded to tell Natalie that she was a sex therapist and that her brother in fact was a homosexual but she had managed to convert him!

Natalie had thought that by now she had heard everything over the last few years of following me around the circuit, but this left her with her eyes out on stalks. When I finished my act, she grabbed at me nervously and told me that she would not be sitting backstage waiting any more. This had been more than she could take, and she never came down to the clubs again – at least not until my status merited my own private dressing room where she could hide away!

Many of the club owners or managers were as colourful as their establishments and none more so than Sandford Goudie, who was in charge of the Fiesta Group of clubs in the northeast, mainly Sunderland. He was to become one of our dearest friends, our two families remaining closely interlinked over the years. He is now the millionaire owner of one of the largest manufacturing groups in that part of the country.

It was Goudie who took me out of my supporting act role and gave me my first 'star' billing. I'll never forget the faith he placed in me and the gamble he took. Had he been wrong it could have cost him a small fortune and done serious damage to his professional reputation. I'm gratified to say that his decision paid off – for him as well as for me; Goudie set the precedent that I was able to use for years afterwards in dealing with the clubs.

After I had attained sufficient status to dictate more of my own terms and had the 'No Strippers' clause written into my contracts, there was still one gentleman who managed to 'catch' both me and my management most successfully. When you read the story you will realise precisely why I have not given his real name, but I am sure he will recognise himself and hopefully laugh!

The first time I played his club, I was told by my agent that it was an exclusive country club, with superb amenities such as squash courts, indoor swimming pool etc., and that it would be a fabulous week, combining work with relaxation.

It sounded too good to be true but I agreed, mainly because I was in one of my 'keep-fit' periods and dreamed of losing pounds, pleasurably, whilst working! I should have known things weren't going to quite work out that way when I had trouble even finding the place. After driving around country lanes asking every walker the way, I finally drew up to the entrance. As I walked into the foyer with Irene Collins, who was by then my manager, she said to me,

'Roger, what are those ghastly stains on the carpet?'

I jokingly replied, having glanced around,

'Probably blood, dear!'

To be brutally frank, the whole place stank of urine and stale beer, barely disguised with a liberal use of disinfectant. Threadbare scarlet drapes hung limply across grimy windows and cheap imitation brass light fittings dangled crookedly on the walls, themselves covered with last decade's flocked paper. The smells, the decor, everything, had the flavour of a Victorian hospital that had been turned into a seedy boarding house.

As I looked around repelled, the opening line from one of Bette Davis's wonderful films came to mind,

'What a dump!'

Irene and I were shown to the cabaret room, where some old drudge was lethargically sweeping away the debris of the previous night's shindig. On the tiny stage one of the other acts was already rehearsing, so Irene and I pulled chairs off a stageside table and sat down to wait our turn. Then the trouble started. Mr. 'A', our employer, came down to greet us, smiling most charmingly. He apologised profusely for keeping me waiting, and said,

'We've only got the stripper to rehearse, and then the time is all yours.'

'WHAT!' yelled Irene. 'You know Roger never works with strippers now!' She drew up all five foot six of herself in front of this massive man, scarlet with indignation.

'Calm down!' he said, smiling and patting her on the shoulder. 'I promise you, her act is the height of good taste!' Irene dragged him away from me to the back of the club where a heated debate ensued.

However, as I was to find out later, Mr. 'A' could charm the devil himself, and Irene returned to me somewhat grudgingly with, 'Well, I suppose this one last time won't matter.'

I was talked around, although firmly convinced that the audience – my family audience – would not sit through such an indignity. But no! He was right. There on opening night were mums and dads, teenagers and grannies, who seemed to take the whole proceedings as a normal occurrence.

Having established that all would go smoothly, Irene departed for London leaving me to enjoy the rest of the 'amenities'. Only there weren't any; no swimming pool, no nothing. Furthermore, the hotel rooms were as pokey and threadbare as the entertainment area. I resigned myself to a thoroughly boring week, but it only took one night to discover that I was in for far more amusement than I had bargained for, or ever want again!

The larger-than-life owner was carrying on a vendetta with his equally large and tough wife, who in turn was being given support by a pair of even larger and tougher brothers. Apparently she had already laid him out cold with brass candelabra on at least two occasions.

He chose the second night of my week to throw a little

117

champagne party after the show – his wife having gone to her brothers'. The guests consisted of him, myself, and eight rather attractive young ladies who were training to be hotel receptionists (but what they were learning there I dreaded to guess!). There was much hilarity and downing of bubbly, until suddenly a stony silence fell across the room. There in the doorway stood his wife, hands on hips, an expression on her face that would have stopped a charging rhino!

'What's going on?' she bellowed.

I have never seen people scatter so fast in my life. That is all except Mr. 'A', myself and the girl next to me who had been over-indulging and was incapable of moving at any pace! 'A' just sat there beaming while the insults flew thick and fast. I think he was enjoying himself hugely, but I was so embarrassed I didn't know what to do next.

As by this time the hour was nearly five in the morning, by far the best escape seemed to be seeing the near-unconscious girl to her much needed bed. So pleading an act of gallantry, I hoisted her to her feet and with one arm supporting her made my exit, leaving husband and wife to fight it out.

What I didn't know was that all the 'students' were housed in caravans at the end of the garden. As the summer dawn light hit the fogged girl's eyes, the excess of alcohol hit her stomach and she dragged me to a patch of nettles to obey nature. But she was so unsteady on her feet that her final lurch sent me spinning into the nettles with her. Every square inch of my face, hands and neck was covered in stings. By the time I handed my violently ill companion to her friends in the caravan, the pain was such that I vowed to keep away from 'A' and his 'parties' and never to return to this particular club.

As I made my way back into the hotel foyer, longing for my bed, I was greeted by 'A', stark naked and roaring with laughter. His wife had tricked him out of their flat and locked the door, leaving him to his own devices.

'Oh God!' I said. 'You can't stand around like that! Everybody will be getting up soon!'

'No problem!' he replied, arm around my shoulder. 'There are two beds in your room, and after a couple of hours sleep I'll send somebody to get my clothes.'

We proceeded to my room only to discover the thin curtains

wouldn't keep out the daylight so we pinned a blanket across the window.

I was just dropping off to sleep when he whispered,

'Have you got a gun?'

'What?' I yelled, sitting bold upright in bed, all vestiges of sleep gone. 'Of course I haven't got a gun! Why?'

'Oh just a thought,' he mumbled, turning over, 'Her brothers might be back later, and we'll be in trouble!'

'*We'll* be in trouble! You mean *you'll* be in trouble!'

'Oh no!' he yawned, 'You too, you were there!'

End of conversation, as he snored his way into a deep sleep. I lay there rigid, waiting for the expected pounding on the door, until eventually the hour, the excitement and the remains of a bottle of champagne enabled me to doze off.

Next morning, his bed was empty. I went down to breakfast – or maybe it was lunch by then and in they came, Mr. 'A' and wife, mooning like lovers, all last night's hysterics forgotten.

The rest of the week was reasonably quiet, but there was always a threatening undertone and a battle of wills apparent in every conversation. By the Friday night I had been lulled into a false sense of security and in all innocence joined him in the bar after the show. Suddenly we had the company of two blondes and two sets of 44D cups.

'This one's for you, Rog!' he offered, generous to a fault, nodding towards a pretty face at my right shoulder.

'Oh no! Don't start that again!' I pleaded, 'Don't get me involved!'

But it was too late – at that exact moment a familiar hush fell on the room. There was Mrs. 'A' with that same thundering look on her face.

'Don't start on me,' I yelled, grabbing my pint of beer and retiring as far from the grinning playboy husband as I could. Fortunately this time she displayed a sense of humour. After a few moments of verbal abuse they left cheerfully together.

I was to work once more for him about two years on, but that's another story which involved Natalie and which I will relate later. My last sight of 'A' on this occasion was of him loading a crate of champagne into my car with a big wink, and a,

'Thanks for a good club week and all the entertainment!'

119

Chapter 7

Keep alive   the   dusty road

MY DAYS OF kindergarten schooling in showbusiness were over. I was now beginning to learn a few hard facts about my professional and personal life – not all of them easy to swallow. Gone were the carefree, irresponsible days of the bachelor performer, a wandering minstrel happy enough with a few coppers in his pocket and a little black book of telephone numbers. I was riding high with the first blush of newly married bliss, but came suddenly down to earth with the realisation that my private life, my family life, was fated forever to take second place to my career. The demands of my profession had first call and Natalie and I would be facing many long, lonely separations.

It is one of the sad faces of our business; a young, starry-eyed girl marries a performer, filled with dreams and expectations, then quickly reels under the impact of a lifestyle far different from that she'd planned. Of course there are men who face similar problems when married to female performers. In either case, it's not surprising the divorce rate in showbusiness is so high. Fortunately for me and Natalie, she'd been involved with show people for several years and knew more or less what to expect. Not that it made the separations or the loneliness any easier; it just cushioned her from any sudden shock.

Immediately after our honeymoon Natalie went back to work. We had no grand design for the future other than to persevere and to succeed and, rather vaguely, to start a large family one day. So it came as rather a startling surprise to be offered the job as surrogate parents for our friend Hal's son, Brett. Following his divorce Hal had been given custody of his son, but now he faced a dilemma. He'd been offered an excellent job on an oil pipeline in Iran, with the stipulation that no wife or children could accompany him. We appreciated his problem; it was a suggestion difficult to refuse, so we agreed that between ourselves and Brett's other godmother we would somehow manage to take care of him. Of course we were in no position to have Natalie quit her job to take care of him full time. However, since he was now in daily nursery school, we arranged for Brett to stay with his other godmother during the week and we would have him at the weekends.

Our tiny flat had only one bedroom, so we developed a routine of putting Brett to bed in our room until we retired, then switching him to a foldaway bed in the drawing room. The routine worked fine and we were all managing happily with the arrangements, until the more-or-less inevitable happened. Shortly after our first Christmas together Natalie announced she was pregnant.

We were overjoyed. Nevertheless, there was no way we could manage in that flat with Brett and a child of our own as well. We sat down one night and, dizzy with delight, began making plans. Prices of property in London were exorbitantly high, so we decided to find a place in the country. In any case Natalie wanted to get out of London. She was already finding my absences a strain, which the anonymity and impersonality of life in a big city only made worse.

'It'll be better for the baby, and for Brett, too,' she said. 'And at least during the summer I can potter around the garden when you're gone.'

All very well, that, but where to get the money? The price of a country cottage then was not unreasonable, but laying our hands on any kind of hard cash was not easy. True, I was working most weeks, but low down on the Playbill with a commensurately low salary. By the time I had paid travelling and professional expenses, there wasn't an awful lot left over. Putting my earnings together with Natalie's, there was still not enough cash for a down payment. And even if I could scrape a deposit together, what bank manager or building society would grant me a mortgage? I was not exactly a good risk.

Perhaps needless to say, the news of an expected grandchild was greeted with much enthusiasm by Natalie's parents and Toby recommended we buy a home of our own as a solid investment in the future. I was too proud to tell him we couldn't afford to buy but, as the weeks went by and we went around in evermore depressing circles, Natalie quietly went away, met her father for lunch, and explained the position. He never hesitated a second. Forthwith I was summoned to his office and he pushed a cheque across his desk towards me, with words I will never forget,

'Here you are, my boy!' he boomed. 'Don't throw good money after bad by renting. You can pay me back whenever. I'm sure it won't be long because you have the will to succeed. I want to see you and Natalie and any children as settled as your business will ever allow.'

I tried to refuse, although I daresay my heart wasn't really in it. Toby, on his part, would brook no discussion on the subject. I took the cheque, thanked him for his generosity and banked it in our 'Fighting Fund'. Armed with Toby's help, I faced my bank manager with new ammunition and got him to listen to our plans. We intended to find an old cottage, perhaps a bit on the dilapidated side, and restore it. This would be cheaper to buy, and we could suit the restoration to our taste over a period of time, which would also help the financial strain.

Natalie meanwhile was feeling fit as a fiddle and told her boss she would continue to work until she was seven months gone. That would bring us to July, at which time Brett would move in with us permanently. We would all stay on at the London apartment until the baby was three months old, then move out to the country to start a new family life together.

How idyllic it all seemed! Not a cloud on the horizon, until the day in June when Natalie returned from a hospital check-up ashen faced. Fighting back the tears, she told me that her examination showed the foetal heart beat to be very weak; her doctor had told her to expect the worst. She was ordered to bed, not in hospital, but at home. For the next three weeks she remained there, following to the letter the doctor's orders.

I was on the road those three weeks. On my return, the doctor called me in after examining her and told me that the baby was dead. Further, Natalie was fighting labour, which was both mentally and physically unhealthy. He told me the only thing to do was induce labour and, since no hospital bed was immediately available, it would have to be at home. Tearfully, Natalie agreed.

When Natalie had recovered sufficiently from the emotional and physical shock, we once again set about looking for a country home. It was the sensible thing to do for Natalie's well-being and in any case we both still wanted to have a large family. While I worked Natalie scoured the countryside and as soon as I had a free day or weekend she'd drag me off to view derelict properties with 'promise'. Some of these properties showed little promise of anything but total collapse. Frequently, after visiting cottages listed for the first time, we would break down in fits of laughter, wondering how anybody could write such incredible lies when describing homes for sale.

A 'third bedroom' usually meant a box six foot by six under the eaves of the loft, where even a midget would have to stoop. 'Slight damp' was a euphemism for streams of water running down the walls. 'Has potential' meant it was time for the bulldozers to come in.

But at last, one drizzly day in November, at the end of a depressing day viewing hopeless cottage after even more hopeless cottage, we passed our 'dream cottage' with a 'For Sale' board outside. We didn't have an appointment, neither were we listed with that particular estate agent, but we decided to take a chance and ring the bell. What could we lose?

We were in luck. The owners were in, and in fact openly desperate to sell. They welcomed our poking and prying into every corner and two hours later, over a gin and tonic, we shook hands on a deal, subject to the usual surveyor's report. Natalie and I fairly danced our way out to the car and, as with any first home buyers, by the time we were half way back to London we'd decided which bedroom was whose and Natalie had chosen the colours of the wallpapers.

Within a few days – the survey having turned up no serious structural faults – that fabulous cheque of Toby's was in the solicitor's hands and I'd found a local country mortgage society willing to take a chance on me.

In the midst of all our excitement about our new home, it occurred to me that the cottage was rather isolated. Well, I thought, a puppy would be just the thing for Natalie and Brett, so off I went scouring the pet shops for a surprise gift. And, since my next engagement wasn't until two days after Christmas, and we would be spending our first civilised

Christmas together, I would make the puppy a Christmas present. So on Christmas Eve I drove out of town on some pretext and returned home with Barney – our first bulldog.

Puppies are wonderful creatures – but maybe not so wonderful in a cramped London apartment. What a mess he made! What energy he displayed! Just watching him and Brett rolling around on the floor in a tangled web of torn newspapers exhausted me. Thus it was with a sigh of relief that some three weeks later we saw our few pieces of furniture loaded onto a removal van, knowing that at the cottage there would at last be a garden for our two energetic pups to romp in.

Our timing, however, was not of the best. January is traditionally dreadful in England, but this one turned out to be Arctic. On moving day we were suddenly hit with a snow storm. As we left for the cottage ahead of the van, I wondered whether the removers would follow or turn back and head for the safety of their warehouse. But as we slipped and skidded towards the final hill before home, I saw the van doggedly hanging onto our trail. Then, just as they pulled up to the cottage and began to unload, the storm turned into a blinding blizzard.

The next few moments were like a reel from an old Mack Sennett silent comedy film. The moving men raced back and forth, from van to cottage to van and back again, dumping the furniture in the first room they came to. They slipped and slid and skidded, hanging precariously onto our few modest sticks of furniture, while Natalie and I stood by helplessly, not sure whether we should cry or fall down laughing.

Finally, leaving furniture, cartons and tea chests filled with odds and ends piled high in the room, the men climbed back into the van and slithered off into the blizzard. In moments they disappeared in a shroud of white, leaving behind just the echoes of grinding gears.

Back indoors, Natalie and I stood contemplating the pile of furniture and boxes, wondering where to begin.

'At the top,' I said eventually, answering her unspoken question, and we set to work shifting cartons and tea chests, trying to bring some semblance of order to the chaos. Little Brett, now six, pitched in too, unpacking such vital items of equipment as mugs and spoons, tea bags and the kettle, and a

Twenty years on. Irene and I did it all on a handshake.

"Save the Children" Christmas Concert at the Albert Hall in the presence of H.R.H. The Princess Anne.
Delight as my "Greatest Hits" goes quadruple platinum and the presentation is recorded on Canadian Television.

After 22 years, another gown and mortar board as I enter the Court of Patrons for the Royal College of Obstetricians and Gynocologists charity 'Birthright' whose research into birth defects is so close to my heart.

Then there were seven...left to right standing: Jessica, Guy and Emily, seated: Lauren and Alexander.
Below: Guy and Jessica caught with me by our intrepid home 'press photographer', Natalie.

B'Nai Brith Awards 1980. Natalie and I meet fellow recipient Kenny Rogers.
Below: Grand Ole Opry debut with Minnie Pearl, Roy Acuff (Mr Nashville) and old friend Chet Atkins.

Left: Safari in the bush with lifelong friend Terry Matthews, 1982.

Right: Congratulations from skipper Pat Hemple. My first marlin and all the action on film!

Below Right: Natalie joins the Masai housewives for a lesson in handicrafts.

Below: With Alan Root, internationally renowned wildlife filmmaker and old school friend plus 'Million', a household pet. "Aardvark a million miles…" His joke not mine!

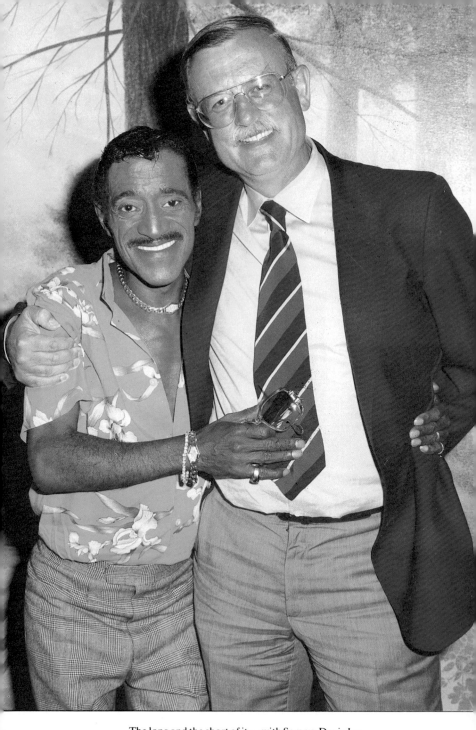

The long and the short of it — with Sammy Davis Jnr.
at Harrah's, Lake Tahoe, Nevada.

box of biscuits we'd thoughtfully packed for emergency rations. Moving the smaller items wasn't too difficult a job, but when it came to shifting beds and large pieces of furniture up the narrow, winding staircase, the struggle nearly brought on two apoplectic strokes. Finally, red in the face from the exertion and thoroughly fed up, we got the job done and returned to the kitchen for a mug of tea.

'Gosh it's cold in here!' chattered Brett as we sipped the tea. For the first time, the cold hit us. Till then we'd been so occupied with our exertions we hadn't noticed. Now we realised that the only heating in the entire house was the fireplace in the drawing room. In the kitchen stood an ancient boiler which we had been assured would provide us with all the hot water we'd need; at the moment it stood empty. In any case, I got the distinct feeling that Natalie didn't know how to work this antique.

'Why don't we light a nice fire in the drawing room and huddle around that with our tea?' Natalie suggested brightly. A great idea, except that when I braved the cold and the snow to go out to the coal house, I discovered that the previous owners had departed with every last scrap of coal. There were no logs either, unless I wanted to chop away at the timbers in our ceilings, an idea that for one fleeting crazy moment I found very tempting in the circumstances.

What a thoroughly miserable group we were! I was freezing and furious. Little Brett was freezing and pouting, his lower lip trembling. Natalie was freezing and trying to check the tears as she searched through the cartons looking for blankets and a hot water bottle. Barney, the pup, was freezing and whimpering, no doubt wondering in his little bulldog brain what tough luck had brought him into the household of these incompetent humans.

'The pub!' I exclaimed. 'There's a pub not far down the road. We can get a hot meal and warm up for a while.'

'It's snowing outside,' Natalie said.

'And it's icicles inside,' I retorted. 'We'll all perish with hypothermia if we don't go someplace warm for a while and get some hot food inside us.'

It was certainly one of my better ideas. The warmth as we entered the pub wrapped itself around us like a blanket. There was a fire in the hearth, the aroma of something cooking somewhere and a buzz of friendly chatter at the bar. And at once we perceived the difference between country living and an urban existence. Maybe it was our forlorn appearance, but I don't think so. We were strangers, but were made welcome by the landlord and the customers. As we unfolded our tale of woe, heads nodded in sympathy and drinks and food pressed upon us. Never did sausages and mashed potatoes taste so good!

After an hour or so we said our goodnights and headed for home, steeling ourselves for the cold, uncomfortable night ahead. But lo! our tale of woe had not gone unheeded. There on the doorstep was a huge bag of coal, a sack of logs and, so thoughtfully, some commercial firelighters. Anonymous gifts from new neighbours. I felt like Bob Cratchett out of *A Christmas Carol*, my family saved from a miserable Christmas at the last moment by a friendly ghost. I felt like shouting out, 'God bless us one and all!'

In a few minutes I had a roaring fire going in the hearth and the three of us plus Barney were curled up on the sofa, snug and safe and feeling a whole lot better about things. Eventually, Natalie put Brett to bed with a hot water bottle, then she and I wearily climbed the stairs to our own bedroom. Undressing swiftly, we threw ourselves under the covers. No sooner had our bodies hit the bed when it began slowly to inch its way across the floor towards the opposite wall. We lay there, clutching each other, shrieking with laughter until we finally came to rest some ten feet from where we'd started. Well, you can't expect a three-hundred-year-old cottage to be built on anything but a slope, can you?

Since then we've moved house twice and I've been clever enough, having learned from experience, to be on the road at moving time. No fool I!

The following spring my personal manager called me to tell me he was leaving on a trip to America with another of his artists, who was then riding high on the hit parade. That was perfectly acceptable, except for one small oversight on his part. Although NEMS Enterprises, particularly Vic Lewis, were my agents, my personal manager had arranged for all contracts and cheques to be sent to his home address. Off he went to

America without altering the arrangements. Three weeks passed, then four . . . then five and six. Not so much as a postcard from him. We knew he was in Los Angeles but precisely where we didn't know; neither did NEMS.

Panic began to creep in. I had just three weeks left of confirmed bookings that I knew about, after that I was in trouble. Not only was I running out of bookings, I was running out of money. Natalie and I drove to his London flat and, peering through the letter box flap in his front door we could see piles of mail on the hall carpet, many of the letters clearly addressed to me – envelopes filled with bookings, cheques! What frustration seeing those envelopes lying there without any way to get at them! I tried NEMS but they said they couldn't help unless I had a list of possible bookings they could follow up and get contracts redrawn. I must say their enthusiasm in my time of need was underwhelming.

I was down to my last week of work. As I floundered about, wondering where to turn next, Natalie's temper snapped. Natalie is a lovely, smiling, more or less easygoing lady, but if you stretch her rubber band too far – look out! Now, with no sign of my elusive manager, no work and little money, she sprang into action like a tigress. First she began ringing around the clubs I had played before, acting as my manager, recouping some lost dates. Then she charged down to the NEMS offices and began badgering them and Vic Lewis to get off their chairs – to put it politely – and do something constructive. Every day she would be down at the NEMS office, notebook in hand, poised like a spider to pounce on poor Vic. He finally tried sneaking into his office through a back door, but that didn't work. Natalie found him out.

One day, in desperation, he called in a young German lady who was then working for Alan Blackburn, his partner, and said to her,

'Try to do something with Roger Whittaker, will you for God's sake, before his wife drives me completely crazy!'

She called me in and we chatted for a couple of hours, during which time I gave her a list of all my engagements to date. Over the next two days she managed to fill in twenty-four weeks of work, which she proudly presented to Vic. He looked at her results, handed the papers back to her and suggested that she take over my career – if she wanted to. She did want to. The young lady's name then was Irene Korff – she is now Irene Collins – and twenty-one years later she is still my personal manager.

Irene's faith in my talent and my prospects is something I will never forget. When we met she had both a secure and well-paid position with NEMS Enterprises but a few months later, after a surprise and secret marriage to Joe Collins (father of Joan and Jackie) she decided to risk everything and devote all her energies to my career. Her courage in making such a decision was as great as were her rewards for the first eighteen months small. On average over that period I handed her the magnificent sum of fifteen pounds a week. She never so much as blinked at these crumbs.

Somehow Irene had seen something in me, an image nobody else had perceived. She knew what she wanted and within days of our new management agreement – strictly verbal – she began remoulding me, something even Natalie had never dared to try. My hair and beard were trimmed to respectable lengths. My faithful old brown suit, the very sight of which had made Joe Collins think his bride had lost her marbles taking me on, was ceremoniously burnt and replaced by a neat pin-stripe. My stage kit, which had given rise to my being labelled a folk singer was quickly abandoned. My new image was silk shirts, well cut jackets and trousers. The truth of my father's old adage, 'You have to spend money to make money!' came home to me for the first time. I saw a dramatic increase in BBC radio and television bookings and my place in the cabaret world rose to new heights.

Watching all this from the wings, Natalie smiled in approval and returned to the country to enjoy home-making, knowing I was in good hands. To this day she and Irene can fight like a couple of wildcats – but it's on a business level. They remain good friends, respecting each other's qualities, and when a particular battle is over it's done and forgotten. It is an amazing coincidence – although I'm sure astrologers would find it no coincidence at all – that these two ladies who dominate my life were both born on the eighth of August. I jokingly tell Irene that had I known her birthday when we'd first met I might not have agreed so readily to join forces. An

Irish 'Leo' and a German 'Leo' is perhaps more than any one man can take!

Bursting with energy, Irene soon arranged a recording agreement with an independent producer, Denis Preston, who was to become my guide during the most formative years of my recordings. My brand of music could never be catalogued under one specific label, but that didn't bother him. What he wanted from me was originality. He encouraged me to write more and more without worrying about the commercial possibilities of my songs. This I did faithfully, producing some of the most diabolical songs I've ever written. Of forty songs, only four or perhaps five were of any value, but at least it was a start in the right direction.

Another of his great inspirations was to record a live cabaret performance. To do this properly and create the right atmosphere he arranged for a live audience to come into the studio, which he'd had decorated as a night club. He then proceeded to wine and dine them and, as the proceedings became ever merrier, I made my appearance. The results of all this faithful attention to detail is one of the most authentic cabaret recordings I have ever heard, enhanced by the superb recording quality that only a studio can produce. The audience of course enjoyed it all thoroughly and to this day members of the Fan Club who were there recall the event and our meeting after the show.

The date of the recording is etched in my memory yet further because of the news I'd received that morning. My elusive – and now ex – manager, after a silence of seven months, was heard from via a radio news bulletin. Natalie and I were driving into London for a rehearsal when the news reader announced that the 'star' and his manager had been arrested at Heathrow airport for alleged possession of drugs. We were so shattered that I had to pull the car over to the side of the road for a moment. When I'd recovered my equilibrium sufficiently to drive off again, Natalie and I argued heatedly over the circumstances that could have led to the disintegration of someone who, however unreliable, had never shown any inclination toward the use of drugs.

We had driven on just a short distance when, to our utter astonishment, we saw at the side of the road the very person. I figured the newscast must have been wrong and stopped to pick him up. For a minute or so the entire situation seemed unreal, as though the past seven months had never happened. But when he started talking about current events, we realised that the radio report had been accurate.

I'd always thought that if ever I saw him again I'd hit him first and ask questions afterward, but now, as I saw this pathetic, broken human being, all anger drained away. I said to him, calmly and unemotionally,

'Before you go on about how all this came about, I must tell you that I now have a new manager and that you and I will never work together again.'

The tale he told us then was as pathetic as his appearance. A typical Hollywood story; all too typical, I might say. As soon as he'd arrived on the pop scene in California, he and his 'star' had been given the 'celebrity treatment'. There was round after round of those nauseating, so-called glamorous parties where nobody really knows you, wants to know you or gives a damn about you, but so long as you remain a 'celebrity' you're invited. At one of these 'spectacular' jollies LSD was slipped into the drinks.

Apparently it was a very heavy dose because both he and his star had to spend some time in hospital; worse yet, he explained, they were hooked. And once hooked, he couldn't escape the habit without long-term professional help. Whether he never got it or never even sought it I don't know. Frankly, driving along in the car was not the best place for an in-depth conversation on such a serious matter. In the event, being 'busted' at the airport turned out to be just what he needed; a short, sharp shock humiliating enough to make him come to his senses.

I believed his story but was nonetheless resolved never to associate with him again. Since then, down the years, we've had chance meetings on the street but no more. I've kept track of his fortunes, however. Although all worked out reasonably well for him in the end, he has been dogged by tragedy and sometimes I wonder whether I'd been a bit too inflexible, too dogmatic with him and should have offered him a hand in friendship when he needed it most. But that's all in the past and with the benefit of hindsight. The past is the past.

Chapter 8

Let me be your sun

'BACK AT THE ranch,' as they say, Natalie was working her fingers to the bone, sanding down beams and learning new skills such as plumbing, wiring and plastering. During the holidays Brett flew to Iran to join his father. We'd send him off, duly labelled, then wait anxiously for news of his safe arrival, each time firmly convinced the airlines would lose him and he'd wind up in New Delhi or Timbuktu. However, although his baggage sometimes did take unscheduled tours to places far and strange, Brett himself was never mislaid.

For Natalie, immersing herself in the building and decorating line was as much therapy as art. Two further pregnancies had ended in sadness until finally, after batteries of tests and even surgery, she was told by a specialist that she could never have a child of her own. We refused to abandon all hope but each in our own way threw ourselves into work to avoid fruitless, morbid dwelling on what might have been and what apparently could not be.

So, while I was on the road, Natalie painted and decorated, wired and plastered, sanded and scraped, doing a beautiful job on the old cottage. She not only worked herself ragged, but to avoid becoming completely housebound interested herself in the fascinating folklore of the area in which we lived – East Anglia. The oldest documented and inhabited part of England, it has many strange stories to tell. Natalie set about researching into these tales, visiting centuries old churches and graveyards, poring over moulding documents, poking about in ancient burial mounds and dust-covered record books.

She began to scribble stories about these ancient folk tales and often, on those nights I was home, we would light a fire in the hearth, put out all the lights to create the right atmosphere,

131

and Natalie would regale me and little Brett with stories of ghosts and ghouls and things that go bump in the night. Brett loved it. Hugging his knees and giggling he would beg her,

'More! More! Tell us more!'

Strange how we all like to be frightened – well, just a little!

Professionally, things were improving, much of it due to Irene's hard work. My writing was also improving, to the point where I was able to record a complete album of my own songs. I even began writing commercial 'jingles', which proved to be very lucrative, if nothing else. So, although I was not exactly setting the world on fire, I was jogging along nicely, thank you, with perhaps a bit more hope than confidence in my heart.

Came the spring of 1967, and the annual Knokke Song Festival in Belgium, to which all the European countries sent a team of five entrants. Just five days before the event the British team's manager, Brian Epstein, (of Beatles fame) found himself an artist short, somebody having fallen ill. Apparently – much to my amazement when I heard it – he'd been following the course of my career and approached Irene about sending me as a replacement.

Irene rang me with a command,

'Meet me *now*!'

She was bubbling over with excitement when I got to her office. Success at the Festival, she said, could launch my career into a new sphere, take me into cabaret on the Continent, open up new markets for my recordings. I must admit that I wasn't as knocked out as she was, although flattered and excited at the prospect. But there was one snag. I was scheduled to be in cabaret in Manchester. If I failed to honour a contract I could be blackballed around the entire cabaret circuit. I could even be sued.

At once Irene got on the 'phone to the club owner and, while I sat there biting my nails, she used every ounce of her charm and persuasive powers. Eventually she got him, albeit grudgingly, to agree to release me.

No sooner had she put the 'phone down than we were off – off to buy new clothes, to meet with Epstein, to find an arranger to orchestrate my music.

Each artist had to sing two numbers at the Festival. I had nothing in my repertoire different enough to make an impression. At the time *Fiddler On The Roof* was playing in London. The music publisher suggested I see it and consider the song 'If I Was A Rich Man', which he thought an ideal performance number for me.

That night as I watched the masterful Topol strut and stride magically about the stage singing the song, I knew I could do it, and would do it well – but I was not Topol. I had misgivings. For my second number I had chosen my own composition 'Mexican Whistler', but it wasn't until our arrival in Belgium that I learned it was considered an orchestral number and that the rules stipulated I had to sing lyrics.

Time was short, too short to find a different song and have the band parts written, so hastily I scribbled some lyrics to my whistling number. I wrote just enough to form one verse and a chorus, bringing the song within the entry rules.

Meantime, totally mesmerised by the speed of events, Natalie waited at home for my news. On the first evening, after rehearsals, I rang her and blathered on vaguely about the big names who were appearing, about the usual chaos of rehearsals and how amazed I was by the amount of attention the proceedings were receiving from the press. As the junior member of the British team I wasn't all that impressed with the Festival's importance; I was more concerned about my pulling out of the Manchester contract and the effects it might have on my cabaret career.

The Festival was a five-day affair. I called Natalie again after my first performance and told her how delighted I was at the audience reaction. Then, on the third day, a BBC producer attending the Festival called Natalie and said to her,

'Do you have any idea of the sensation your husband is causing?'

'Well,' she replied, 'Roger did say they seemed to like him.'

'Like him!' said the producer. 'He's in line for the Press Prize!'

Natalie mumbled something about how nice that would be. It didn't mean much to her and, frankly, when she told me about it, it didn't mean much to me, either. A scroll or whatever, I reckoned. But I was a bit bemused by all the faces around me smiling mysteriously at me and the 'thumbs up' signals I was getting from complete strangers.

I remained completely in the dark until after the final Gala Show. Suddenly, as I was returning to my dressing room to change and return to my hotel, people were grabbing at me, slapping me on the back and yelling at me to go back on stage. Bewildered by it all, I stumbled onstage to meet a battery of popping flashbulbs and was at once surrounded by other artists and members of the orchestra shouting congratulations. I'd won the treasured Press Prize!

The Press Prize, I discovered, was the award given by the entire press corps at the Festival to the artist considered 'Most Likely to Succeed'. By the flurry of excitement going on around me I understood this must be a more prestigious award than I'd at first appreciated. I was pleased, flattered, embarrassed, flustered, bewitched, bothered and bewildered – all at the same time. It was one o'clock in the morning before I reached a telephone to tell Natalie the news.

I awoke early the next morning, Sunday, with too little sleep and a kind of emotional hangover, a 'downer' after the excitement of the night before. I'd won the coveted Press Prize. Great, I thought. But what does it mean, in the real, hard, world of show business commerce? I showered and dressed quickly; Irene and I were due to fly back to London in a few hours. Then the 'phone began to ring . . . and ring and ring and ring. One of the calls was from Irene. She'd cancelled our flight and booked us out for Monday. We had meetings today, lots of meetings. Everybody and his brother wanted to talk to us, talk about tours, concerts, records – the works!

I 'phoned Natalie and as casually as I could told her there'd been a delay and I'd be home on Monday and asked her to meet me and Irene at the bar at Heathrow airport instead of the arrivals gate. She assumed from my request that we'd have a quiet drink with Irene before she returned to London and we went back home to our little cottage in the country. I didn't disabuse her of that notion. Not, at least, until we actually met at the airport.

'I've only got a couple of hours,' I told her, after a quick kiss and a cuddle. 'I'm off to Paris to cut some singles. "Rich Man", "Mexican Whistler" and a couple of "B" sides.'

Tuesday morning I was in the studio in Paris, cutting the records. On Friday, the two singles were released throughout

Europe. By the following Tuesday I found myself in the Number One and Number Two spots in four different hit parades: France, Holland, Denmark and Belgium. To say that I reeled under the onrushing tide of these events would be putting it mildly indeed. I was staggered. On the continent of Europe I was an overnight sensation, an instant star. In Britain and elsewhere in the English-speaking world nothing had changed but there I was most definitely Top of the Bill. A *Star*!

Star. Funny word, that. The traditional dictionary definition is 'a brightly burning heavenly body of great size'. Of course the more modern sense of the word is listed as meaning 'to have as main performer'. In other words, the person most likely to draw a crowd, fill a theatre, a cinema, a nightclub.

There are, of course, 'stars', and then there are the true stars, the international superstars, such as Frank Sinatra, The Beatles of the 1960s, among others, who could pack a concert hall or football stadium anytime, anywhere in the world. To me the title of 'star' has been so misused and overused it has become almost meaningless. The majority of so-called 'star' performers are main attractions in limited parts of the world; but a 'superstar' is a household name worldwide.

I confess that luck plays a part in true stardom; a matter of being in the right place at the right time to get your break. There are many fine artists around the world whose talents are equal to, perhaps greater than those who have achieved international recognition, but for one reason or another they have never made it big. I confess, too, that I am well aware of my own particular luck, and that I have been blessed with finding my own niche in this very complex and fickle business.

The ladder of success goes down as well as up in show business, a business that more than most is hounded by insecurity and uncertainty. Sudden failure dogs your every footstep, waiting to bite you in the ankle and send you crashing down into oblivion. It's a business in which your career is to a large extent held hostage by the public – a public famous for changing its tastes and its heroes as rapidly and inexplicably as the shifting winds.

I don't think there can be an entertainer in the world, however well established, who like myself hasn't thought on occasion their careers were at an end. Doors open and close with such rapidity that you jump every time a hinge squeaks. You dash through every narrow opening that beckons, afraid the door might shut on you forever. Even now, when I'm blessed with a track record that allows me a certain freedom to pick and choose, I agonise over every opportunity rejected, wondering whether I'd made a mistake, should have accepted the offer of a tour, a concert . . . perhaps they won't ask me again . . . perhaps people will forget about me if I'm offstage too long.

And so, very much aware of these demons of insecurity that come to haunt show people in the middle of the night, when my success at Knokke opened those Continental doors for me I sprinted through and grabbed every offer in sight. My stomach was in knots with a mixture of excitement and fear; excitement over the prospects and the opportunities open to me, fear over the prospect of failure. I knew that this was my big chance, and that if I blew it, another might never come; I'd be a supporting performer in the cabaret bill forever.

With my change of status on the Continent quickly came the understanding that all my hard work on the cabaret circuit until then had in fact been fun and games by comparison. The pace changed from rush to frantic, from drive to overdrive. I not only had to change my lifestyle, but my style of performance. My onstage time doubled from an hour to two hours. Further, I was no longer playing second fiddle to food, booze and gambling, singing and strumming over a hum of activity going on all around me. I now found myself facing a sea of faces concentrating on me!

On my very first concert night I bounded onstage, in my ignorance filled with confidence and rushed through three or four up tempo numbers until I came to the first quiet number. As I paused it suddenly got to me that I'd never heard so much silence in my life. I was so thrown out of gear by the quiet and the audience's rapt attention that when I finished the number my mind went completely blank. I hadn't a clue what to do next.

In that momentary flash of blind panic I discovered the virtue of working with my own back-up band. They came to my rescue by playing the intro of the next song twice, until I gathered my senses. When I concluded the concert, to round after round of applause, I felt ten feet high. My elation at the audience reaction was heightened by the fact that my own material seemed to have gone down best of all. Denis Preston's insistence that I persist in writing my own material was now paying off.

Backstage, amid the congratulations, my elation gave way to quaking knees. The body's natural adrenalin that helps see a performer through, faded away and left me a bundle of shredded nerves. These days I can handle it better but, prior to a performance, no matter how cool and controlled I appear on the outside, inside a volcano is bubbling away. Of course stress creates its own kind of stimulation and I feel it's an essential ingredient in a performer's art. But where it takes its toll is in your personal life. The pressures of performing and travelling tend to strain your relationships with the people around you whom you love, but sometimes cannot deal with. Before my success at Knokke sent me spinning around the Continent like a drunk in a revolving door, I'd had the time between cabaret dates for a few days at home every week or so. Suddenly I found myself away for as long as six weeks at a time without taking a break.

We therefore decided that wherever possible Natalie would join me on tour and when next Brett went off to his father for a holiday she met me in Belgium. The change in my status came as quite a shock to her. She was not used to the consequences of my becoming a 'star'. Inevitably I was now encumbered with an entourage, some necessary, some just 'hangers-on', who seem to be part of every star's baggage. More difficult to cope with was public recognition. In Continental cities I was no longer just another face on the street and we found the adulation just a bit disconcerting.

The crunch came one night in Brussels. We'd arrived there, some nine of us, about one in the morning, starving hungry after a drive of two hundred miles and nothing to eat since breakfast. The local promoter told us there was just one large restaurant open that served until two. We dashed over but found the place absolutely crammed with late night revellers, many of whom had been waiting a long time for a table. The proprietor recognised me immediately, however, and with a great fuss and to-do insisted – despite my protestations, I must say – that we jump the queue and gave us the first available table.

Since there were nine of us in the party, sorting out our orders from the menu took a bit of time. As the waiter began scribbling them down a group at an adjoining table came over and asked for autographs. That started a stampede. Before we knew what was happening a great crowd had surged around us, maybe fifty or a hundred people, shoving and pulling and shouting, thrusting menus and pieces of paper at me. Our waiter disappeared in the crush.

By the time the crowd drifted away, happy with its autographs, the head waiter appeared and, apologising profusely, told us the chef had gone home and the kitchen was closed! We were all more than a bit frustrated, exhausted and groaning with hunger, but Natalie became loudly furious, cursing the rudeness and thoughtlessness of the autograph hunters. I was totally embarrassed and felt she was behaving like a spoilt child. And I told her so.

'Those ''damned'' autograph hunters you're cursing so loudly are the same people who are paying for all this and all the bills! Don't ever let me hear you react like that again!'

It was the only time I've ever had to 'put down' Natalie – before or since – and her face crumpled. For both of us it was an awakening to a new experience of how quickly you can come to resent the public attention you yearned for all along; like a suitor, having at last won the heart of his beloved, suddenly finding she's become a pain in the neck.

There are plenty of performers around who feel that way about their fans. But not me, and not Natalie. After that incident we swiftly became humble, sincere in our acceptance of the reality that without the fans interrupting our privacy, without the autograph hunters and all the rest that goes with success, there wouldn't be success. The late American President, Harry Truman, commenting on political life once said, 'If you can't stand the heat, stay out of the kitchen.' That can just as well apply to show business. If you want to remain a private person, become an accountant. To this day we remember this incident and use it now and again when we feel it necessary to remind our children, gently, that what they have is courtesy of Dad's fans, thank you.

Not long afterward another incident in Belgium gave me pause to thank success for my now familiar name and face. Late one night, on some dark road in the middle of nowhere, Natalie and I were asleep on the back seat of a car, being chauffeured to my next tour stop. Suddenly the car screeched to a halt, and angry voices shouted in Flemish. Sleepily, we tried to see what was going on but the glare of headlights all around made it impossible. Suddenly our driver's door was jerked open, he was hauled out bodily and through the open windows on both sides of the car guns were poked at us. Natalie froze. My reaction was to grab the gun barrel resting against my head and shove it up against the roof of the car. (Since my Army days I'm paranoid about guns. I just saw red.)

We still couldn't see anything because torches were being shone straight into our eyes. Amid the confusion I heard our driver shouting out my name several times, his voice hysterical with fear. The guns withdrew. The torches went out. Our doors were opened and we were helped out politely. Natalie could barely stand from shock. Our driver rushed over and explained that the men were plain clothes police manning a road block. There'd been a bank robbery nearby during which three people had been gunned down and the police were taking no chances.

The police were around us now, smiling and nodding. From somewhere somebody miraculously produced a bottle of brandy to revive us. While I tried to explain to the policeman why I'd rather foolishly grabbed at his gun, a photographer appeared and began taking pictures. I then had to sign autographs all round as the policemen laughed and joked and patted me on the back and shook my hand. I suppose it was funny to them but for me and Natalie (and for our driver!) it was a nightmare. All this excitement was too much for Natalie and she left for home the next day.

Natalie never really enjoyed those early tours. She'd spent too much of her childhood uprooted and globe-trotting with her father, an obsessive traveller. She's a creature of order and organisation. She hated – and still does – living out of a suitcase. However, following two highly successful Continental tours, a major European airline came up with an offer even Natalie couldn't refuse – two weeks filming in Russia.

Chapter 9

I've had the great good fortune to journey where I please

THE IDEA BEHIND this public relations exercise to Russia was the promotion of that particular airline's Eastern Bloc travel, with me and my wife visiting all the sights. Fabulous! Except that we soon discovered my 'wife' was going to be portrayed by a professional actress; Natalie would be allowed a small part as an extra in the crowd. I expected a storm of justifiable protest from Natalie, but actually she didn't mind at all, preferring to enjoy the perks of the trip without appearing in the limelight.

There was one further complication. There was no way Irene was going to miss seeing her 'star' appearing in such an interesting production; the problem was she was expecting a baby! The exclamation mark represents surprise all around. Irene had once vowed never to have children. As for Joe Collins, he already had three grown-up children; a son, Bill, and those two famous ladies, Joan and Jackie. At 66, Joe was not all that keen on going through sleepless nights, wet nappies and all the other disruptions that a baby creates. However, to no one's stupefaction, Irene confessed her delight at the prospect of becoming a mother, provided she could continue her career, and Joe, caught up in Irene's happiness and the good wishes of his friends, was soon bursting with pride and stocking up on cigars.

Toby, Natalie's father, was a bit nervous about her going to Russia. He'd been in British Intelligence during the War and afterward, and he knew he was 'listed' in Moscow. The Russian Embassy granted her visa without question, but Toby cautioned her to keep a low profile and to behave while she was there.

Off we went, a motley crew of pregnant manager, 'star' with blonde, buxom 'wife' (even on departure we were filmed, with

140

Natalie playing an extra) several extras from I didn't know where and a film crew I can only describe as wild, funny and, as it turned out, terribly irresponsible.

On the flight, which took us first to Warsaw, we were advised by a Soviet official of all the rules and regulations – and there were plenty of them. We were told where we could go and where we must not go, what activities were permitted and which were forbidden. Most important of all we were warned about currency regulations, the Russians being constantly on guard against black market activities. I'd been told by people who'd been there that Muscovites would buy the clothes off your back for pots of rubles – and anything else Western you cared to sell them. But if you were caught you'd be in big trouble.

We were also warned about exchanging our money – it had to be only at official agencies and at the official rate, which was a small fraction of what you could get for it on the street. In any case, all transactions had to be recorded and the papers kept; you had to declare all money of any kind you brought into the country and all items of value such as jewellery, watches, cameras and so forth. And by golly you'd better still have all those items when you left and a precise accounting of what you spent and what you had left over – or else!

As the Soviet official droned on I kept thinking, 'surely they can't be as strict as all that?' However, on leaving Warsaw we were joined on board by another 'extra' – this one not employed by our producer. Even before we reached Moscow this gentleman was sweating profusely as the film crew just couldn't take him seriously and pulled his leg unmercifully. He kept denying he was Russian, so we decided to play along and pretend we believed him.

When we got to our room in the hotel, it took Natalie all of ten minutes to find the microphone. Out of the window went all her father's warnings as, fuming, she broadcast right into the 'bug' exactly what she thought of her unseen listeners, their phobias, their ancestors if any and informed them, colourfully if somewhat vulgarly, that they'd better switch off at night if they didn't want to be embarrassed. I calmed her down eventually, suddenly quite sober myself after all my joking about spies and rules and regulations, chilled by the realisation that everything we did would be observed and overheard.

We were assigned two charming lady interpreters by the Ministry of Tourism and given instructions that we had to stay in groups with either one of these ladies whether filming or relaxing. All the while, our extra 'extra' tagged along with whichever group he considered most in need of watching. It was a bad state of affairs because we had all come with genuine interest in observing an orderly, happy, equal existence for a people who, there is no doubt, had prior to the revolution suffered considerably from gross oppression. What we concluded was that one oppression had been replaced by an even more oppressive authoritarian regime and that the stories we had heard had solid foundation.

The ordinary men and women in the street were fascinated by our filming, but if we attempted to get into conversation with them, gentlemen in heavy overcoats appeared from nowhere and our audience meekly faded away. Snatched contact with people in the street showed them to be as warm and friendly as ordinary folk anywhere else in the world, and it was extremely sad that we were unable to really get to know them. We had read as much as we could about Russia before our trip and were quickly absorbed in the fascinating places we were allowed to visit and film. The evenings, however, had to be spent in designated places of entertainment – most ordinary bars and restaurants being out of bounds. That way, the authorities could keep all foreigners under supervision.

After a couple of those evenings, we decided to spend a quieter time in a bar where most of the foreign press congregated. It was quite small and only some hundred people were ever in there at one time. We were sitting in a circle of crew and foreign journalists when an inebriated and huge Russian pushed his way into the circle and plonked himself down beside Natalie. The conversation instantly died as he leered at her, then shot his hand under her skirt (one-track minded and straight to the point as I observed later). Trying to push him away, Natalie frantically whispered, as I reached boiling point,

'Don't start anything! Get the waiter to get rid of him!'

But before I could summon assistance, another even larger figure loomed behind the Russian's chair.

'Eez theez man giving you any problems?' boomed a character with a thick accent and, as I nodded my assent, the offending Russian seemed to rise from his chair as a massive fist sent him flying through the air. It was like a scene from a cowboy film. His body literally ploughed its way through the tables and chairs, breaking and scattering them in all directions until he came to rest unconscious against the far wall. Horrified, we sat like zombies expecting the police to appear and cart us all off to Lubianka. But nothing happened except the Russian's friends bundled his unconscious form out and the barman quietly cleared up the mess. Grinning and rubbing his knuckles, our protector picked up the fallen chair and sat down next to Natalie putting his arm around her shoulders. Then, as an afterthought, he enquired of me,

'Your wife?'

'Yes!' I replied, still stunned by the events.

'Oh, so sorry!' he said removing his arm.

'Are you Russian?' one of our group tentatively asked, to which he threw back his head and roared with laughter.

'One of *them*? Never!'

He proudly told us that he was Finnish and, to our anxious questions about being arrested, he laughed even louder. Russians, he informed us, never fight with the Finns. He was the only person who seemed not to care in the slightest about the authorities. We stayed talking for hours and he told us all so much of the history of the Russian/Finnish situation that when I eventually visited Finland in later years, I was able to understand the Finnish people in much greater depth.

While Natalie, Irene, the actors and I did our very best to avoid problems, certain members of the film crew seemed determined to create as much trouble as possible. Two cameramen in particular had been to Russia with other film units in the past, and were under the impression that they could beat the system and knew all the loop-holes. Their naïveté nearly cost us the film and our freedom. Most of their pranks were pure fun – or so they thought!

One night, one of the guys picked up two women in a bar – a Russian and a Swede – and took them both back to his room. Of course the 'Tricoteur' at the head of the staircase noted the fact and called the security guards. Those frightening grey men gave the gentleman and the ladies sufficient time to get the party going before they burst in, catching all three stark naked and cavorting in a most undignified manner. The three were made to stand against the wall with only their hands to cover their confusion, while a lecture on morals in Russia was duly administered. Apparently it is considered quite acceptable for a man to take one woman to his room (although prostitution is not officially admitted) but two women is most decidedly against the State rules on moral behaviour. He had to choose which lady to keep. Diplomatically he kept the Russian girl and discarded the Swede, who was then ordered to dress, and leave Russia on the next plane. The men escorted her out, leaving the cameraman with the Russian girl. The party had lost its flavour, however, and he paid the girl her fee – an alarm clock!

This and other tales were told with great ribald humour, and we all went along with the laugh. What would have worried us sick, had we been aware of it, was the film crew's flagrant disregard of currency regulations. They had managed to smuggle in various foreign currencies which they then exchanged for rubles on the open market (Russians were desperate for hard currency). In retrospect I believe the authorities were allowing the crew to be lulled into a false sense of security, playing a cat and mouse game, waiting for the most propitious moment to pounce – our departure!

We had hired a private plane to take us and some journalists back to Belgium. As we waited for final clearance at the airport, having handed in all our documents to the authorities, the film crew found their usual gathering place – the bar. The airport was packed with people. We sat around waiting, flushed with excitement and anticipation for the flight but tired after fourteen days of filming under strained conditions. We were ready to go home.

All our Russian money had been returned and exchanged and our documents examined so that the numbers tallied with expenditures. You are not allowed to take rubles out of Russia. At the bar, one of the crewmen bought a round of drinks and paid for them with rubles he'd collected on the black market, which he had of course not declared and which, had he had his brains together, he would not have flashed at the bar.

It was just the moment the police were waiting for. No

sooner had he paid, than our planted 'extra' gave a signal, a squad of uniformed men appeared and forthwith the entire crew was marched away. Our 'extra', who until then had been fluently multilingual, suddenly spoke only Russian. He shook his head blankly at all pleadings in English, French and German. A few yards away we watched all this, unable to help, unwilling actually to become involved and frankly alarmed at this turn of events. When the flight crew arrived the captain and the co-pilot were also marched away.

More police arrived. Our papers were inspected minutely. I found my hands were shaking and my palms sweating as I fumbled for my exit documents. We weren't sure what was going on, what the implications might be for all of us. We had all heard that the Russians were adept at trapping foreigners in compromising situations, jailing them and using them to exchange for Russians held legitimately in Western prisons. Eventually, to our immense relief, the police seemed satisfied that our papers were in order. We were ushered together to a corner of the departure lounge and ordered to remain there and wait for the flight crew.

From there we could see into the glass-walled cubicle where the camera crew was being held and questioned. Their faces were ashen, all the tomfoolery and bravado gone. They were obviously scared witless and with good cause. Half a dozen plainclothes police surrounded them, bombarding them with questions which we of course could not hear. Their pockets and hand luggage had been emptied, the contents strewn over a table. For two hours we waited and watched this frightening mime, until finally the offending cameraman was taken away, sandwiched between two policemen. Our pilot was then taken in to talk to the others. When he emerged he was as white as a sheet. He took us to one side,

'Listen!' he said, 'this is extremely serious. There's nothing I can do for the guy under arrest except contact the Embassy and get them to help. But they caught another man with a few rubles – not a lot but enough to prove he broke the regulations. They're threatening to hold us all until they check back into everything we've done over the past two weeks. They could hold us here for weeks and trump up no end of charges!'

Horrified – and, I may add, terrified – we sat and listened to his plan for a quick getaway. His co-pilot was prepared to try to bamboozle them with a trick. Wishing him luck we held our breath as he marched back into the holding room, then watched in awe and trepidation as a play unfolded worthy of a couple of Oscars. The co-pilot (as the pilot had explained) had managed to grab an extra currency declaration form while all the initial chaos was at its height. He'd filled it in to account for the few extra rubles in the man's possession and forged a signature. Now he barged into the holding room, shouting loudly in French and, as shouting seemed to be the only language the Russians took note of, they were thrown into confusion for a moment – long enough for the co-pilot to say to the petrified cameraman,

'Is this what you were looking for, you bloody idiot?!' as he flashed the forged document like a magician with a deck of trick cards – now you see it now you don't.

'You left it on the desk, you bloody fool!'

Given the pressure the man was under, his thinking was quick as lightning.

'Oh, thanks!' he exclaimed with relief. 'They wouldn't let me explain that I might have dropped it somewhere.'

All this in French, mind you, and knowing full well the Russians understood them perfectly. But the ploy worked. The police, now thoroughly confused themselves by all the Gallic shouting and gesturing, gave the man back his passport and told them all to leave. Captain, co-pilot and cameraman walked over to us, the latter much abashed and embarrassed by our dirty looks. The captain then said quietly,

'Pass the word. As soon as my assistant is through currency control you all move to the gate and run for the plane. I'm going to get the engines started and as soon as you're all aboard we're getting out of here!'

'Are we cleared for departure?' I asked, bewildered by his conspiratorial attitude.

'No!' he said. 'But it won't take them long to discover that currency document's a phoney and that'll be curtains for all of us! So when I say "move" – you *move*!'

By now we all felt as though we were in a movie, a spy thriller of some sort. Surely this couldn't be real?

As nonchalantly as we could we gathered together our hand

baggage and sauntered casually toward the exit. It was no mean feat. We were as nervous as an atheist in church. Our 'extra' was still with us, too, keeping a watchful eye on our movements. At a signal from the captain we started walking fast, then broke into a run down the exit ramp. Our 'extra' gave a shout and ran after us, grabbing at our arms, trying to stop us. But nobody was stopping for anybody! We rushed onto the tarmac and scrambled into the plane – our 'extra' still with us. The door slammed shut and the plane began taxiing down the runway.

'Fasten your seat belts for immediate take-off!' came the order.

The Russian gave a resigned shrug and buckled himself in.

'Okay, okay, I might as well stay with you a bit longer!' he shouted.

Once airborne the captain announced that we might still have to go back if they sent fighter planes after us. What a thought! For some twenty minutes we sat there in total silence, frightened out of our wits. Not that we thought they'd shoot us down, but if they forced us back to Moscow after all this, it was to the salt mines for the lot of us! Finally, after a while, the stewardess suggested we all have a hefty drink or two. As far as I was concerned it was the best idea I'd heard all day. About an hour later, much alcohol having hit many a fluttery stomach, we were all feeling a lot better. Even our Russian 'minder' had to admit it looked as though Moscow didn't think us important enough to chase. By the time we landed at Warsaw to refuel we were still shaky but congratulating ourselves and our pilots on a narrow escape. In the transit lounge, our Russian friend bought us a round of drinks and wished us luck.

'Here's to you all,' he said, raising his glass, 'and I hope I never see any of you ever again! *Zdarov'ye!*'

With that he threw back his vodka glass and drained it with a gulp. Poor chap, I guess he needed it as much as we did. With a look of utter relief on his face, he waved goodbye and disappeared into the bowels of Warsaw airport.

But our troubles were not yet over. The captain gathered us together again and said he wanted to get out of Warsaw as soon as possible because the Russians could well persuade the Polish police to hold us. However, there was one small snag. All reachable Western airports were fogged in and accepting no incoming aircraft. He asked us to take a vote on whether to hang about and take a chance on being arrested, or fly out at once and take a chance on finding an open airport – a definitely dangerous option. We did not hesitate a moment. We voted instantly and unanimously to get the hell out of there and take our chances with the weather. The way I saw it, if the pilot was willing to chance it, so was I.

As we took off again, we were a much subdued crowd compared with the laughing, excited group that had landed at Warsaw airport just two weeks before.

Airborne, the captain said he'd keep us informed about his destinations. First he tried Frankfurt but air traffic control refused him; landing was impossible. Other possibles on his list came and went as we flew blindly over Europe until he told us,

'We're nearly out of fuel, we'll have to land somewhere. Prepare for a forced landing!'

A few of the ladies were crying by this time, and I was becoming terribly concerned for Irene, worried that with all this she might lose the baby she was carrying. We began to descend then, all of us clutching the pillows and blankets placed on our laps. We heard the creak of the undercarriage being lowered and we knew the crucial, life-or-death moments were upon us. Yet the sudden, shouted command – *emergency positions!* – caught us by surprise. Quickly we assumed the crash positions we'd rehearsed, hearts pounding, teeth clenched, minds silently screaming.

There was a sudden flashing of yellow lights and we felt the wheels hit, bounce, grip, the engines roar into reverse thrust, the brakes catch . . . and we began slowly to taxi down the strip. A great cry of joy and relief came from our throats. Tears, too. Out of the windows we could see nothing but fog. We had been talked down through the pea soup right to the last second, with visibility of just sixty yards.

There came to us the shaky voice of our captain.

'Ladies and gentlemen – welcome to Antwerp!'

Knees trembling we disembarked from the plane to be met by a gathering of fire engines, ambulances, newspaper photographers, reporters and TV crews. Our flight had been monitored all over Western Europe shortly after we'd left

Warsaw. Our pilot, who had broken just about every rule in the book to get us out, was whisked away by Belgian officials to give an account of the entire incident.

All this because of the stupid, illegal activities of one man who paid with six months in a Russian jail, and the stupidity of a second man who was lucky enough to get away with it. We discovered later that the entire sum involved amounted to fifteen dollars! Just for that had an irresponsible person put at risk all our freedoms and indeed our very lives.

While writing this Russian episode, Natalie and I reminisced about the events and concluded that at the time we were anxious and worried, but perhaps not as frightened as we should have been. It was only afterwards, when we realised how close we had come to vacationing in Siberia or being killed in an air crash, that we nearly died of heart failure!

Natalie murmured something about,

'Wasn't it around this time that people in the business started saying, "stick around the Whittakers and anything and everything can happen!"'

Too right!

Chapter 10

What makes a woman act so mean

THERE WAS ONE incident during our Russian tour I omitted to mention because it leads so beautifully into another aspect of my new-found success. An unashamed and inveterate womaniser before my marriage, I now found that the tables were turned. Suddenly the hunter became the hunted. Even in the sub-zero temperatures of a Russian winter!

During our trip we were struck by the singular lack of attractive Russian women. If they existed they were hiding somewhere, because all we came across were dowdy, decidedly unfemale females. If they wore make-up at all they wore it badly, garishly; bleached blonde hair was harsh and brittle, cut in the European styles of the 1950s. Their clothes, too, were twenty years behind the times. Buxom figures were encased either in shapeless sacks or squeezed desperately into outfits two sizes too small. The latter was the sight that greeted us as we sat down to our first breakfast in Moscow.

A bored and aggressive waitress began taking orders from the film crew seated around our large circular table – bored that is until she came to me. Not a word of Russian was spoken by any of us so there must have been something about my expression, because before I could say '*Nyet, nyet!*' (No, no! I've learnt since!) my head was clamped to her ample bosom and my hair ruffled as though I were a small child. Natalie made no attempt to come to my rescue, nor did the crew, whose leers and lascivious remarks needed no translation.

From then on breakfast was total embarrassment. The next morning she appeared at our table the shocking epitome of that expression, 'let it all hang out'. Her black uniform dress was cut down to the navel, with a tiny apron tied about her waist. She apparently refused steadfastly to serve any table but ours and when not on a trip to the kitchen hovered behind my chair, waiting for my coffee cup to empty. My draining the last drop and replacing the cup was her signal to step forward, drape one huge boob over my shoulder and dip the other orb into my empty cup, at the same time fondling my hair and crooning soft words of Russian into my ear.

It didn't stop there. As soon as we'd finished our meal and headed for the exit, off would come her apron and she'd rumble after me in hot pursuit. Natalie would march straight ahead, choking with silent laughter, as I would try to disentangle myself from her octopus arms – no mean feat as she was built like an Olympic wrestler!

By the third day I was debating whether to miss breakfast entirely or don a false beard and moustache. Bravely, however, I took my place at the table, braced for yet another onslaught. To my intense relief, but to the disappointment of everybody else at the table, whose mornings were being made ribaldly risible by my discomfort, my admirer was gone. I suspect the management had decided her conduct was too decadent even by capitalist standards. In her place was yet another gorgon, this one the complete opposite physically, a pinch-faced matron, thin as a pipe cleaner. She giggled incessantly whenever she filled my coffee cup, apparently having gotten the Word.

The phrase 'the trouble with women . . .' began to take on new meaning for me. I am not alluding here to the wonderful female fans whose constant support means so much to an entertainer (no disrespect to my male fans!). However, if trouble is going to come, you can be sure it will be from that small portion of women who react in the craziest way when they come into contact with a personality in the public eye, be he entertainer or politician. Sometimes problems occur because of these fantasies, but at other times there is a more sinister method behind the 'madness'.

I have never seen myself as a performer with a macho image; a Tom Jones, for example. I'd be totally dumbfounded if some lady thrust a pair of panties at me onstage! Nevertheless on several occasions I have been left shocked and confused by the attentions of amorous females.

Until my success at Knokke I had never been a target.

Suddenly, having made the front pages of many Continental newspapers and magazines, I became 'desirable'. I suppose I was a bit naîve, considering my years in show business, but I wasn't yet hardened or cynical enough to expect the worst from people, or suspicious enough of their intentions. Traditionally, I've always been ready to pose for family snapshots after a concert or during the signing of autographs. Most performers will oblige. Soon after Knokke, however, I experienced my first 'set-up' and it was so well done that I didn't realise I was being set-up until hit with a sledgehammer the next day.

After one particular concert on the Continent I was approached, among the crowd of autograph seekers, by a positively gorgeous young lady of perhaps seventeen or eighteen, accompanied by her mother. There was the usual banter during the signing of the autograph and then the mother asked me if she could take a picture of her daughter with me. Of course I obliged, and as the flash went off the girl smothered me with kisses. I laughed, a bit embarrassed, but thought nothing further of the incident until I was rudely awakened the next morning by a telephone call from my hysterical press agent.

'What on earth were you thinking about?' he screamed down the 'phone.

Still half asleep I hadn't the slightest idea of what he was talking about. But the tone of his voice jolted me awake.

'What's wrong?' I asked.

'What's wrong? What's wrong?' he shrieked. 'Have you seen this morning's papers?'

'Of course not,' I said. 'It's seven-thirty in the morning. Anyway I don't read the foreign papers!'

'You'll read this one!' he exclaimed. And he went on to explain that his 'phone hadn't stopped ringing ever since the early morning edition of the paper had hit the street. He was besieged by demands for a follow-up story to the front page leader which came complete with a large picture of me in passionate embrace with a young starlet – guess who?

The headline read,

'ROGER WHITTAKER IN AMOROUS EMBRACE . . . ?' And it got worse.

The girl's mother was her press agent!

My first and only worry at that moment was that the British press had got hold of the story and telephoned Natalie, asking for comment. I didn't bother about a denial, leaving it to the man paid to do that job, but called Natalie at once. Fortunately, being wise to the ways of some of the gutter Continental press, the British newspapers had completely ignored the story. As for Natalie, she knew me and the ways of wily women well enough to raise not an eyebrow in surprise. But she did suggest I keep somebody at my elbow in future to prevent a repetition of such shenanigans.

Thank goodness I heeded her advice. Just a few days later, following another concert, I was approached by a beautiful blonde wearing a thin silk dress that left nothing to the imagination. There was a fellow with a camera behind her and she asked if she could have a picture taken with me. I confess I was about to say 'yes' when my minder literally swung me off my feet away from her while taking a swipe at the guy with the camera.

'Lucky I was here!' he exclaimed. 'She's one of the most notorious porno artists in town!'

I was beginning to understand. To this day, unfortunately, I have to keep a wary eye on photographers. It's incredible the things some journalists will do to photographs to concoct a story with a whiff of scandal.

Those two incidents soon after the Knokke Festival were my initiation into the ways of women with trouble on their minds and greed in their hearts. But to tell the truth, that kind of woman is comparatively easy to handle. I can even understand the motivation of the woman who seeks nothing but publicity for herself. What I fail to comprehend is the motivation of those women who seem hellbent on getting into your bed, by any means fair or foul. Most of them are so coldblooded about it one wonders what on earth they would get out of the experience did they in fact succeed. Perhaps it would be an ego trip for them to be able to boast they made it with a 'star'.

The first determined effort of this kind I can recall was actually relayed to me by my own wife! In fact, now I think of it, just about every time something nutty happens to me Natalie is somehow involved; it's impossible to disentangle her completely from such events. On this occasion she joined me halfway through a tour and found me complaining bitterly about the promoter's girl friend. She was obviously 'on the make' and I couldn't discourage her. She was a nuisance, following me everywhere, even entering uninvited into my dressing room before a performance, a time when I need to be alone to psyche myself up for the evening.

Finally I persuaded Natalie to take the girl out for dinner one evening and keep her out of my hair. Tired as she was from travelling, Natalie readily agreed, seeing an opportunity for an early night. So when I returned to our hotel room in the early hours, expecting her to be fast asleep, I was surprised to find her sitting up in bed, a mischievous grin on her face.

'Boy, have you got a problem!' she said.

Apparently it had been quite an interesting evening. At the bar in the restaurant Natalie had offered the girl a pre-dinner drink. Either the bartender got a bit heavy-handed with the spirits in the cocktail or she was not used to drinking, or both; in any case, that one drink annihilated any inhibitions the poor girl might have fostered. To the amusement of all and sundry at the bar and to the astonishment of Natalie, the girl leaned forward and in a whisper that bounced off all four walls of the room she asked Natalie's permission to go to bed with me!

Temporarily lost for words – no mean feat in itself – Natalie finally blurted out that the girl had better ask me herself, since I was the subject in question. Mortified, the girl took great pains to explain, much to the fascination of all at the bar, that she had only linked up with the promoter in the first place as a means of snaring me. But, she said, she didn't want to upset Natalie, hence the request for permission. Nonplussed by this direct approach, but actually feeling sorry for the girl, Natalie gently talked her into returning to her hotel room to sleep off the impending hangover, assuring her it would all turn out right in the end.

'I didn't know how else to handle it,' Natalie said. 'She was on the verge of hysterics.'

The strategy did not work. Far from being subdued, next day the girl bounced up to me brightly and asked me right out, had I thought the matter over? As flummoxed as Natalie had been, I decided the only course of action was to give her the kind of lecture I would have given my own daughters.

Chastened, she took my advice on the chin, I'll give her credit for that, but cheerfully she told both of us she'd remain a friend forever. Much to our surprise, she did. For years she would appear in the most unexpected places all over the world but never behaved in anything but the most proper manner again.

Not all such situations are so easily reconciled. On the road again, and after an energetic afternoon playing squash, I returned to my hotel and dived straight into the shower. Squeaky clean and refreshed I turned off the taps and grabbed a towel. A rustling noise from the bedroom made me pause. I peeped around the door of the bathroom, for in spite of the 'Do Not Disturb' signs I invariably hang outside my door, hotel maids religiously ignored these requests for privacy. I did not want to prance out of the bathroom and surprise one of them. The surprise, however, was on me. There on the bed, making herself at home, plumping up the pillows, was a not very attractive but very naked lady.

Quietly I closed the door and turned the shower taps back on again while I considered my next course of action. I had it! Natalie! She'd know what to do! Poor Nats, I knew I was asking a lot of her but silently I picked up the telephone handset in the bathroom, hoping to hell the sound of the shower would drown out my conversation, and dialled home.

I was not warmly greeted. A decidedly distraught Natalie answered the 'phone, her voice the jagged edge of a rusty tin can. In the background I could hear the unmistakable screeching of a child in the throes of rebellion; in this case, I was told icily, our Emily, aged ten months, was in the process of redecorating herself, Natalie and the kitchen with her afternoon feed. (I tackle our brood in a later chapter.)

'Well, speak up!' Natalie shouted down the 'phone, trying to provide counterpoint to Emily's howling.

'I can't,' I whispered.

'Oh, no, don't tell me you've lost your voice. I'd better call Irene and tell her to cancel tonight's show.'

'No, it's not that,' I said. 'There's a naked woman in my bed.' I felt just as foolish saying it, believe me, as it reads.

'So, what am I supposed to do about that?' said my wife, not sounding as perturbed as I thought a wife ought to be in such circumstances. 'Do you know who she is?' came the next

155

question. Ah, curiosity at least!

'Yes. She's the wife of one of the guys in the hotel,' I replied.

'Well in that case the answer's simple. Call down to the desk and have her removed, but don't bother me with your problems!'

Hmm, most unsympathetic, I thought. But as our conversation was obviously at an end, I hung up and sat down on the edge of the tub, mulling over the problem.

Natalie was right, of course. The thing to do was have her removed. However, the question was how to do it without getting myself caught in the middle of a husband and wife battle. Would he believe I was just an innocent party? Would she drop me in it to protect her virtue? I sat there so long the lady must have thought I'd disappeared down the plug hole, what with all that water running. Fortunately she never ventured into the bathroom to investigate the longest running shower in the world, giving me time to find a solution. And at last it dawned! I would pretend I didn't know who she was. I grabbed the 'phone again and dialled the front desk.

'Sorry to bother you,' I said, 'but I'm faced with a delicate problem. I've just finished my bath and discovered that a lady has obviously mistaken my room for hers and has in fact gone to sleep in my bed. I wonder if a maid could quietly wake her and save the lady embarrassment. I'll remain in the bathroom until this is done.'

I could almost hear the man wink as he said,

'Of course, Sir, I'll see to it immediately!'

The shower still running, I put my ear to the door and a few moments later was rewarded with the sound of voices coming from the bedroom. Then came the sound of the room door closing and with a sigh of relief, I closed down Victoria Falls and emerged from my hiding place. Natalie and I had a good laugh about it when I got home but, as a result of that experience, a few years later the last laugh was on Natalie. Here's how it happened.

Although at this time I was working in Britain, my schedule had been so tight I hadn't been able to get home for six weeks and Natalie was becoming fidgety. As women will do when they're restless, she decided to go to the hairdresser and do some shopping. Passing a lingerie shop she spied a stunningly sexy nightdress and on impulse bought it. On the way home she stopped by our offices and showed the acquisition to Joe and Irene.

'Pretty!' said Irene.

'Pretty damned useless,' grumbled Natalie, 'with nobody to model it for.'

'Well,' said Joe, 'why don't you just take off and go and join Roger? The children will be perfectly all right with the nanny and I'm sure Roger will be delighted to see you!'

What a wonderful idea, thought Natalie. And since every marriage needs a bit of excitement I won't tell him, I'll just drive up there and give him a surprise. So after telephoning our nanny to say she wouldn't be back until the following evening, she set off to drive the hundred and forty odd miles to where I was performing.

I was out when she arrived about seven that evening. But after showing the desk her driving licence she persuaded them to let her into my suite. She also persuaded them to say nothing to me when I arrived, since it was all to be a big surprise. By this time it was all a wonderful joke and, laying the flimsy garment across the bed, Natalie hid herself in the bathroom, ready to jump out when she heard my key in the lock. Unfortunately, the door had a very silent lock and she didn't hear my entrance. Seeing the nightie on the bed I thought, 'Bloody hell, not again!' and quietly closing the door behind me, seething with anger, I found the hall porter and explained the situation.

'Leave it to me!' he announced grandly and with me at his heels he marched back to my room. Crossing the bedroom he yanked open the bathroom door and shouted,

'Excuse me, madam, I think you are in the wrong room. Would you please leave immediately!'

A scarlet-faced Natalie emerged, blurting out that she was my wife. Angry, surprised and disconcerted, I shouted out my confirmation. Natalie burst into tears. The obvious embarrassment and confusion of the hall porter, who no doubt thought he'd stumbled into some marital tangle, only added fuel to my already boiling temper. And as he backed out of the room I yelled at Natalie,

'Don't you ever do that again! It is not funny and I do not

157

need that kind of surprise in my life!'

Poor Natalie! Her wonderful plan had come to this! Her evident distress cooled me down and I tried to comfort her. Soon we were giggling about it and we did make the most of her brief trip. But to this day she will never appear without notifying me first!

One incredible encounter came not face to face with the lady concerned, but on tape. The Fan Club had been running for a couple of years, but not all the mail sorted out by Clodagh, Natalie's secretary, was from fans. Sometimes songwriters would send in cassettes of their songs, sometimes cassettes came from well-wishers. So Clodagh regularly listened to the openings of the tapes before sorting Natalie's mail from mine.

'Mr. Whittaker,' she said one day, 'I'm not sure how to deal with this cassette. Perhaps we should just ignore it,' she said handing me the tape.

'Hi Roger,' the tape began, in a pleasant, cheerful female voice, 'my name is . . . and I have been a fan for many years . . .' and then there followed in the same tone, the most unrepeatable stream of filth I've ever heard! Aghast, I stopped the tape and asked Clodagh to throw it away, but after a few minutes called her back. The woman was clearly disturbed and the fact that she had given her name and even her address posed the problem of how she would feel if ever she should regain her equilibrium and remember what she had done.

I will never know if I did the right thing but I decided to return her tape, with a message to the effect that I was sure she had mistakenly enclosed the cassette, and to save her discomfort I was returning it to her to destroy. We never heard another word but it left us wondering.

Not all approaches come from strangers. I remember the time Natalie's engine boiled over when one of her childhood friends, with a penchant for married men, decided I was going to be her next victim.

Natalie was then spending a lot of time in and out of hospital for a series of nasty operations and this dear, devoted 'friend' would merrily send her get-well flowers and cards while at the same time placing herself in my path at every opportunity. Worse still, she exercised not the slightest bit of decent discretion, but blatantly offered me the keys to her apartment.

Totally undeterred by the presence of Irene or anyone else or for that matter undeterred by my constant rejections, she persisted. In order not to aggravate Natalie's condition, Irene and I decided to keep this nuisance a secret from her.

What neither of us knew was that this 'friend' was able to keep track of my movements and Natalie's hospital visits via Natalie herself. During the course of cleverly devised girl-to-girl chats, she got from Natalie precise details of our personal life. Just as the situation was reaching crisis point, when I concluded there was nothing for it but to tell Natalie the truth about this two-faced 'friend', the woman made a miscalculation.

Fed up with hospital beds, Natalie had checked into hospital for tests merely as an out-patient, in order to spend the night with me in London, where I was doing cabaret. As we entered the ritzy restaurant where I was appearing, the head porter hissed at me as he passed me my mail,

'That woman is here again!'

Natalie and Irene were already halfway to my dressing room; as I pursued them I thought rapidly of what I could do to head off a collision. I caught up with them just as they were entering the dressing room where, in full view on the table, was a large bouquet, two bottles of champagne, and an open message.

'How nice,' said Natalie, smiling as my heart sank, and reached for the note which she presumed to be from a well-wisher. Irene tried to make a grab for it, but too late.

Scanning the message quickly, a message I knew would be filled with ridiculous, amorous outpourings, Natalie's smile vanished.

'I see,' she said, through clenched teeth.

Hurriedly, Irene and I explained the situation. Fortunately, Natalie was well aware of her friend's predilection for other women's husbands.

'Let me handle this,' she said. 'I will leave no doubt in that woman's mind that she'd better try it on with some other woman's husband!' Of course Natalie's language was a bit stronger than than, but you get the drift.

From experience at that particular venue, Irene and I knew what the woman's routine would be that night. Habitually, after my performance, she would swoop past the guard at the door and make a beeline for the corridor to my dressing room, where I'd be talking to other guests. She would plonk herself down in a chair and wait patiently for their departure before making her move. So that night we made sure there was nobody in the corridor but me and Irene (with Natalie hidden behind a large marble pillar). Seeing just the two of us, the lady propelled herself at top speed towards me, arms outstretched.

'Roger, darling!' she exclaimed.

I retreated a couple of steps as Natalie, with a malicious grin, emerged from her hiding place holding bouquet, champagne and note in her hands.

'Yours, I believe,' she said deadpan to her ashen-faced friend, who turned and fled so quickly she left scorch marks on the carpet.

All this may sound as though I'm a bit of a 'goody two-shoes'. Actually I'm as human as the next guy, I really like women, and if my flirtatious nature appears to be going a bit over the top my normally understanding wife quickly administers a figurative clout over the ear. However, I am not the only one to suffer from unwanted attentions, as Natalie has discovered on more than one occasion. Some years ago a male fan for some reason switched his allegiance from me to her and as time went on he appeared to become increasingly jealous of our marital harmony. His letters became so wild we eventually had to consult the police. There was little they could do, they said, unless he actually tried to carry out any of his lunatic threats. For security, we hired round-the-clock bodyguards when in his neighbourhood. Fortunately that particular gentleman was all threat and no action.

Natalie and I have always worked closely together. That's not necessarily a good thing in show business but every time she decides to disassociate herself from my work she becomes annoyed at some mishandling of the business side and returns to the fold to put the matter right. When she involved herself in organising and boosting the Fan Club little did she realise the task she'd set herself or the pitfalls awaiting her. Ninety-nine per cent of the fans enthusiastically welcomed the personal approach she put into encouraging their friendship but there was that tiny one per cent minority who seemed to resent her relationship to me and, in a sense, her acting as a barrier between them and me. The first time Natalie came face to face (or rather foot to leg, as you'll see) with this jealousy it proved a painful experience.

As I've pointed out, my friendly manner with women can sometimes be misinterpreted. I know I ought to be more careful of how I react but that is *me*, and it gets me into a lot of hot water. One evening, while I was on tour in Britain, Natalie and I were scheduled after my show to attend a reception given by the mayor and council of the city. Irene having decided to remain in London, it became Natalie's job to make sure I appeared on time. After my performance a delightful group of people gathered backstage for autographs, including two barely nubile but very attractive teenage girls. While Natalie waited in the dressing room I chatted and signed, unaware of the passing of time. Finally just the two girls were left and it was obvious they were in no hurry to leave. I suppose I was a bit enchanted and didn't rush them. Natalie however, watching the clock, twice came out of the dressing room to remind me I had to change for the reception, and we were running late. The third time she emerged to remind me, one of the girls screamed at her rudely,

'Bloody wives . . . f--- off!'

This is not a remark to address to a lady with a fabled Irish temper. She stormed up to the girls, pointing to an exit sign and bellowing,

'Right, scrubbers – out!' At which point one of the girls took a flying kick right at Natalie's shin. It was perfectly aimed and strongly dealt; you could hear the crack, like a branch snapping off a tree. Natalie staggered backward and slid down the wall, howling in agony, as the girls fled.

We never did make that reception. Instead we spent the next two hours in the emergency department of the local hospital as Natalie's purple, swollen leg was x-rayed and treated. Fortunately no bones were broken but my poor wife limped for a couple of weeks.

'Remind me never again to get between you and your groupies,' she commented wisely. These days she talks only to known members of the Fan Club backstage and keeps well away from me!

161

When show business folk get together and swap stories we all realise that our experiences are by no means unique; certainly not our experiences with women and with fans. Back in the 'good old days' of cabaret clubs, largely due to the nature of our work and our lives, those experiences tended to be a bit naughtier than they were later on. Besides, I wasn't married to Natalie then!

Anyway, I remember the time I was doing cabaret in the north of England and three well-known comedians were at nearby clubs. We were all staying at the same hotel, and arranged to get together after the final Saturday night show before moving on. Compared with the technique of one of those lads, my approach to women took on all the innocence of a Salvation Army conversion job! He was forever getting himself entangled in complicated situations, hoist by his own knavery. On this occasion, he had been stringing along one of the little cocktail waitresses in the hotel bar all week. On the Saturday night, as the rest of us ordered our drinks prior to the traditional exchange of latest gags and showbiz tales, he waltzed in with a silly grin on his face and announced,

'Count me out tonight, fellas, I'm on a winner here! She's asked me back to her place – don't wait up for me!' And, with a lewd wink, he departed.

In those days we were all endowed with a hell of a lot more energy than we can muster today and it was not unusual for us to sit up all night, drinking and talking, then pile into our cars and go our separate ways. At four o'clock that morning the hotel lobby door burst open and a furious comedian marched to our table and threw down his car keys.

'What do you think happened?' he exploded. 'Not only did she live sixty miles out in the middle of nowhere, but when I got there I discovered she had invited all her friends and relatives round to meet me! I had to sit there all bloody evening eating bloody sardine sandwiches, drinking endless cups of bloody awful tea and signing a hundred bloody autographs!'

Religious conviction is a very personal matter and over the years I have resisted all attempts to convert me to one sect or another. I never thought that religion would lead to the strangest encounter – to date – of my career; I pray I never experience a weirder one.

Throughout the world, in many cities, I get requests from small publications for interviews on my attitude toward family life, world problems, ethics and morality. Most of these requests are vetted in advance by my press agent before an interview is granted as it's all too easy to step into a pothole and land up to your neck in trouble if you're not careful with your public utterances on matters moral. However, occasionally the odd 'nutter' slips through the net and I find myself sitting on the edge of my chair, in a cold sweat, wondering how to end the conversation as soon as possible without giving offence.

On this particular day I had consented to give such an interview in Australia. Always nervous about these things, I was unnerved yet further by the appearance of the lady reporter, a woman dressed sombrely in black and pale of face. She spent the entire time with eyes downcast, fixed on her notes, never once looking at my face until the interview appeared to be at a close. Then she looked into my eyes and said,

'One final question. So many of your own songs have such deep messages it could almost be said, couldn't it, that you have been sent as a messenger from God?'

Now that is quite a remark, not to be fobbed off easily with a witty reply. So, as lightly as I could (and praying my road manager would swiftly escort the lady out) I mumbled something to the effect that I was merely commenting on my own experiences in life and that I very much doubted there was any Divine intervention in my art.

She got to her feet, her eyes gleaming.

'Bless you,' she said, 'you still haven't realised who you are – how perfect! May I touch your hand?'

By this time I had an icy river running down my spine.

'Of course, of course, and thank you for your time,' was all I managed to croak.

A brief, feathery touch of our hands and she started to leave, stopping briefly at the door; then, with a beatific smile over her shoulder, she said,

'We will meet again, and you will come to realise that you are His envoy.' And with that she disappeared.

'Jesus!' I exclaimed as the door closed behind her.

'Don't take your Boss's name in vain,' grinned my road

manager, Ken, facetiously.

'Why didn't you rescue me?' I snarled. 'From now on no more fringe interviews, anywhere. Okay?'

'Okay, okay!' he said. 'How was I to know she was that kind of a kook? Anyway, we won't see her again, thank goodness!'

But he was very, very wrong.

Show after show, concert after concert – she was there, in evermore weird garb, quietly smiling as I talked backstage with members of the audience who wanted to meet me. She never said a word to me, just watched and smiled. It made me feel extremely uneasy and I kept feeling my eyes being drawn to hers over the shoulders of the people I was talking to.

Natalie then joined me on this Australian tour, accompanied by Emily, aged three and Lauren, aged one. Unsettled by the long flight and the time differences, the children were a bit fractious and so Natalie remained in the hotel suite with them for the first few nights. Finally, leaving them with their nanny, she joined me backstage one evening. We were chatting to some friends and members of the audience when I saw 'her' beginning to move towards me. Ken placed himself strategically at my elbow. But this time it was Natalie she addressed.

'Lady, you are blessed,' she murmured, taking Natalie's hand and, to her consternation, kissing it.

'I beg your pardon?' said Natalie, backing away.

'Don't worry,' said the apparition, 'I am one of your husband's disciples. I just want to be near your blessed presence. I will follow!' she said and floated away, leaving not only Nats, Ken and me, but everybody there totally dumbstruck.

'Good grief!' exclaimed Natalie, sinking into the nearest available chair, 'where did she come from?'

Ken and I explained about the interview, which everybody thought was very funny.

'Thank heavens,' I began, to groans all around at my inadvertent expression, 'no, seriously, we'll shake her off when we start the one-nighters in two days.'

No such luck.

In every town, at every concert, there she was, always strategically seated in the front row so that at some time during my performance she could rise from her place and reverently place a sheaf of flowers at my feet. By now everybody's nerves were beginning to twitch and on a couple of occasions during a performance I nearly lost track of what I was doing. Several times Ken tried talking to her, gently trying to persuade her to go home, wherever that was. But he gave up when she clasped his hand in hers and said to him,

'You are so close to him that his aura is upon you! Let me be near you and thereby closer to him.' She scared the hell out of him. But maybe that's an inappropriate phrase in the circumstances!

Eventually we consulted the police, but short of taking out a court order to stop her molesting us, there was nothing we could do. Legal proceedings were out of the question – that kind of wrangle and the ensuing publicity no artist needs. So we all decided to ignore her completely and maybe she'd go away, vanish in a puff of smoke or something.

The lady refused to comply and in time she just blended into the background, became part of the scenery. I'm sure many an audience believed she was a 'plant', part of the show. Finally, the long concert tour was coming to an end. A sumptuous farewell lunch had been laid on for the day after the final show, with Natalie and I guests of honour. It had all been splendidly organised at a hotel with long banks of tables leading to the head table on the dais, where Natalie and I were seated. Magnificent bouquets and garlands of flowers were everywhere.

The luncheon proved to be a most enjoyable, relaxed affair, with good food, free-flowing wine and not too many long-winded speeches. There was that general hum of conversation and laughter one gets at these lunches – until just before the coffee. Suddenly, the conversation died away, the laughter stopped. All eyes turned to the door of the banquet room.

And there she stood in a flowing white gown, a massive bunch of lilies cradled in her arms. I was hypnotised, paralysed by this ghostly figure gliding as if on air towards us.

'Help,' whispered Natalie at my elbow, 'is nobody going to stop her?'

The room was as silent as a tomb as slowly she climbed onto the dais and made her way around the table to where I was seated. No doubt many of the guests believed this was some kind of original presentation, an award of some kind. I saw smiling faces below me, faces looking up expectantly.

The apparition stopped by my side.

'You are the risen Christ!' she shouted suddenly. Then, turning to Natalie, she dropped the lilies in her lap and, sinking to the floor, began to kiss her feet. For a second or two the entire place was held in a freeze frame. Then Natalie leaped to her feet, shrieking,

'Get her away from me!'

That broke the spell and started the action again. Dimly I heard shouting from the guests below and from nowhere two burly gentlemen appeared, lifted the woman from the floor and began carrying her, kicking and screaming, from the room. Her last words as she disappeared forever from my life were,

'Mother of Christ, don't send me away . . .'

A buzz of nervous conversation began again. Natalie had to leave the room to be sick. Ken apologised for failing to stop the woman in time, but I just shook my head. It wasn't his fault. It wasn't anybody's fault. It was just a sad, unfortunate incident, the inevitable climax, I suppose to a very strange story. The woman was arrested on a public nuisance charge and was sent away for psychiatric examination.

There's little more to add to this tale, except that for a time this affair, on top of all my other experiences with religious fanatics, affected my song writing. Each song I wrote I examined carefully, analysing its contents for anything that might be misconstrued as a religious message. It took me quite a while to get over it.

To end this chapter on my troubles with women on a lighter note, I must relate how towards the end of one particular tour, a promoter shattered my reputation for being, as he put it, 'up tight, puritanical and without a sense of humour.' The joke he played on me I considered at the time to be a bit over the top but later I was able to have a good laugh about it and even now, when I find myself taking things all too seriously, I think about his 'cure', relax and enjoy myself.

How did he do it? Well, during one year of touring I featured as part of my act a Zulu wedding dance song, using two female backing singers. In all its pristine glory, when the

Zulus ruled a good part of what is now South Africa, this wedding dance was a spectacular sight, with thousands of maidens dancing bare-breasted in front of their prospective husbands. The scene was magically done in the film *Zulu*. All this I explained to my audiences before my number, and then jokingly invited some of the ladies sitting in the front rows to join me on stage and help out my backing duo. There were always a few willing to take up the challenge.

On this particular night, when I issued the dare, there was a great movement from the front rows and dozens of the most outrageously dressed, scantily clad women of all shapes and sizes piled onto the stage and with cleavages bouncing in all directions proceeded to accompany me in the wedding dance. My initial reaction of discomfort and embarrassment quickly changed to hysterical laughter as during the course of that wild song and dance some of the 'ladies' danced right out of their dresses and became topless! The house was in an uproar! My musicians could hardly continue playing, in fact like a bunch of sailors on leave could barely restrain themselves at the sight of all those bouncing and heaving bosoms.

As the number finished to a standing ovation from the audience, the ladies filed off, kissing me avidly as they departed and I wondered first of all how I could get the auditorium back into some semblance of order, and second who the hell had set up the whole thing. A glance at the wings told me. There was the promoter lounging against the sound desk, grinning and winking at me.

Well, I never did regain decorum that night. The audience wouldn't let me and the evening took on the air of a private party. It was without a doubt the craziest concert I ever gave!

When finally I staggered backstage, the show over, a few of the more bountiful 'maidens' were gathered around the promoter and the party began all over again, one which went on all through the night and into the dawn. It turned out that the promoter, fed up with my serious, straightlaced approach, had hired a couple of dozen inmates of the local whorehouse and filled the first two rows of the theatre with them!

Which reminds me of another story . . . but no, there are some stories best left untold. Suffice it to say that anything and everything can happen to you in show business.

Chapter 11

The joys of life weren't rare till this moment

SHORTLY AFTER OUR return from the Russian adventure, Irene resumed scheduling my tours. This meant splitting the year between the Continent and Britain – the Continent because I was so successful there, Britain because I had still to prove myself in my own home country. Naturally this meant I was away from home a good deal of the time, a situation that somehow lasted ten years. Financially and professionally these were ten rewarding years but I can say with hindsight – that most acute of senses – that I made a mess of them. I overextended myself and lost sight of my true values. In particular, it seemed that whenever Natalie needed me most, I was somewhere else.

She had become a real trouper at coping by herself, but that is not the point. For example, soon after the Russian trip Natalie fell pregnant again and once again miscarried. I was somewhere on the Continent while she was in hospital, being told by her specialist not to try again and that any further pregnancies were absolutely out of the question.

No woman likes to hear that, and she rang me, naturally upset. 'I am not going to give up!' she shouted.

It is not easy to console a weeping wife over the telephone. I mumbled something about the possibility of adopting. She stopped crying. 'Would you really consider adopting?' she asked. 'I've never brought up the subject before because I was sure you would never accept somebody else's child.'

I assured her I had no reservations and that as soon as I got home we would look into it.

What, on the surface, seemed to be a simple solution, turned out to be one of the toughest problems we have ever faced. Being in the right age group and not having been married before, with a home of our own and the experience of having taken care of Brett all those years, we thought it would all be plain sailing. However, the first three adoption agencies we approached rejected us within moments of the interview starting.

'Show business!' one lady sniggered, 'hardly the kind of life we wish one of *our* babies to be brought up to.'

'Totally impossible – there is no stability with your life style,' another sneered.

But the final and most unbelievable rejection came from one of the Irish agencies. They did not even consider us married! As Natalie was a Catholic, and I a Protestant, we had not had a full nuptial mass at our wedding, and consequently as far as that adoption organisation was concerned we were living in sin. Natalie was so annoyed that she immediately rang the priest who had married us, Father Barrett, and told him of the conversation. He roared with laughter and immediately asked why on earth we hadn't gone to him in the first place for advice. Before we knew it, he had arranged an interview for us with another agency and the wheels were in motion.

Other adoptive parents will understand what I am talking about when I say that what followed was equal to the most difficult 'pregnancy' ever undertaken. We both bristle when couples, who have had no problem in producing endless offspring, tell us 'what a lovely easy way to have a family.' Far from it! Every aspect of your life is microscopically examined. Every moment of your family history and your personal past is investigated and no question is too embarrassing that it can be left unanswered. Your home is inspected, every corner poked and pried into, and you begin to feel that your very soul is being x-rayed. Friends, doctors, bank managers, police – all are questioned, until finally the agency is satisfied you are proper people to be given the responsibility for a child's life.

We were particularly fortunate in having a wonderfully warm and kind adoption officer, who later became a great personal friend and in whom Natalie felt she could confide. We were constantly aware of the problems created by my travelling and that Natalie would, in all certainty, play the role of lone parent on many occasions. However, I must have convinced them that I was as keen, if not keener than Natalie to take on the role of fatherhood to the best of my abilities, and as soon as possible. Finally they accepted our application and we found ourselves on the waiting list, having been duly warned that it might be at least a couple of years before the right baby came along.

The first week of May we were all over the moon that Irene had happily and safely produced a beautiful baby daughter called Natasha. Joe Collins and I celebrated in time honoured fashion and suffered the consequences. Within a week Irene was back home and already at her desk with the baby in a carry-cot at her feet. I must say at this point that her determination to carry on both her career and motherhood with equal ability has never wavered and she has succeeded marvellously in combining the two.

Convinced that motherhood was a long way off for her, Natalie went back to work part time while I continued to rush around the world. Both of us were quite sure it would be at least a year before we had to swot up on formula-making, bottle feeding and nappy changing.

The house was quieter than usual, Brett having joined his father for an extended summer holiday, camping and tramping around the Iranian oil fields. The dogs looked lost without their romping companion, and Natalie found she had a lot of time on her hands. However, a few weeks after we'd been finally approved by the adoption agency I got home for a short visit and one day, as we were happily engaged in revamping our small garden, the 'phone rang. Natalie stopped digging and went inside to answer it.

A few moments later she reappeared, white and shaking. For one terrible moment I thought she'd received tragic news, as she just stood there, gesticulating at me, unable to speak. I rushed past her and grabbed the telephone, to be greeted by the cheerful voice of the adoption officer asking me whether it would be possible for us to collect our new daughter the following week!

Pandemonium! As I put the 'phone down Natalie and I grabbed each other and danced around in a circle like a pair of silly school children, laughing and singing, and crying. We fell to the kitchen floor, hugging each other with joy and disbelief. We spent the rest of the day making plans.

The first item on the agenda was to inform our parents. Thus far we had not told them anything, unsure of their reactions. Since my parents were shortly due to arrive to stay with us, we thought it best to telephone both sets of prospective grandparents right there and then and give them the news. Both reactions were negative. In no uncertain terms. Natalie and I were disappointed, but in time we came to understand their own disappointment at becoming as it were adoptive grandparents, instead of enjoying the propagation of their own bloodlines. It was a natural reaction and as time went on they overcame it handsomely.

Undeterred by our parents' initial reaction, Natalie and I rushed to London to create an instant nursery. In a large department store we filled basket after basket with baby clothes, nappies, bottles, sterilising equipment, everything we could think of. Then we went on to buy a pram, a cot – the list seemed endless! The sales lady was open mouthed and kept glancing curiously at Natalie. Finally, unable to contain herself any longer, she whispered as discreetly as she could that it was extremely bad luck to buy everything at once, in advance, and looking pointedly at Natalie's flat stomach, enquired when the baby was due.

'Next week!' announced Natalie brightly.

The poor woman was so dumbstruck it seemed only fair to let her in on our secret. She was so obviously happy for us, in contrast with the gloom of our own parents, it really made our day. Our next problem was collecting the baby, since I had to go up north for a cabaret date, but we resolved this by arranging for Natalie to meet me up there the day before we were due at the nursery so that we could go together. The rest of that week dragged on interminably and every day we spoke on the telephone, the excitement growing with each passing hour. By the time Natalie arrived at my hotel on 'collection eve' we could hardly speak. Certainly we hardly slept a wink that night and were on the road at dawn.

At the nursery the adoption officer asked us one more time whether we had any doubts whatsoever. Sitting there on the edge of our chairs, unable to drink the coffee they'd brought us, we forced ourselves to answer calmly and patiently, when all we really wanted to do was tell him to stop talking and bring us our baby. Finally, a nurse arrived carrying a little bundle wrapped in a white shawl, which she put into my arms.

There, in front of my eyes, was a tiny, red-faced, dark-haired, sleeping angel. Her eyes opened for a few seconds. She yawned and stretched her little body. I just clasped her to me and said,

'Come on little lady, we're going home!'

And home we went, with our tiny treasure, Emily.

Natalie's father, Toby, was the first to meet her. We went over there one fine Sunday for lunch so Emily could be introduced to that side of the family, aunts and uncles and all. As we were having a quiet drink before lunch, Grandad went for a walk, pushing the pram before him through the orchard. Through the open doors we could hear him chatting away to Emily, obviously delighted with her and hoping for a gurgle in reply. We smiled at each other, for we had known he wouldn't be able to resist her and when my parents met her they, too, fell quickly under her spell.

Toby and Emily went on to develop a special relationship and affection for each other. He would have been immensely proud of her today, for it appears she will be the one to follow most closely in his footsteps, with a career in journalism and politics.

Somehow, the arrival of Emily gave me new confidence and inspiration. One evening, rehearsing for the Mike Aspel television show, I was asked to create something different. The theme of the programme was the ability of song writers to produce (or not produce) songs at a moment's notice. So when I found a moment I picked up my guitar and began strumming a tune. Words began to form in my mind. Aspel stuck his head around my dressing room door, saying,

'That sounds nice. What is it?'

'It's something I've just written. It goes like this . . .'

'It's great!' said Aspel. 'We'll do it on the show.'

I played and sang it on the show, but didn't think much more about it. Most of the songs I'd written to date had been eminently forgettable. This one was called 'Durham Town'. Shortly after that show EMI put it out as a single, and subsequently I performed it on radio but I had no high hopes for it. There was another song I'd written at the time, 'This

'Moment', that was closer to my heart for it described how I felt about the arrival of Emily.

A month or so later, in April, 1969, I went to Helsinki for the first time. Finland was rather a shock to me, compared with other European countries I'd visited. Although later I developed an abiding love affair with Finland and the Finnish people, that first trip proved to be one of the loneliest of my life. Few people I met spoke English and it was only at the restaurant where I was performing that I met anyone I could converse with.

With nothing much to do for a few weeks except perform in the evenings, and with my loneliness sharpening my perception, I began scribbling lyrics for a musical I'd had in mind for some time. It had a working title of *Walls*, the 'walls' being those of prejudice and bigotry, an emotive subject. One of the titles born during that exercise was 'New World in the Morning'.

Meantime Natalie telephoned almost every day and during my second week told me that 'Durham Town' was beginning to move in the shops, with most retailers re-ordering twice. I was not terribly impressed. I'd heard it all before and seen sales suddenly fizzle out to nothing. About three days before I was due to return home Natalie rang again and said, 'Now we're getting solid sales figures and it looks as though by the time you get back you'll have entered the Top Thirty!'

Sure enough, when I got back I found Natalie's prediction had come true. I couldn't believe it! It was one thing to have had hits in foreign countries but now, at last, I had a hit record in Britain! There wasn't much I could do to exploit the success, however, tour schedules being what they are. After a short break at home I was back in France working on radio and television. 'Durham Town' had already been translated into French and was going to be released there shortly but I was now thinking ahead and developing the song I'd begun working on in Helsinki, 'New World In The Morning'.

Now into my life came Alain Vallat, later to become my manager for France and all French speaking territories in the world. To say that Alain was one of the best looking men I'd ever met in my life would be like describing the Mona Lisa as a painting or the Taj Mahal as a white building. Any attempt at description of Alain becomes gross understatement. His fatal attraction for women undoubtedly helped further my career. He had only to smile to get himself through any female barrier in radio, television or the record business. On the other hand, his way with the women could and did get me into very hot water occasionally.

To give Alain his due, he was more than just an 'operator'. He was extremely bright, knew our business and had an imagination that worked overtime; he got me to try to do things of which I never would have thought myself capable.

One afternoon we were listening to my small tape recorder and I played him 'New World In The Morning'. His reaction was immediate.

'I think this is a great song, Roger,' he said, 'and I am going to get it to the organisers of the Rio Festival.'

I didn't even know what the Rio Festival was and told him he could do what he liked providing I had the time to perform there. He played the song to a French publisher, Claude Pascal (who later became a great friend) and offered him the publishing rights if he could get me into the Rio Festival. Most countries had by then submitted their entries, but since the organisers of the festival liked the song they decided to do a bit of juggling. Britain already had Malcolm Roberts going to Rio so I needed a country to represent. Having been born in Kenya, I was able to represent my homeland. It was all settled.

The Festival, however, was not until the latter part of the year and there was a lot of water yet to flow under a lot of bridges before it would take place. My full schedule offered no breaks for holidays, so it was with the greatest of pleasure that I accepted from Alain a series of bookings for the south of France that summer. It meant that Natalie and Emily could join me in the sunshine and make the work load more tolerable. I thoroughly enjoyed working in France and with the help of Alain's boundless enthusiasm and charm was able to organise most of my year into a series of 'home and away' tours between France and Britain. On one of my home visits I got together with Dennis Preston and played for him the material I'd put together for the *Walls* musical I still had in mind. Before I knew it he had me down in the studio and recording an album. The musical never did come to anything, but every one of the titles on that album went on to become a hit.

Alain's penchant for variety never ceased to amaze me so I was not terribly surprised when he came to me with an offer to appear in Iran, both in cabaret and at private parties given by the Shah and Empress Farah. It sounded fascinating and I accepted at once. At the time the Shah was trying to bring the social structure of Iran up to Western standards, which apparently included the introduction of Western style music; hence my invitation. However, the clashes of culture were still very much in evidence, as I discovered when Alain and I arrived in Tehran. Iranians considered entertainers fairly low down the social scale, so instead of being put up in style in a certain luxury hotel, we were given rooms in a dilapidated annexe building adjoining the servants' quarters. Instead of air conditioning the room had open brickwork venting. This arrangement was rather interesting acoustically since all sounds passed easily from room to room. I soon found out just how far Alain's energy could go when dealing with women.

The day finally arrived when I was to perform for the Royal Family. A private plane came to collect us and landed us on the shores of the Caspian Sea. There, at the summer palace, I was to entertain Empress Farah and the royal children. It meant quite a change in repertoire. For the past week or so my Tehran cabaret stint had been a bit on the earthy side, which I wasn't crazy about but which the Iranian promoter had insisted upon, but now I entertained with children's verses and folk songs. The many and varied cultures of the East and Middle East are rich in folk music that combines instrument, voice and movement to tell stories, an art lost to the West. Fortunately my own music has tales to tell and I knew a great many folk songs so my performance went down well. It was a most intriguing experience. These days when I see those children all grown up and in exile in France I recall the occasion fondly.

On our last night in Iran I was asked to perform before the Shah and the Empress at a Gala Evening. It proved to be a fascinating evening, but as far as my performance was concerned I might as well have stayed home for all anyone seemed to care. Everybody continued to eat and talk throughout my show. I didn't take it personally, because they

175

all did exactly the same thing during everybody else's performance.

The trip was a pleasant enough diversion, I'll say that for it, but it did nothing for my career. I confess I was really wrapped up in my heavy work load, dashing about Europe, performing here for one night, there for a couple, back to England for a few days then returning to France or Germany or wherever. I was enjoying the exaggerated attentions and show business *schmaltz* that came along with hit records. In fact I was becoming rather blasé about it all, a bit inflated with self-importance. I needed puncturing and I soon enough got it, at the hands of a Dutch audience in Amsterdam one night.

Considering myself the star turn of the evening, I insisted on having the closing spot, despite protestations from producers and promoters alike. They pointed out that there were many big names on the programme and advised that I'd be better off closing the first half of the concert. I was deaf to their pleadings. I was the star and I was going to have the prestigious top-of-the-bill closing spot. These Dutchmen were not going to put one over on me, getting me to warm up the audience for their own favourites to follow! Eventually they shrugged and capitulated.

The show was going along nicely and when I came on I got a terrific reception from the crowd. Delighted, cocky, I swung into my opening number. Thunderous applause. I went into my follow-up and then I hit them with song number three. More applause. And then, to my astonishment and horror, as I got ready for my next song four thousand people got up and walked out.

I couldn't believe my eyes! For several seconds I stood there onstage watching it all happen, the entire audience hustling out of the concert hall. When there was nobody left out there but me I ran backstage and threw a temper tantrum at the producers, demanding an explanation.

'We tried to explain to you *before* the concert,' one of them said. 'But you were so insistent you should have your important spot we decided to teach you a lesson. You should listen to the people who organise a concert and who know their own market. So now we'll tell you. All the last buses and trains leave in ten minutes and so does the audience – every week!'

Thoroughly chastened and feeling very foolish, I picked up my guitar and followed in the wake of the departing audience.

The Dutch not only taught me to respect the advice of people in the know, they also proved to me, albeit unintentionally, that I was not the superb physical specimen I believed myself to be. I'd always prided myself on being in good physical shape, reasonably fit, keeping in trim by playing at such strenuous sports as squash whenever I got the chance. So when a Dutch TV producer asked me to open a show by jumping up and down on a trampoline while singing 'Up, Up and Away' I agreed, although I did have a misgiving or two. Performers are often asked to do the most ridiculous things to 'make a shot' for the camera. To me this smacked of stupidity, with a hint of danger, but everybody concerned assured me there'd be no problems. They would even lay on a Dutch Olympic coach to give me lessons and rehearsals.

Well, I thought, what the heck? It'll probably all be good fun and I was certainly athletic enough to do the stunt. Under my instructor's guidance, I actually began to enjoy the sensation of bouncing around, controlling my movements. After a couple of lessons he told me I was ready to try a forward somersault. Up I went, my entry into the movement perfect, but coming down I knew the split second I hit the canvas that I had got it all wrong. I felt the pain shoot up my spine like a bolt of red hot lightning and I lay there, moaning in agony, unable to move my legs at all.

In a panic they rushed me to the hospital, where a slipped disc was diagnosed. Fine, I thought, not too bad at all, they'll just pop it back into place and I'll be raring to go again. Alas, Whittaker the deluded optimist again! A succession of orthopaedic specialists, osteopaths and finally even an acupuncturist came and went and did their thing and failed miserably in their attempts to get me mobile again.

Some days later, nature and rest having done their work, I was able to walk again, although my twisted, crablike gait could have won me the lead in *The Hunchback of Notre Dame*.

I struggled to complete the doomed television show, but insult was added to injury. Two guys were helping me with the simple task of getting my socks and trousers on, when the producer marched into my dressing room on the attack.

'You needn't think of suing us. Others have tried but they have never won. We shall just assume that you had a damaged back before the incident and nobody can prove otherwise, so it will be a waste of your time and money!'

I suspect my face probably turned purple with rage and pain, for he had the good sense to take a pace or two back as I growled,

'Listen! I don't give a damn about suing, but if you want a show you'd better find somebody to straighten me out.'

Yet another osteopath was brought to the studio and to my intense relief, and that of the production staff, he worked a miracle. With the smallest of clicks, I found myself upright once more. For safety, the studio insisted he stay around in case of a relapse, which thankfully never occurred, and during breaks in the taping he re-educated me in the use of my body. The producer apparently had not been far wrong with his bluff about a previous back injury, as on my return to England and a check-up in Harley Street, it was discovered that one of my legs is longer than the other and as a result there had been gradual but progressive wearing of the vertebrae. I still make mistakes and overextend myself physically, but the slightest twinge puts a quick stop to all thoughts of behaving like a young colt!

The Rio Festival finally loomed on the horizon. In truth I didn't expect much out of Rio, considering it another interesting sideshow in my career, much as the trip to Iran had been; fascinating, fun and marginally useful in stirring up local interest in me. The trip did not get off to a good start. Nobody was at the airport to meet us. Alain and I made our own way to our hotel, and amid the total confusion in the lobby I began to wonder whether the whole Festival was going to be a major catastrophe. A little later the girl who was supposed to have met us at the airport turned up at the hotel, blushingly apologetic. She explained that since I was listed as representing Kenya, she had been looking for a black man at the airport.

She was not the only one in Rio without a clue who I was. And with good reason. Within an hour or so of our arrival Alain and I discovered that somebody had released an EP of 'Mexican Whistler' on the French market and it had found its way to Brazil. All very well except that the record sleeve bore no photo of me, just four West Indian steel drum players! The release added a further complication. My original intention had been to perform just 'New World In The Morning', with something for an encore up my sleeve. However, since 'Mexican Whistler' was now being heard in Brazil, the Festival organisers suggested I perform that as well.

The Festival programme was scheduled to last a week. Malcolm Roberts, the British entrant, told me the Rio audiences were something special. If they didn't like you they made things pretty hot for you, but if they did they'd let you know in the most enthusiastic way. That piece of information did nothing to steady my nerves. At rehearsal before the first night I sang 'New World In The Morning'. I wasn't sure how it went down, but backstage afterwards a gentleman knocked on my dressing room door and introduced himself. It was Henry Mancini.

'That's a very fine song you have there,' he said, and told me he'd like to feature it in his next album. I'm not certain he ever did, but that night I was much encouraged that someone of Mancini's stature should be interested in one of my own songs.

Nevertheless I felt more confident about my old standby, 'Mexican Whistler'. I told the musical director I'd like a percussion section for it. Well, I certainly got one all right! They were Brazilian and they were brilliant – half a dozen first class conga drum players, half a dozen marimba, swimba – all kinds of musicians. I ran through 'Mexican Whistler' for them and they loved it, getting it right in five minutes. They were all knocked out by it, never having heard whistling like that before, particularly to a South American rhythm. ('Mexican Whistler' is based on the music of Paraguay and its flute players.)

On the first night of the Festival, with some 40,000 people in the audience, I saw what Malcolm Roberts had meant about unfriendly Rio audiences. A few of the early entertainers who didn't make a hit were jeered and hooted at and pelted with rolled up programmes and tight little balls of paper. It is not easy to whistle when you're nervous, but to my astonishment when I had finished 'Mexican Whistler' the audience stood and whistled and cheered and clapped. As the week went on I found that taxi drivers would draw up beside me and try to get

179

me to whistle. Strangers too, would stop me in the street and babbling away in Portuguese would also ask me to whistle.

On the final night I was told that in addition to the local audience there would be 360,000,000 people watching the programme on television, all over the world. Until then I hadn't appreciated how important the Rio Festival was, just as I'd underrated the Knokke Festival. As it turned out, I did win medals that night but I was not in the top three, so it was a bit of a let down.

However, on returning to England I discovered to my amazement that 'New World In The Morning' was receiving a big play on radio in the United States. It demonstrated to me once again what a funny business show business is; you just never know what's coming next and from which direction. You get excited about something that comes to nothing and you shrug off something else that proves to be terribly important.

Back home for a few days I caught my breath before flying off to Helsinki again. For some reason I have never been able to comprehend (apropos of that last paragraph) I'd become very popular on the cabaret circuit there. Since so few people spoke English, I found this very curious. I had been there just about a week when Alain Vallat rang to tell me he and Irene had organised a trip to French speaking Africa. I was thrilled with the thought of returning to Africa, even though it didn't include Kenya, but it also meant that unless I could get Natalie out to Finland for a visit I wouldn't be seeing her for nearly three months.

I telephoned her at once and persuaded her to come over with Emily. Tom Hertell, the Finnish promoter, gave us part of his house to live in. It was a beautiful house in a suburb of Helsinki, set in a wooded area beside a sparkling lake, and was completely surrounded by a high, wire fence with huge entrance gates. Tom had eight dogs, ranging from a tiny terrier to a great dane, all of whom would rush out to greet you, noisily and enthusiastically. The first thing I told Natalie when she joined me was that if she went walking with Emily at no time were the dogs to be let out of the main gate or the compound that led down to the lake. At that time of the year the lake was frozen over and each morning, for some reason, a man broke the ice in great patches from one end of the fence to the other.

One morning I went into town to visit Tom at his office, leaving Natalie and Emily with Tom's housekeeper. It was a bright, frosty morning and Natalie told me she'd probably take Emily for a walk. Cautioning her once more about letting the dogs out, I left for Helsinki. When Tom and I returned that evening, Natalie told us how much she'd enjoyed her little walk in the woods with Emily. Tom's jaw dropped.

'The only problem was,' said Natalie, 'I was quite convinced I'd accidentally let the dogs out because there were all these scufflings and growlings behind us all the way!'

Tom now blanched.

'My dear Natalie,' he said, a bit shakily, 'those were probably wolves. Why do you think we keep the dogs in, and have a high fence and have the ice broken all the time? Because without all that the wolves would come in and kill all the dogs! You must never walk in those woods on your own again!' Now it was Natalie's turn to blanch.

Six days before I was due to leave for Africa Natalie flew back to England. Alain then called to tell me about a few things he'd forgotten for the trip – such as the necessity for visas and inoculations! Actually, as an East African I should have thought of those things myself; nevertheless, with just a few days remaining, I found myself dashing all around Helsinki to the various African embassies involved, arranging for my visas and my shots.

The pressure was on, because although all the contracts had been signed, the trip was on only if I could organise everything in time . . . IF . . . it was a big 'if' when you were dealing in Helsinki with embassies not famous for speed or terribly interested in your urgency. I spent four frantic days in endless paperwork, muttering if this . . . if that . . . if not . . . driving myself mad in the process.

But from what strange sources comes inspiration! All these 'ifs' gave me the idea for a song, one that became a big hit for me, 'I Don't Believe In 'If' Anymore'. It is one of my most treasured compositions.

Off then to Africa eventually, complete with tropical gear, jabs here, there and yes, there, too, and appropriate visas. In Ghana we had a three hour stopover to make a flight connection and I used the time to wander about, lapping up the sights and sounds and smells of Africa. I was hit by a wave of nostalgia and for a moment felt a twinge of homesickness, a longing for the carefree days of my youth in Kenya, running around barefoot, at home with the wildlife, at one with nature.

How different was my life now! It was food for thought.

As the tour progressed I fed into my programme some of the African music I remembered from those early years, much to the amazement of my European entourage and to the delight of my audiences.

According to French colonial tradition, audiences were multiracial. I was so overwhelmed by it all and so cocooned by the organisers of the tour that for a time I forgot there was another face of Africa. The face of violence.

On more than one occasion during the tour we were forced to hole up in town while yet another futile and bloody skirmish was going on in the next village. And yet, amid all the chaos, amid all the killing and the burning and the looting, somehow a kind of normalcy remained and, as though becalmed in the eye of a hurricane, we played on, to audiences that cheered and applauded and welcomed us warmly. Perhaps, in a way, we were their lifeline to sanity in a world gone mad.

The insanity of it all came home to me brutally one day when wearily I checked into a small hotel in a town in – it matters not where. It was a hotel much like any other in that part of the world. A few ancient wicker chairs in the lounge, a bar, an indifferent desk clerk. In my room a ceiling fan hummed quietly, barely stirring the heavy, humid air; a mosquito net neatly tied above the bed.

As I put my suitcase down on the floor I nearly retched. The carpet was hacked to pieces. The desk was scarred with machete slashes and covered with bloodstains. There were bloodstains everywhere . . . on the walls, in the bathroom. The damned place was a slaughterhouse. Sickened, shocked and repelled, I demanded to see the manager. When he came up I pointed around the room. Almost hysterical I shouted angrily at him, asking him why in Heaven's name he hadn't had the mess cleared up?

He shrugged with Gallic resignation. 'Monsieur, why bother? I would go bankrupt if I tried to clean up and repair all the time. Next week, next month, they will be back and do it again. When we hear they are coming we go away. We come back when they are gone. Each time I just pray they have not burned it down!'

I did not sleep well that night.

In that atmosphere it was small wonder that imaginations ran riot, especially among the European musicians who had never set foot in Africa before. Just a couple of days before the tour ended I was sitting in the bar of a hotel when three of the band rushed in, green around the gills, clearly unnerved. Ordering double brandies they knocked them back and told the barman to leave the bottle. Hands shaking, one of them said to me,

'Sweet Jesus! I'd thought I'd seen it all but that's more than I can take. They're boiling babies in a vat on the corner of this street!'

For the moment my brain refused to register this information. But by now in that strife-torn country I could believe anything was possible, even probable. I went outside to have a look. On the corner, sure enough, a group of locals were huddled around a large, steaming vat. As the contents bubbled and boiled, I caught a glimpse of a tiny bleached skull and then a wrinkled arm as it floated to the surface.

Monkeys.

Monkeys, looking for all the world like infant corpses, an understandable mistake in the circumstances for new visitors to Africa. A few nervous giggles greeted my explanation when I returned to the bar. But I'm not sure the lads were really convinced.

Two days later, thanks to the miracle of modern day air travel, I went from the pits to the sublime, to my first major appearance in Paris. As I checked into my posh, plush, oh so civilised hotel, I felt as though I'd travelled through a time warp. It was hard to believe it was the same century, the same planet. Africa was a million light years away, a bad dream, a nightmare. True, there had been many a moment of pleasure during the tour, of satisfaction of a job well done, a performance, a song well received. But all in all it was a shattering experience, a shocking, albeit valuable lesson in what man can do to another man.

Chapter 12

Time can change the faces of   the   mountains

EVEN IN THE depths of winter Paris has its own special aura of gaiety and romance. As my taxi took me around the heart of this wonderful city, I reflected upon my recent experiences in West Africa and realised what a lucky man I was. Christmas was but days away and the Champs Elysées was festooned with tiny silver fairy lights strung from tree to tree. Crowds of chic women and well-dressed men scurried in and out of fashionable shops, their arms laden with brightly wrapped parcels.

In my reverie we almost passed the Olympic Theatre but just in time I shouted to the driver to stop. There over the entrance, in neon lights three feet high, was the announcement: 'Christmas for two weeks . . . Mireille Matthieu – Silvie Vartan – Roger Whittaker.' Roger Whittaker! I swallowed hard. It would be my first time as a headliner in one of the major theatres of the world. My reflex reaction of delight lasted but a fleeting moment before an attack of nerves suddenly hit me as I realised the test before me. I was the sole foreign star on the bill and I would be singing in French, a language few but the French themselves can speak with confidence. With a heavy sigh I told the driver to take me to the apartment I'd rented.

There was one significant factor in my favour. Natalie would be in my corner for this engagement; she and Emily were due to join me in a few hours. It would be our first Christmas together as a real family.

For the next few days we enjoyed an idyllic 'second honeymoon'. Between rehearsals we explored Paris, scoured the markets for decorations, bought a Christmas tree, sets of brightly-coloured lights and armfuls of presents for each other

184

and for Emily. The December air was crisp and refreshing, bringing a glow to our cheeks. Paris was beautiful, lovers embraced in doorways and the accordions played 'Sous les Ponts de Paris' in the little boîte we found in Montmartre. All augured well for my debut at the Olympia.

For the opening night Bruno Cocatrix, 'Mr. Olympia' himself, had arranged a star-studded audience. Much of that night was a blur for me then, so I can hardly remember all the details now. I sang 'Durham Town' and 'New World In The Morning' in French, then a native French song called 'Un Éléphant sur mon Balcon' ('An Elephant on my Balcony') and 'Rich Man' from *Fiddler On The Roof*. The audience loved it all. I was called back for an encore and then again, just to do 'Rich Man'.

Backstage after the show a party got under way. The crush was enormous as international stars and their minders pushed their way into the dressing rooms and an army of press photographers crowded the narrow corridors. Flash bulbs popped in my eyes, blinding me, so that half the time I didn't know whose hand was pumping mine up and down in congratulations. Over the hubbub somebody would shout in my ear, 'Roger, Johnny Halliday' or, 'Roger, Gilbert Bécaud', then 'Roger, Francoise Hardy.' Finally a voice shouted, 'Roger, your wife!' I'd forgotten about Natalie – almost! She told me it had taken her half an hour to get through the crowd and said, 'If I can find a patch on your face that isn't smothered in lipstick I'll give you my own kiss of 'congratulations!'

The evening was pure magic and long after we got back to the apartment and collapsed into bed I lay awake replaying the events in my mind. Tossing and turning, I began to worry about the critics. The audience had liked it, my show business colleagues liked it – but critics are something else. When my doorbell rang the next morning it was a bleary-eyed Roger who opened the door for Alain. He grabbed me in a bear hug.

'You are zee heet!' he grinned as he chucked a pile of newspapers on the floor. He went through all the notices with me and indeed I had rave reviews from the critics. The significance of all this became immediately apparent. Offers flooded in from all over France, for concerts, festivals, radio and television. I was now regarded – at least in France – as more than just a singer. I was an Entertainer. Irene and Alain had their hands full trying to juggle my commitments for the year ahead.

Suddenly Britain began to sit up and take notice. Early in the new year, after appearing on a TV show with Engelbert Humperdinck, I was offered my own network TV programme – but a children's show! Working with children is a prospect most entertainers view with terror, but I loved it and the show turned out to be tremendous fun. The children's reactions to my antics fed my own innate sense of the ridiculous and before long the whole thing took on a completely zany air. And I won over a new generation of fans!

All too soon I had to say goodbye to England and dash off again to the Continent. My schedule called for appearances at the Cannes Film Festival to be followed by a summer open air concert tour of the French Riviera. It sounds great and most of it was, but now and again it proved to be something less than wonderful. I have mixed emotions, for example, about the Film Festival. In many respects it was like a big circus. Dionne Warwick, Nana Mouskouri and I were faced with the difficult task of trying to entertain a rather different kind of audience – film stars – who were really not interested in anything but the awards and being seen in the company of the 'right' people. We battled valiantly to entertain, but none of us will ever know if we won.

Having been treated rather shabbily, we enjoyed a modicum of malicious satisfaction from the awards, watching faces in the audience turn from anticipation to disappointment as the winners were announced. Of course there was elation, too, for the winners, accompanied by the inevitable hugs and kisses. It was all so predictable – until that very unpredictable lady, Vanessa Redgrave, climbed the stage steps to receive her award, a magnificent crystal statuette. As she mumbled her few words of acceptance, the statuette slipped from her hands and shattered into a thousand pieces across the stage. The audience was stunned to silence but she, with hardly a blink or hint of discomfort, left the podium and the next award was announced.

To this day I can't remember who the next winner was. As

the entire auditorium rippled with laughter, from under the elaborate backdrop a ghostly broom appeared, wielded by an unseen hand, which blindly swished it from side to side in an attempt to clear the shards of glass but succeeded only in tripping up anyone unwary enough to get near it. This farce went on for several minutes, with the famous trying gracefully to accept their awards while hopping from foot to foot to escape the broom. Finally a red-faced official shot round the backdrop and the broom disappeared as quickly as it had arrived. Up to that point it had been a very stuffy event, but with the ice – or rather the statuette – broken everybody relaxed and the rest of the evening was good fun.

All festivals have this vague atmosphere of hysteria about them. For so many people, stars as well as starlets, hopefuls, writers, producers, directors, wheelers and dealers all, a festival like the annual one at Cannes can be a time of make or break. Business is conducted everywhere and anywhere and at any time; in bars, restaurants, hotel lobbies, wherever you can nobble the people you want to contact. Here, too, is the press, photographers in particular, thick as flies on a sugar bowl, desperate to fill the columns of their journals with news and pictures – preferably of the sensational kind. Photographers, notably the Italian papparazzi, would pop up in the strangest places, looking for an 'exclusive'. I can tell you it is positively unnerving trying to have a pee with a microphone stuck under your nose and a flash bulb popping!

Even your own bedroom is not sacrosanct, as Natalie and I discovered when we were in Juan les Pins that summer. I was doing my bit at a festival there, in the delightful company of Cliff Richard, Olivia Newton-John and Petula Clark. Olivia, who sang only in English, dubbed me 'Mr. Onky Onky' after hearing me struggle through 'Un Éléphant sur mon Balcon'. I guess my attempts at good nasal French left something to be desired. In spite of the frenetic pace we had a wonderful time. Emily, with nanny in tow, was able to wander about and go down to the beach, which was barely a hundred yards from the theatre.

Occasionally we were overcome by the heat and fatigue. One afternoon, after four hours of rehearsals, Natalie and I ran the gauntlet of journalists permanently encamped in the hotel lobby and fled upstairs for a couple of hours siesta in the cool of our room. It was an extremely hot August and when we reached the privacy of our suite we stripped naked, slid into bed and pulled the sheet over us. I then rang room service and ordered tea, cold drinks and a bucket of ice.

'I'll leave the door unlocked,' I said to Natalie, 'so we won't have to get out of bed when they deliver the drinks.'

We were just beginning to doze off when there came a tapping at the door.

'Entrez!' I called out, assuming it was our waiter. The door swung open. In dashed a lunatic shouldering a running television camera, followed in hot pursuit by a reporter, microphone in hand and half a dozen sweaty minions in his wake. Instantly wide awake, Natalie pulled the sheet up to her neck, which was just as well, as the man with the mike plonked himself down on the bed next to her and began the interview, while the man with the TV camera raced from side to side like a demented ferret, trying to find the best angle. He almost got more than he bargained for; the reporter, bouncing up and down on the edge of the bed in his excitement at managing such an informal interview, was pulling the sheet lower and lower, while Natalie kept sliding farther and farther down the bed, trying to stay with it and under it.

All the while a jabber was going on in a foreign language I could not make out. Finally Natalie hissed at me, through clenched teeth, that the mob was from Swiss television and some joker had assured them she spoke Schweizerdeutsch – Swiss German.

'Get me my dressing gown,' she said to me, 'unless you want a TV sensation!'

Still in bed next to her, I whispered back, 'You'd better hang onto the sheet. Remember I don't have anything on either!'

To add further absurdity to this bedroom farce, the waiter then appeared with our drinks. If he had turned out to be Peter Sellers in disguise I wouldn't have been a bit surprised. As the waiter approached the bed, ignoring the crowd scene, the interviewer with the mike clapped his hands in glee.

'Wunderbar!' he cried, stopping the cameras for the moment. 'Vee vill haf zem haf ze tea in bett!' Our waiter, trying desperately not to crack up with hysterics at this,

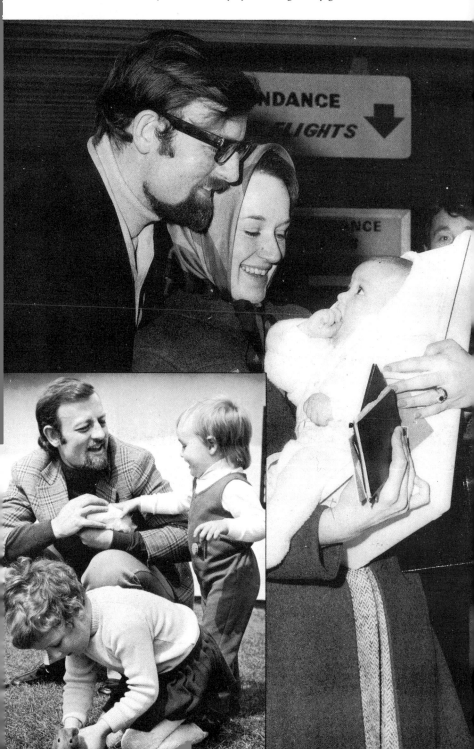

Leaving Paris with Emily after my Season at Olympia.
Below: Emily, Lauren and I play with our guinea pigs.

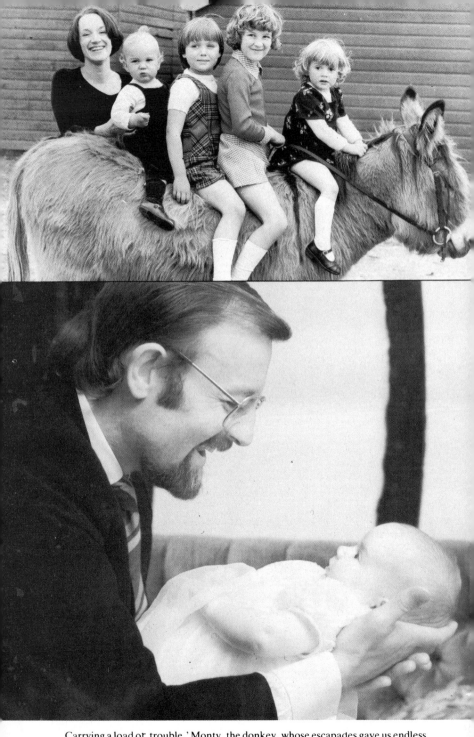

'Carrying a load or trouble.' Monty, the donkey, whose escapades gave us endless humorous memories.
Below: Hello little lady! Jessica 1973 and I am now surrounded by women...

"If I were a rich man" was my first major hit record and I got the chance to act out the part for Dutch television, 1975.

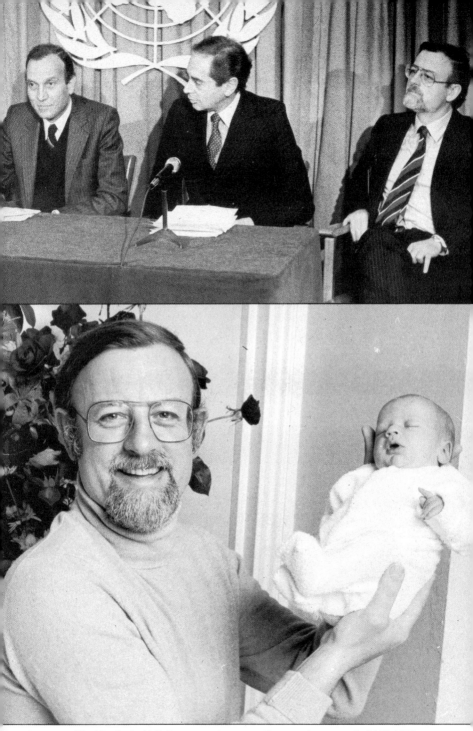

Working in the U.S.A. more and more. — Press conference at the U.N. 1980 to judge the UNESCO competition for the Year of the Handicapped Child.
Below: In 1978 Natalie presented me with Alexander, earlier than expected!

Meeting President Jimmy Carter in Portland, Oregon,
on one of my mammoth U.S. tours.

Two gentlemen to whom I owe so much: Ed Preston (centre) President and Manager of Tembo Records (Canada) and John Ford, Vice President of RCA for U.S.A. and Canada. *Below:* A welcome visitor to our present home. David Soul.

I've been set up! Caught well and truly by Eamonn Andrews for "This Is Your Life".

proceeded with straight face to pour our tea into dainty cups and serve us.

'One lump or two, Madame?' he asked Natalie, bowing from the waist in the approved manner.

He handed her the cup and saucer, but Natalie shook her head. There was no way she was going to let go her two-handed grip on the edge of the sheet. 'I don't drink tea,' she said.

'Cut!' yelled the producer. Then, to Natalie, 'You must haf tea. All ze English haf tea.'

At that Natalie lost her cool. Clutching the sheet around her and swinging her legs off the bed – almost exposing me – she snarled,

'I never drink tea and I never conduct interviews in the nude!'

For a moment there was stunned silence; then the entire Swiss crew burst into peals of laughter as for the first time they realised our state of undress. The interviewer went scarlet, the cameraman wiped a tear of laughter from his eyepiece and the troupe backed out the way they had come in, bowing and smiling and mumbling something about finishing the interview at a more convenient time.

I've had some extraordinary press calls in my time – in the rear seat of a car at high speed, upside down in an airplane, even backstage caught with my trousers down around my ankles during a quick change. But that particular incident wins first prize in the loony interview stakes!

After a lovely, golden summer touring the south of France I returned to England, still uncertain of my niche there. Despite the undoubted successes of 'Durham Town' and 'I Don't Believe In If', somehow the status I'd achieved on the Continent still eluded me. Variety had always been my goal so when a twenty-six week radio series was offered I jumped at the chance. For years I had been telling myself, and anyone who would listen, that there was a vast untapped source of talent out there and the radio series gave me the chance to prove this point.

On the very first show I invited listeners to send me their lyrics or even poems to which I could put the music. Then I sat back to see the reaction. Within days the producer and I realised the flood gates we had opened. During those twenty-six weeks over one million entries were submitted. The task of sorting them meant not only that the BBC had to employ dozens of extra staff, but that our little cottage was stacked to the ceiling with cardboard boxes stuffed with paper on which were written words, some terrible, some indifferent, some possible and some occasionally exciting. Between recording days, I worked every available hour, sifting and sorting, occasionally yelling 'Nats – come and listen to this!' and she would be subjected to snatches of musical ideas to go with prospective songs. Titles such as 'Why and Wishes', and some very complicated lyrics by a jeweller from Birmingham by the name of Ron Webster entitled 'The Last Farewell' were quickly and quietly arranged for the following week's radio show. There was such a variety of material that none of us ever felt we could do real justice to some of the beautiful pieces submitted, therefore a final show was added to the series, consisting entirely of songs sent in by the public. A panel of judges was organised and the winner announced. 'Why' by Joan Stanton was the winner, not only with the panel of professional judges, but also in the poll taken of the listeners.

We all felt it was a shame for the songs to be born and then quickly die when the series ended, so it was decided that we would choose the twelve best for an album. By the time it had been cut, 'Why' was a single and in the charts. The album quickly followed and sold equally well. What to follow it with, was the next problem. I had little time to write, so one of my French publishers came up with a song that he assured me had only been covered by a Spanish group called The Top Pops. This is an 'exclusive' promise that is often handed to singers only to find it has been given 'exclusively' to all and sundry. Such was the case this time. I believe in fact that it had over forty 'covers' all over the world. The twist in the story was that I got to number one in Spain with 'Mammy Blue' but it only crept into the low twenties in England.

Trying to keep a proper sense of perspective when so much is going on all around is extremely difficult and often my priorities got away from me. For me, my family has always been a warm and welcoming sanctuary and, despite the separations, Natalie and I were able to share our dreams and together begin to see them take shape. Down through the years we've cherished whatever home we've lived in and left a little bit of ourselves behind when we moved on.

Behind closed doors, we are like any other family in the world – slopping around in jeans, lounging around in front of the television, squabbling and laughing over the silly day-to-day problems as they occur. In the early days, with little money for luxuries, we delighted in doing all the home alterations ourselves, but I found myself in trouble on several occasions when, due to my inconsistent visits, I started heavy manual jobs, and then dashed off to work, leaving Natalie with the clearing up! Our first little cottage had been 'vandalised' by previous owners who had painted over the three-hundred-year-old oak beams with gloss paint. The sight of these became such an irritation that, whilst I was on the road, Natalie tore her hands to bits, sanding and scraping from room to room. The results were marvellous but as the true character of the old place became more obvious, I realised that the central architectural feature of the house was in dire need of correction. The massive inglenook fireplace in the living room, framed by huge beams, had been filled in with rough brick work and a hideous and inefficient Victorian coal burning stove cemented in. I could stand it no more, so while Natalie was busy painting upstairs, I bought a sledgehammer and set about opening up the fireplace.

The crashing and shuddering that reverberated around our little home went on for about twenty minutes before Natalie, unable to contain her curiosity any longer, came down. The volcano erupted! What I failed to remember in my enthusiasm was that normally in these circumstances one covers all the furniture with dust-sheets. In those few minutes I had managed to raise a sandstorm, liberally covering everything in the room with fine brick dust, including the newly exposed beams! Natalie stormed out of the house trailing a torrent of expletives, with the ultimatum that she would not return until all the mess was cleared up. Unable to get a word in edgeways, I followed her to the car trying to tell her something. But she wasn't listening and drove off down the hill, leaving me to finish the job – and I was determined to do so. Four hours later, a very cold and much abashed wife crept back in.

'Where did you go?' I asked, grinning.

191

'The bottom of the lane,' she grudgingly admitted. 'Why didn't you tell me the car was playing up? It conked out after four hundred yards!'

'I was trying to tell you when you flounced out,' I replied.

Natalie's famed temper cools as quickly as it boils and we wound up with both of us grabbing tools and smashing open the fireplace. Finally, sometime after midnight, we pulled the cork on a bottle of wine to toast our discovery of the most marvellous inglenook, big enough to sit inside, that was to become a focal point of that home.

We worked like beavers on that house, getting enormous pleasure out of working together, never thinking that we might one day move. Just as we got the place perfect, my career was really taking off on the Continent, and I found myself collaborating with a French writer. Emily was still only a baby and as time at home was so precious, rather than go to France to write, I invited him to stay with us for a few days. My wife was less than amused when not only the writer turned up but also Alain, our Parisian publisher and another writer to boot!

Expansively I offered my hospitality, the nearest hotel being fifteen miles away. As we only had three bedrooms, we managed with one guy sleeping on a camp bed in the dining room, another on the sofa, and the other two occupying our diminutive guest room. Typical of songwriters, we tended to work from early afternoon until well after the midnight oil had burned, emerging mid-morning to review our achievements of the previous day.

Had they only stayed the few days we had anticipated everything would have been all right, but after two weeks of having to cook meals, climb over sleeping bodies whilst trying to keep a teething baby quiet, Natalie became impatient for their departure. One day, after she'd returned from another shopping trip for the mountain of food needed to keep five hulking men going, I told her that we'd finished and that I had organised a party for that night. Nats was exhausted but rallied to the occasion. It was a swinging party; around four o'clock in the morning she staggered upstairs to retire and leave us to our revels, only to find our bed was occupied.

'That does it!' she stormed at me. 'Get rid of them *now*!'

Feeling no pain, I grinned at her and mumbled something to

the effect that we would spoil everybody's fun. I was being so drunkenly obtuse that she stood there with clenched fists, seething, until one of the female guests, so plastered that she really could hardly stand, stripped off her top, exposing ample bosom encased in the flimsiest of lace and asked me to autograph that part of her anatomy. As I lurched forward to oblige, Natalie leaped forward also, whipped off my glasses and proceeded to do the Mexican hat dance on them! Astounded, we all sobered up like lightning and, perhaps needless to say, the party quickly disintegrated!

The next day, all of us were nursing gigantic hangovers. Sloth-like we crawled around trying to clear up the shambles we'd created. Natalie was not speaking to any of us. Hang-dog would describe any of us five fellows! When we'd finished she appeared carrying a tray of reviving antidotes and as we took tentative sips, she began to laugh – then we all did! But as we packed the last of our visitors into a cab, she told me the house was too small if I was going to invite the world and his friend to work at home. Still feeling extremely sorry for myself, I shambled to the local watering hole for another 'hair of the dog' and to a sympathetic audience announced,

'We have just got the house as we want it – and now she wants to move!'

Before I could take a breath, a list of all the available houses in the area had been given to me. Only one was in the price range we could afford. Armed with this information I returned home and told Natalie that if she was really serious, then while I was away for the next few weeks she should look at new places, including the aforementioned house. Two days later, still suffering from an aching liver, I left on my travels.

When she sets her mind to something, my partner in life can move with exceptional speed, but I was nonetheless astounded to hear that in one short week she had viewed that one house, put in an offer, put ours on the market and sold it to the first prospective buyer. She was bubbling over with excitement. Shrugging my shoulders at the rapidity of events, I resigned myself to moving, actually quite enamoured at the prospect myself when over the telephone she painted the picture of our new home to me.

'It's four hundred years old, beamed, with a thatched roof,

four bedrooms and about twenty acres of land!' she enthused. 'Mind you, it needs some repairs!' she casually threw at me as an afterthought.

I could hardly wait to inspect everything myself so on the morning I got back, with a builder in tow, Natalie drove us over to the next village. Set in a hollow, with a tangled, overgrown garden, the initial impression was that of a picture postcard ideal of an English country cottage. A magnificent heavy oak door opened into our new home, and there the dream shattered! As I stepped over the threshold into the hall, I found that I couldn't stand upright, the ceiling was so low!

'I suppose you think this is funny!' I growled. 'This is impossible.' I should have noticed the builder had stepped back a few yards.

Brightly, Natalie replied, 'Not at all. You see, it needs new foundations, so we are going to jack the house up and sink the new floors another two feet!'

'What?' I yelped. 'But we've got to move in two months, and besides it will cost a fortune.'

Sunnily she replied, 'That's no problem! The house was under a Demolition Order and I got the whole place, land and all, for a song. So we have plenty of money to rebuild with.'

Resigned to the situation but with a great deal of trepidation, I continued round the house. The next room we entered charmed me instantly; a beautiful inglenook fireplace dominated a long, beamed room with a very attractive ancient paved floor. In the gloom it took my eyes a few seconds to take it all in, but when I did I took the arm of the builder in a vice-like grip,

'Did you really persuade my wife this was possible? What's that?' I asked pointing to the vegetation growing through the paving.

'Oh, that's only because there are no proper foundations.' he reassured me and, taking a pickaxe, proceeded to lift a large piece of the floor to show me the sand beneath, at which point water welled through!

'That will go, too,' he cheerily told me. 'The house was built on an underground spring, but we can channel the water around it while we do the foundations.'

'You're mad!' I ranted at Natalie, but in vain. Not for one

moment did her sights waver. Over the next few weeks, gangs of workmen jacked up the main beams of the house yard by hard, sank new foundations, replastered the walls and attended to the other rebuilding needs. As usual, I was away when the move finally came, which was just as well since in spite of all the whip-cracking, only one end of the house was habitable.

The need for Natalie to take possession of a building that still only vaguely resembled a home was twofold. First, having sold our other house, we had to get out as per contract. Second, to our unmitigated joy we had been accepted as parents of yet another gorgeous baby daughter. By law we had to go through all the formalities of an investigation again, but this time we knew what to expect and were confident we would pass inspection.

Emily was still very small, but big enough to begin asking questions now and again when faced with pregnant ladies in their final months. In simple terms we explained about babies and told her we had 'chosen' her and that fact made her very special. When we announced the news that her sister was going to arrive soon she was thrilled, but adamant that she must help us 'choose' the baby. In a moment of confusion we found ourselves agreeing – to the consternation of the adoption officer when we told her.

'Oh, no!' she groaned. 'The last time parents said that, we had a hysterical two-year-old on our hands determined to take home a baby already placed with other parents and of the wrong sex!'

'Whoops!' said Natalie. 'How do we get around this?'

'Don't worry,' said the adoption officer, 'we'll sort something out. But I'm glad you warned me!'

When the great day dawned we drove off in the car with Emily, all of us excited and chattering away. Emily was babbling as only a two-year-old can, telling us of all the plans she had for her new sister. We had already chosen her name – Lauren Marie Whittaker. And we knew by then there'd be no problem with Emily's 'choice'. The adoption officer had come up with a perfect solution: when we arrived at the nursery all the other babies were out being fed. A long row of empty cots lined the room and Emily rushed from one to the other until she found the one that was occupied.

'Here she is!' she called to us. Then, to the baby, 'Hello, Lauren! I'm Emily, your sister!' Beaming from ear to ear, she stood on tiptoe and reached into the cot, touching the little pink fingers. Lauren, four months old, gurgled back a greeting and a bond was instantly forged. Natalie and I stood quietly, gulping back the tears, allowing the two sisters to become acquainted.

Finally Natalie stepped forward, picked up the baby and cuddled her. 'Look at her eyes and mouth!' she exclaimed, and we burst out laughing. We'd named the child after Lauren Bacall and there before us were the most sensational eyes and mouth very much in the mode of her namesake and a face with the promise of equal beauty.

On the way home Emily insisted we strap the carry-cot right up against her, and all the way she talked and crooned to the baby, although Lauren was asleep most of the time. A few days later, when the grandparents came around for the first time, Emily announced to them,

'Look at what we chose!'

That word 'chose' was to provide us with a good deal of amusement later on, but for the moment our thoughts were wrapped up in our complete little family, in our new lovely home, and in our little world that seemed so rosy.

Hal's son, Brett, was still with us, too, and just as excited as any of us about Lauren's arrival. He was quite the little man about the house when my travels took me away, always the first to answer the telephone and regale me with stories about his two 'sisters'. However, the time came when Hal remarried and naturally wanted Brett to join him in Iran. Sadly we said goodbye to the boy; but what we thought surely was a 'last farewell' turned out to only be a goodbye for a year. Hal soon realised that the standards of education in Tehran left much to be desired and asked us if we would care for Brett again. With open arms we welcomed him back a year later, grubby shorts, scraped knees, runny nose and all.

But wait – that was not a year I can dismiss in passing for it was then that my world all but turned upside down.

Chapter 13

When you move with the changes

ONE SMALL CHILD is easy enough to take along on your travels, two tiny tots are another matter entirely. Therefore Natalie and I decided that except where long separations would be intolerable she would remain at home with Emily and Lauren when I was on tour. We'd both seen too many show business children who had been dragged around the world by their parents, their lives in disorder, their health and their confidence badly affected. Children need roots and stability in their lives. They need a place they can call home, a rock on which they can feel secure, safe, and loved. As a result of this decision, of course, our separations became more frequent. I would dash home for a few days whenever possible and when I did I shut myself in and the rest of the world out until once more it was time to pack and be on my way.

A twelve-week tour of Australia and New Zealand was coming up, which would include the Christmas period, and we decided to go as a family preceded by a week in Manchester which seemed to present an opportunity to acclimatise the girls to travelling, to hotel rooms, and all the other inconveniences they might experience when we all went 'Down Under' together. We employed a nanny to help with the children on the tour but for the Manchester week Natalie wanted to manage on her own.

Each night Natalie remained with them in the hotel, helping them into their strange beds in a strange room, while I performed. However, on the final night there was an important dinner at the hotel when I needed Natalie at my side. We couldn't arrange for a babysitter but the hotel had a 'listening service'. As we dressed for dinner, with the children tucked into their beds, Natalie showed Emily the microphone between her bed and Lauren's cot, explaining, 'If you wake up and need anything, just talk into that and the lady listening in will come and get me.'

Down we went to dinner in the main ballroom, where as guests of honour we were seated at the head table. All through the first course Natalie kept whispering to me, 'I think I ought to go up and check on them.'

'Stop worrying,' I said. 'They'll be okay. If anything was wrong they'd tell us.'

No sooner were the words out of my mouth than a rumble of laughter began at the back of the room which spread quickly and became a veritable gale. And there, walking towards us, came a red-faced maître d'hôtel leading by the hand a stark naked three-year-old. Equally scarlet of face, Natalie leaped to his rescue.

'Thank you, Madam,' the poor man muttered, and marched away with as much dignity as he could muster.

'What on earth are you doing here?' Natalie whispered to Emily as she led her toward the exit.

'I thought I'd just come and see how you were!'

In the foyer Natalie met another gentleman, smartly dressed in a business suit.

'Ah, I see she found you. So glad,' he said. 'She seemed to know exactly where she was going but I thought I'd better wait around and see.'

Apparently our little stripper had met the man outside the lifts on our floor, walked into the lift with him bold as brass and asked him to press the button for the ballroom as it was out of her reach. He, with typical English *sang froid*, did as he was asked, despite the fact that the request was coming from a knee-high, bubble-haired, naked little girl. On reaching the ballroom floor, he had handed her over to the maître d'hôtel for delivery. Never again did we leave the children with an electronic babysitter.

Off we went to Australia. It is a long flight, with a couple of stops along the way, and we were dead worried that the children would become fractious. But they were angels, responding to the long hours aboard better than we did. We soon discovered, too, that our worries about their adapting to new surroundings and strange people were needless. They loved it all! They also became thoroughly spoilt by all the attention they were getting and took press calls in their stride. But there was one incident I recall in which little Lauren almost gave us both a heart attack.

We had rented an apartment in Sydney, which suited us better than a hotel and which gave the children a semblance of normalcy. It was a beautiful place, overlooking the beach at Bondi. The only disadvantage was that we were on the top floor of an apartment block with lifts, in the fashion of the time, in the open on the outside of the building. As we left the apartment one day and were about to get into the lift I remembered I'd left something behind.

'Hold the lift for a moment,' I said to Natalie, dashing back towards our front door.

'What?' said Natalie, taking her eyes off the children for a second. In that instant Lauren was out of her pushchair and into the lift and the doors closed!

Total panic! We could hear Lauren screaming as other residents pushed the lift buttons, taking them up and down in the building. We couldn't believe people were actually getting into the lift with a screaming child and doing nothing about it. Telling Natalie to wait there with Emily and the nanny, in case by some miracle Lauren appeared on our floor again, I began racing down the stairs, trying to catch the lift, trying to figure out where it was by the screaming I heard along the shaft.

Finally some intelligent person decided to take her out of the lift and shouted up the shaft what floor he was on so I could come and get her. Poor Lauren was hysterical and Natalie had been close to hysterics herself until I brought the child back, safe but sobbing. It was many weeks before we could get Lauren to enter a lift again without clinging like a limpet to Natalie's neck.

Seeing the world through a child's eyes is a never-ending revelation. During those weeks on tour I got a tremendous kick out of watching Emily and Lauren, seeing them grow up day by day, grow wise the way only a young child can when confronted by new experiences. Which leads me into an anecdote about Emily and how she showed us the beauty of a child's simplistic view of life.

Bo Biddell, our Australian representative, had been born

with one of his arms ending just below the crook of his elbow. In spite of this disability he was determined that he would do everything an unhandicapped person could do. When I met him he'd already served as a police officer for a time and been Australian junior squash champion. It is difficult sometimes to know precisely how to handle such a situation: do you ignore the handicap or do you make a point of discussing it so you get it out of the way? Natalie and I ignored it but we were concerned lest the children embarrass Bo and us by asking questions. Fortunately, as the days passed, the children appeared to be ignoring the handicap too.

One day Bo invited us all out to a picnic in the bush. He chose a lovely open area so the kids could kick their ball around in safety while he attended to the barbecue. But Emily didn't want to play. Instead she positioned herself at Bo's side and insisted on helping with the cooking.

'I can be your other arm,' she said casually, as we held our breaths. Then she said, 'By the way, what happened to your arm, Bo?'

Bo seemed not in the least upset by the enquiry, coming as it did from this innocent tot and it seemed to us his reply had been carefully rehearsed. No doubt he'd been through these enquiries before. 'Arm? What arm?' he said. 'Oh, that. I lost it one day.'

But that did not satisfy a child's curiosity.

'But where did you lose it?' Emily asked.

Digging himself in deeper Bo replied, 'Oh, I think it was on a picnic, like today. I don't remember. But don't worry about it, it doesn't bother me.'

After stuffing ourselves with steaks and other goodies we adults sat back and relaxed in the sun, while Lauren curled up and went to sleep and Emily began kicking her ball around. Farther and farther she kicked the ball until finally it disappeared into some scrub.

'Come back, don't go in there!' shouted Natalie, concerned about spiders and snakes. Emily kept on going, however, with Natalie and Bo in hot pursuit. The ball was quickly recovered but Emily delayed, peering around her.

'What have you lost?' Bo asked her.

'Nothing,' said Emily, 'I was just wondering if this is where you lost your arm?' Bo appeared rather upset by this. 'Well, it was a long time ago,' he said. 'There's no point in looking for it now.'

All these explanations obviously did little to satisfy Emily; on the contrary, they bothered her. At story time that night she seemed distracted and unwilling to listen.

'Daddy, we've just got to go and find poor Bo's arm,' she begged. That did it. As soon as I turned out her light I went back into the drawing room where Bo was chatting to Natalie.

'Bo, you've got to tell her the truth. I know she's only tiny, but she has always been told the truth and it must come from you.'

'I realised that as soon as I had opened my big mouth,' he agreed, 'I promise to tell her first thing tomorrow.'

After breakfast the next day he took her off for a walk and as we watched the tiny girl and huge man stroll off hand in hand, we wondered at the outcome. On their return, Emily hopped and skipped back into the apartment and went off to play with her sister. Bo sat down heavily, and announced, 'What a kid!'

He had carefully explained that what he had told her had been a silly story as he had not thought her grown up enough to understand, but that in fact some quirk of nature had meant that he had been born with half of his arm missing.

'I nearly cried,' he said, 'as she flung her arms around my neck and said, 'Poor Bo! But never mind, you've got two good legs, haven't you?'

That trip was like old home week in a way. At every hotel, city and airport we seemed to meet another familiar face: Harry Secombe, Spike Milligan, Cleo Lane and Johnny Dankworth, just to name a few offhand, were apparently on the same circuit and even on the same hotel list. As Harry was checking out, I was plonking my bags next to his and checking in; as I was leaving Cleo and Johnny would be arriving and Spike and I seemed to be going round in revolving doors together. It would have been great fun if we ever could have gotten our acts together, as the saying goes. But we never seemed to be playing the same city on the same dates, largely because we were often following each other from venue to venue, one act in, the other one out of the same club, theatre or TV engagement.

Once in Sydney I managed to get together with a fellow artist. Neil Sedaka and I were each doing an hour-long show at the St. George's League Club and afterwards, which meant long after midnight, we'd try to rustle up something to eat. In those days they rolled up Sydney's pavements at 11 p.m. After four days of trying to persuade the porters at Neil's hotel to find us some sandwiches and coffee we decided to try our luck on the streets. So with our wives in tow one night, or rather early morning, we set off to find a certain bar our musicians had told us about that remained open all hours – strictly against the law.

Down a dark and forbidding alley we crept until we came to a dimly lit doorway. The door was locked. In response to my battering, a hatch opened (shades of the old gangster movies!) and a pair of eyes looked out at us suspiciously. Some fast talking and a palm crossed with Aussie banknotes got us in. In the gloom we were led to a table and instantly served with a lot better refreshment than we'd been getting the past four nights. Somewhere in that Stygian darkness a piano was playing beautiful, lilting jazz. We all stopped to listen. Aha! I thought, an 'undiscovered talent'. Always on the lookout for that rare species, I rose and made my way through the tables to the piano.

Undiscovered talent my hat! There, wrapped up in a world of his own and playing to himself, was Dudley Moore! Nobody had even recognised him, which was presumably the way he wanted it. Anyway, I brought him back to the table and we had a drink and a good laugh about it. Neil and I even offered to book him for the odd wedding or bar mitzvah!

From Australia we went on to New Zealand, where we spent Christmas. Natalie and I instantly fell in love with the country and the people. The atmosphere was so gentle and so peaceful that we seriously considered the possibility of my returning to a teaching career there, supplementing my earnings with an occasional performance. We went so far as to begin negotiations to buy a house.

With these thoughts in mind we returned to England. When I told Irene of our plans she smiled and said, 'That's nice,' obviously humouring me until my sanity returned. 'But first,' she said, 'we have to get through the tours already booked and then do the television series. That'll give you time to think about it.'

'Television series?' I asked. 'What television series?'

'Oh, didn't I tell you?' she said, all innocent and wide-eyed and trying to suppress a jubilant grin. 'Thames Television want you to do a twelve-week Saturday night series. You can have a free hand choosing your guest stars.'

All thoughts of peace and quiet in New Zealand vanished instantly from my mind. I actually did jump for joy, swinging my fist in the air with delight. 'Fantastic!' I exclaimed and at once began to make a list of all the people I had long admired and with whom I had wanted to work.

I have mentioned that it was through my successes in France that I crossed the Atlantic. On one of my TV appearances in Quebec I'd worked with a wonderful French-Canadian singer named Ginette Reno. She could put across a song better than anybody I'd heard recently, albeit in French, and I proposed that this lady join me to help present the show and take a regular spot. Much to my amazement the producer agreed without a murmur of protest. More amazing still was that the powers on high approved every name I mentioned.

I was so elated I didn't notice that during rehearsals my ideas for the structure of the show had been significantly turned around. I was so wrapped up in my own numbers and my guests that when we came to our first run through on the set I was aghast! The original set design had been replaced by what appeared to be a building site! Weird and wonderful scaffolding arrangements had replaced the comfortable layout I had designed, and from the bars hung a dozen scantily clad go-go dancers who opened the show by swinging down from this structure and throwing themselves into wild gyrations to heavy rock music. John Williams, my first star guest, looked more than a trifle bewildered when he had to follow this heavy pop sequence but you could have heard a pin drop as he fingered his way through a beautiful piece of classical guitar.

One unavoidable fact became apparent during that rehearsal – the march of time had caught up with me! An invisible voice, high up in the massive arc lights overhead, bellowed, 'Ere Rog – you'd better get some powder on top!' My hair was getting so thin that the top of my head was reflecting the light. I had never worried about the encroaching baldness, but I have never seen such panic on a studio floor. Telephones became red hot as a wig maker was sought!

That namby-pamby wig (I could use stronger words) nearly ruined the shows over the following weeks. It felt so unnatural. I kept worrying about the damned thing and I'm sure it affected my timing. I never got used to it and it was ceremoniously burned after the last show was taped. Never again, I vowed.

Go-go dancers and wigs notwithstanding, the show was a success, packed with international stars and lots of excitement. Old friends like Nana Mouskouri and Rolf Harris appeared several times, and each week guest stars from abroad were brought in. No expense was spared. Sacha Distel, Stefan Grapelli, Cliff Richard, Shirley Bassey, Mireille Matthieu, The Bee Gees, Nina, Sandie Shaw, Matt Monro, The Tremeloes, The Fantastics, Slade, Lulu, The Dubliners, Val Doonican and Roy Budd all appeared. I can't mention them all but certain incidents stand out.

One Saturday we never thought we would get the show out. The entire proceedings came to a standstill when all involved, crew, audience and fellow performers were doubled-up with laughter. The offender – Dudley Moore! Apart from his solo number, he had offered to act as piano accompanist to Sandy Shaw. She, barefoot as usual, was to saunter down a catwalk, singing her latest hit, to where Dudley at the piano on a lower level would play the melodious 'middle eight', gazing adoringly into her eyes. The problem in rehearsal was that Dudley could hardly see over the end of the catwalk, and proceeded to bob up and down to see how far Sandy had got, pulling the sort of faces that only Dudley can pull. The result was that rehearsed walk after rehearsed walk ended with Sandy still only halfway down the catwalk hysterical with laughter, totally unable to continue singing. Rehearsals were one thing, but by the time the audience was in and could catch his performance on the monitors, their laughter made the situation worse. In desperation, the producer yelled, 'This is a take – get it together!' Everybody took a deep breath and Sandy started her walk again. Quite innocently Dudley raised himself just enough to see where she was – and raised his eyebrows. That did it! Sandy started to giggle her song, then laughed out loud, as did the audience. Finally she made it to the end of the catwalk, crawling on her hands and knees with tears of laughter running down her cheeks. Dudley, thinking it was going to be a throwaway take, really hammed it up. The place was in an uproar, the producer himself shaking with mirth. As the camera cut he announced, 'If it can make me laugh at a moment like this we'll keep it in!' And that's just what the viewers at home saw on their screens three hours later.

Jerry Reed had long stood head and shoulders above many of the American stars I'd admired from afar, so it was an immense thrill to have him on my show not once, but twice, as special guest of the week. He arrived wearing some sort of old bush hat, walked straight to his podium and started to play. The crew, who normally just go about their business setting up, making their noises no matter who is rehearsing, suddenly stopped to listen as Jerry ran quickly through three numbers. We all watched and listened, astounded.

'Just tuning,' Jerry said, with an embarrassed grin, for the first time realising he'd had an audience. He was a pleasure to work with, relaxed, unassuming, always ready with an ad lib and a joke; the shows we did together were among the best of the series.

One of the extra bonuses I earned working with so many different artists was a lesson in what true professionalism means. It was taught to me sharply by Keith Michell, then in the middle of filming his epic television series, *Henry The Eighth*. Keith is not only a fine actor, he is also the owner of a singing voice of near operatic quality. He is every inch the epitome of the professional. As for me, I'd always come on as a relaxed performer (though a bundle of quivering nerves inside) and during the series, working with musicians and comics, I'd work vaguely from the script. Sometimes we'd forget the lines, miss a cue or whatever, but turn the situation around and get a laugh out of it.

So during my first rehearsal with Michell I was not exactly word perfect with my script and fed him a line which was met with a blank stare. 'I know *my* lines,' he said. 'I don't know yours. But I am waiting for the word that gives me my cue and if you don't give it to me, then it's not going to be any *bloody good*! So I suggest,' he continued, 'that you read and learn your script and then we'll be able to communicate.'

Terribly embarrassed, I apologised and retired to my dressing room to study. When I returned we got to work again and the actual taping of the show was first rate. After the recording Michell leaned back in his chair and grinned at me. 'See,' he said, 'it's so much easier if you have got it all at your fingertips. Nobody's time is wasted.' And off we went for a drink together.

That sharp lesson stuck with me and to this day if I have to rush into any appearance, whether it be as host or guest, I get hot under the collar if I'm anything less than perfectly prepared.

Chapter 14

Hold on tight to those you love

WITH EVENTS MOVING rapidly after the end of the series, Natalie busied herself in homemaking while I skipped from country to country. More than ever, we knew it was essential that our home life be as far removed from show business as possible. Rural living offered the escape we were seeking, and Natalie, a keen horsewoman since childhood, persuaded me that riding would be good exercise during my fleeting visits home. Stables and paddocks were added and we acquired two beautiful bay mares. But it was the donkey she insisted on for the children (remembering her own childhood in Ireland) that was to give us the most fun. Only the Whittakers could go to a donkey farm, where they had the most beautiful pedigree donkeys of every description from piebalds to jet blacks, and come home with the most disreputable, moth-eaten donkey in sight. He instantly endeared himself to the whole family, and home he came to be joined in the stable yard by chickens and the cats we kept to hold the vermin in the hay barn at bay.

We had endless cats, all long-haired gingers! The tribe was started by one incestuous relationship between brother and sister, who perpetrated the transgression before the vet's knife could stop it. The tom then disappeared, the cad, and good riddance, we thought. In the end we wound up with twenty-three ginger cats, who poured out of every nook and cranny at evening feeding time. We were convinced they understood every word we uttered, because at the mention of 'the end of weaning' and the 'adolescents visiting the vet' the fecund females would vanish, only to reappear weeks later, waddling from side to side and ready to deposit a fresh litter of kittens in the hay.

As all the toms had been duly doctored we were at a loss to

understand where the continuing strain of ginger was coming from – until the long lost and presumed dead original incestuous brother wandered into the yard one day and cleared up the mystery. Enough was enough, we decided, and took the entire lot down to the vet for an assembly line snipping job. And before any of your cat experts tell us, as did my father-in-law, 'There is no such thing as pure ginger, long-haired female cats!' I can assure you there is. We had fourteen of them! What is supposed to be genetically impossible the Whittaker cats disproved. Our poor bulldogs, meanwhile, were being driven to distraction my our marauding ginger gang but Monty, our ridiculous donkey, adored them, allowing them to share his straw on cold winter nights.

Monty was an escape artist of the first calibre. Eventually we had to fence every paddock with heavy posts and put special locks on all the gates after the havoc he wreaked in my studio. For days I'd noticed him watching the other donkey (his own reflection) in the patio windows of the studio, braying loudly, annoyed at the lack of response from his fellow captive. At last, totally frustrated by being ignored, he carefully chose his moment to go snooping. After a busy morning recording with eight musicians on a hot summer's day, I left the patio doors open to circulate some fresh air. As soon as we had all left for lunch Monty made his move. I swear he had been planning it, because the paddock gate presented no problem and he was in! The first we knew anything was amiss was a yelp from one of the musicians who had returned to collect some music. Investigating, I caught sight of him leaping through the open patio doors as Monty took a quick nip out of his fleeing rear.

Yelling for help I dashed over to the studio. The place looked as though it had been hit by a cyclone; overturned music stands and drum kit, microphones scattered all over the floor, sheets of music strewn everywhere and, worst of all, the precious guitar of one musician neatly pierced by a hoof. Getting Monty out of there was no easy task, either. Tempting him with food buckets proved useless. A stream of invective hurled at him by my drummer didn't move him, either. Finally, six of us had to manhandle him out.

After that incident we secured all the exits from his paddock. At least we thought we had. During haymaking we moved the horses and Monty to fresh pastures, checking the fencing most carefully. No gate this time, but three sliding bars at the entrance. Three days in a row Natalie and I rode the horses out for exercise only to get half a mile up the road before being joined by a braying donkey. We searched endlessly for a gap in the fence and in desperation we decided to 'stake-out' the field to find his escape route. You would have thought we were dealing with a rational human being, the way he behaved! As soon as he thought we were out of sight Monty stuck his head through the top two bars, looked around, listening for humans (I presume) then, withdrawing his head, he lowered himself onto his stomach. He then began to inch his way under the lowest bar, for all the world like a limbo dancer, and puffing and panting wriggled out onto the road. Natalie leapt out from hiding and yelled 'Gottcha!' What a picture it was to see Monty being led back to the field, head hung low like a naughty schoolboy.

Our menagerie finally got a little out of hand when I foolishly gave the children two guinea pigs, who I was assured were both males, only to discover too late that one of our new additions was hiding her light under a bushel! As they proceeded to reproduce prolifically over the next three years, we had to build a special shed to house the fifty odd guineas, each addressed by name. Natalie was faced with junior rebellions at the suggestion of selling each new litter.

Natalie and I have often said those years were the most idyllic of our lives. We had so much going for us. We were so happy. I was successful, beyond perhaps even my youthful dreams, with that success still growing. Brett was now back with us and the house was packed with children. True, I was away from home rather too much but Natalie said what with the children and the menagerie, she never had time to be lonely. Often, too, with Brett in boarding school and the girls still young, she was able to pack up and join me on a tour.

But life is never that simple. The winds shift and circumstances change. I'm sure I'm not alone in fantasising how nice it would be if you could take a time of your life and capture it eternally in a freeze frame. However . . .

Three years had now passed since we'd adopted Lauren. We absolutely adored both our little girls but despite our doctor's negative prognosis we were still trying to have a child of our own creation. Eventually Natalie changed doctors. The new doctor operated on her three times until finally even this optimistic surgeon told Natalie she should forget about it. She would never conceive again.

Six weeks later, Natalie and the girls were with me in Sweden when she told me she felt 'odd'.

'How odd?' I asked her.

'Pregnant odd,' she said.

Immediately she flew back to see her specialist, who said she was right! We were delighted and amazed but also apprehensive, considering her past history of misfortune. At nine weeks she began to haemorrhage and the doctor put her to bed. She spent the best part of the next seven or eight weeks in bed, until four months pregnant the danger appeared to be over. What should we tell Emily and Lauren? We had always been frank with them, answering their natural questions about where babies came from and, as soon as each was old enough, explaining that we had adopted them because 'Mummy couldn't have babies of her own.'

Choosing the moment to tell them was a bit of a dilemma but as is so often the case, the moment chose itself. One morning they bounded into the bedroom and bounced on the bed in their usual manner of greeting.

'Don't jump on your mother, she isn't well,' I scolded.

They had never asked why Natalie spent so much time in bed but now, as I saw their worried faces following my remark, I realised that this was the time for an explanation. As Natalie and I cuddled them we explained as gently as possible that the doctors had been wrong and that Mummy had a baby in her tummy.

How wonderfully trusting little children are. How easily they accept our fumbling attempts to unravel life's mysteries for them. What is so complicated to adults is so simple to children. What we felt was a bit embarrassing was quite natural to them. Why shouldn't Mummy have a baby in her tummy?

They laughed and cheered and hugged and kissed Natalie and deluged her with questions. What was it a boy or a girl? When was it coming out? What was its name? Would they be able to play with it? Where would it sleep . . . ?

We could answer the When, but as to the other questions we had to tell them 'Let's wait and see. It'll be a surprise.'

As they bounced out of our room and back to their own, we sighed with relief and listened to their chatter relayed to us over the baby alarm. Lauren sounded a little confused, so Emily did her little mother act. 'Oh, listen silly. The baby's growing in mummy's tummy.' More mumbles from Lauren. 'No, no!' came Emily's clearly exasperated reply. 'They chose us specially. This time they don't even know what they're getting!' From then on there were no more questions, only impatience about when Natalie was going to finish 'cooking' the baby, as Lauren put it.

There was a momentary upset when, two weeks before the birth, Natalie was told that the baby would have to be delivered by Caesarian section. She was deeply disappointed. She had looked forward so much to a natural birth after all those years of struggling to have a baby.

On that February 14th, I was as nervous and excited as Natalie as I walked beside her to the theatre. I don't think either of us spoke. I just gripped her hand as hard as I could until the staff prevented me from going any farther. When the doors closed behind her, I returned to her room. I had only been seated a couple of minutes when a nurse stuck her head around the door and announced, 'Congratulations – a beautiful baby girl!' and the door closed behind her.

I sat there for a moment trying to take in the speed with which everything had happened and the fact that I had a third daughter. Soon another nurse came to the door and asked, 'Would you like to see your daughter? Your wife won't be back for about an hour.'

I followed her to the nursery. 'Put this on,' she said, handing me what looked to be a plastic shower cap, so I stuck it on my head. Doors opened all around and nurses came out laughing and pointing their fingers at me. 'They're for your feet, silly!' the nurse exclaimed. Apparently this was a time-honoured joke for new fathers. Finally gowned in a sterile robe, I was allowed into the nursery to see my daughter. There she lay, with her tiny little wrist band announcing her name and sex and the fact that she weighed just five pounds. I stood and gazed at her, examining her minutely from top to bottom, my heart in my mouth. She opened her huge eyes, looked at me and then went back to sleep.

I was so elated, so excited. When Natalie was returned to her room, she regained consciousness long enough for me to tell her that she had another daughter and that the baby was absolutely perfect. She smiled and then she, too, went back to sleep.

Natalie in her usual efficient way had given me a full list of phone numbers and people to call so I rushed back to Joe and Irene's and found them already on the third bottle of champagne. Somehow I managed to call all the friends and relatives on the list and vaguely remember inviting all of them to join me that night for a dinner in a West End restaurant. We painted the town red! Natalie looked at me most strangely the next morning when, bleary-eyed and extremely tired, I arrived to spend some time with her and the new baby.

Long before the birth, Natalie had insisted that the very first people to see the baby, after myself, were to be the girls. That morning, accompanied by nanny and brimming over with excitement, two little girls came to meet their new sister. As they ran into the room, they didn't even give their mother or me a glance, but ran straight to the cot and stood there mesmerised, touching the baby's face and hands gently with their little fingers and gazing at her in rapt attention. Then the age old question, 'How did the baby get out of mummy's tummy?'

'Was it like that book at home?' asked Emily, the book being one of those delightful cartoon 'facts of life' books for kids.

'Ah, not quite!' said Natalie. 'I went to sleep, and then they opened me up and took Jessica out!' The usual 'did it hurt?' and intimate anatomical questions followed until Lauren pulled back the bedclothes and said, 'Can we look?' They peered at Natalie's tum, then shrugged and turned their attention back to their new and now yowling sister. However, the best child's explanation from this diversion from normal delivery came when Lauren bounced into nursery school, and a small boy told the whole class he had a new baby. Lauren, brimming over with excitement, announced that she too had a new baby sister, but that, 'Mummy didn't have her properly, they just unzipped her.' Natalie was to be 'unzipped' twice more. Nineteen months later for Guy, and three years after that for Alexander.

Trust old friends to do just the right thing at just the right moment. Shortly after the girls left, Rolf Harris turned up with his wife, Alwen. Instead of bringing the traditional flowers or champagne, Rolf brought a movie camera and lights to record Jessica's first day of life. I'd always been a great admirer of Rolf's timing; this, however, was his best effort ever. No sooner had he set up his lights than by sheer coincidence the paediatrician walked in to put Jessica on stage for a remarkable performance.

Considering past events we were a bit concerned about whether or not Jessica was truly perfect. The paediatrician, therefore, had decided to show us her primary walk and crawl. Apparently all newborn babies can do this just once, then not again until they reach the toddler stage.

A towel was put across a trolley, Jessica laid face down – and we waited. She struggle to raise her little head, then pushed with her knees and elbows and moved forward. The doctor then put a finger in each of her tiny fists, which she grasped strongly, and raised her to her feet. Instinctively her legs moved forward in a walking motion. Perfect! It was an incredible, unforgettable moment. And Rolf got it all on film.

Never before, and perhaps never since, have I experienced such a sense of excitement, felt such strength and warmth from friends and relatives alike as I did when Jessica was born. So many of them had shared with us the years of struggle, the disappointments, and I felt at peace knowing they were now sharing our joy. I knew, too, that although my work would all too soon take me away again to the other side of the world, I would be leaving Natalie in good hands, and with three beautiful daughters.

Just one note of sadness tainted our bliss at that time. Brett returned to his father, this time permanently. For nine years he had been so much part of the family, but now Hal had settled in Canada with his new wife and two children and naturally wanted Brett there. We had always known it must happen one day but nevertheless the tears came unchained when he had to say goodbye.

Chapter 15

If you   can't   keep   the   pace   up

EVERYTHING WAS COMING up roses. I was happy, Irene was happy, my record and concert promoters were happy, my accountant was happy – even the taxman was laughing! To my consternation, the only person around me who didn't appear to be as happy as I would have hoped was Natalie. On my return from the Australian tour shortly after Jessica was born, she seemed moody at times, morose. I put it down to fatigue, having three small children to cope with. However, one remark she made to me kept going round and round in my mind. 'Don't start to believe your own publicity,' she said one day. 'If you do, I'll be down on you like a ton of bricks.' I thought it highly unlikely I'd ever forget who I was, but filed her message away in the back of my brain.

I was, in fact, feeling superbly fit. I wasn't smoking, I wasn't drinking and I was taking regular exercise. The rapid tempo at which I had to live my life simply fuelled my creativity and my performing. I was positively thriving on hard work and a jet-setting tour programme. I was really travelling in the fast lane! I also thought there were no surprises left for me until Irene rang me one afternoon at home.

'I've just heard you've got a record in the Top One Hundred in America!' she said excitedly.

'What?' I gasped. 'How could it be? I don't even have a recording contract there. It lapsed last year.'

'You're right,' said Irene. 'I'd better look into it.'

When I hung up and gave the news to Natalie she said, 'Which song?'

For a moment I was struck dumb. 'You know, I didn't think to ask. I'll call her back.'

But Irene had also forgotten to ask! I said to her, 'It must be

214

one of the Canadian chart hits, probably "I Don't Believe in If".'

She agreed. 'I'll find out and let you know,' she said.

A few hours later she rang again. 'You want to hear a story?' she said, laughing. 'It's one of the songs from that radio series. You remember "The Last Farewell"?'

Four albums had come and gone since the radio series and indeed I was hard pressed to place the song.

Even now I find the story of 'The Last Farewell' incredible. It is a story of monumental good luck, coincidence, timing and show business fairy tale all wrapped up into one. Of course it was also a damned good song! What happened was this:

The wife of one of the programme directors at radio station WSB Atlanta had gone on holiday to Canada, and a friend introduced her to my albums. She fell in love with that particular track, took the album home with her and asked her husband to play the song at a particular time of the day when she knew she'd be stuck in traffic and could catch it on her car radio. Listeners started to phone in about it and soon it was being played on other WSB programmes. Then other radio stations began to pick it up. Before long the thing began to snowball. RCA had to import the record from Canada to keep up with the demand. All this was happening, mind you, without our even knowing about it. Several weeks had passed before the news got to Irene when she rang me that day.

As I mentioned, I barely remembered the song, since it had more or less sunk without a trace after its recording. Now I discovered that I didn't even have the album at home. The night of Irene's phone call Natalie and I had to rush over to a friend's house to listen to my 'new hit'. We sat till two in the morning playing the record over and over again, mesmerised by events.

In six weeks it raced up the U.S. charts, finally coming to rest at No. 6, where it remained for several weeks before sliding back down. Meantime in Britain EMI quickly put it out. Like lightning the song bolted to the No. 2 spot where for four months it threatened to topple Rod Stewart's hit 'Sailing' from No. 1, just a couple of hundred sales a week making the difference. By now, too, 'The Last Farewell' was in the Top Ten in just about every English-speaking country in the world.

The surprise didn't stop there, either, for it was shooting up in the German charts!

That hit had a profound influence on my life, both personally and as a performer. All else I had accomplished professionally till then was relegated to the shadows; that's what a hit at the top of the charts can do for you, whether you like it or not. For the first time even my parents were impressed as relatives in England regaled them with tales of their 'star' son. Irene could hardly keep up with requests for personal appearances. It was positively bewildering. I said at the beginning of this chapter that I was travelling in the fast lane. I was now completely off terra firma and breaking the sound barrier in the stratosphere!

Looking back I can see now that in our innocence we believed living in a country cottage miles from the nearest village protected us from intrusion and from unwanted publicity. With hindsight I'd guess we could have remained more anonymous amid the hurly-burly of London. What I gained in fame with 'The Last Farewell' I lost in privacy. I do not say that in complaint; that's just the way it was. I have never for one moment resented being stopped on the street or in a restaurant by a fan or an autograph seeker; I've said before that I bless my fans for giving me and my family all the good things in life we possess. But in my own home, within my own four walls, I am no longer a singer, just a family man with a wife and kids. So I did resent it when my Sunday lunch or a game on the lawn with the kids would be interrupted by yet another merry band seeking autographs or a friendly chat.

However, the spotlight, the glare of publicity, the fame, make a personality a target for much worse than just well-meaning fans.

One day the children's nanny opened the door to a man dressed in a sober business suit. He asked if he could speak to me. She quite naturally assumed from his appearance that it was something to do with the house or with my business. It was not unknown for me to totally forget about an appointment and disappear for a game of golf, which was where I'd gone that day. Relegating to Natalie the task of making excuses for me she went to call her, the man following her into the house. Natalie appeared and began talking to him. From the outset it was obvious that he was not there on business but wanted to talk to me personally, as a famous singer. Natalie apologised but said that I was away.

'Well I'd better explain the reason for my visit to you then,' he said, and proceeded to show Natalie one of his hands, which was terribly mutilated.

'See that . . . see that?' he began to babble, becoming excited. 'I got that in an accident at work.'

Shocked at the sight and trying not to show it, Natalie uttered some word of sympathy, which seemed only to enrage him still further. Eyes bulging and spittle running down his chin, he grabbed her neck in a vice-like grip with his good hand and began to throttle her, shaking her like a rag doll and shouting, 'I said I would get one of you! Capitalist pigs like your husband owe me a living!'

Hearing the ruckus, Nanny ran back into the room and tried to pull the man away but he was much too strong for her. In a panic she ran screaming down the lane. There were no neighbours anywhere near us and I shudder to think what might have happened had not two workmen just returned to the stable area to collect some tools. They pelted down to the house and a running battle ensued. They got him away from Natalie but they couldn't hold onto him and he escaped to his car parked down the road. The workmen noted the registration number, called an ambulance for Natalie then rang the police, who were there in minutes. Tracing the car proved no problem and the man was in custody within the hour.

All of this I knew nothing about, of course, until I came home whistling merrily to be confronted by the police. They told me the man had only recently been released from a mental hospital, having convinced the doctors that he was cured.

One may well imagine Natalie's state of mind as the result of this attack. The shock and the fright did not easily wear off. Despite the fact that the man was of course put away again, I immediately called in security experts to fit special locks, chains and an elaborate alarm system all over the house. I gave orders that nobody was ever to open the door without first identifying the caller; if unknown, the chain was to be kept securely in place.

Suddenly, just like that, our happy, private little bubble of a world burst wide open. Suddenly the atmosphere in the little village near us changed. Natalie and I had always been the target of some lighthearted teasing about our show business life style – mine in particular – but we moved freely about the community just like anyone else. Now the teasing was no longer lighthearted. Stupid and malicious snippets of gossip filtered back to us about wild parties at the house and when Natalie tried courageously to socialise within the community during my absences she was branded a scarlet woman – to give it the polite old fashioned term. The more famous I became the more exaggerated became the stories about us until finally Natalie refused to go anywhere without me.

You might think it was just typical village parochialism, or a sudden outbreak of jealousy at my newly-won fame. Not so; where we live now, many years later, we are still the targets of the same kind of malicious gossip and Natalie is determined to return to live in London as soon as our youngest child, Alexander, is in boarding school. As she puts it, 'at least I can get a boil on my bum without the whole area knowing about it!'

At first we made the mistake of trying to deny the stories. That never works, we now know. Then we took my father-in-law's advice and laughed at it all. This at least denies the gossips the satisfaction of knowing they've hurt you. What's the point in trying to pillory people when all they do is laugh at the worst things you say about them? The first time we fought back publicly, with laughter as our weapon, we found that many of our neighbours laughed along with us.

It happened at a local planning meeting, which we attended. A farmer, with land adjoining ours and incensed at our building a swimming pool, recording studio and guest cottage, decided to make things hot for us. At the meeting he harangued all and sundry with a list of complaints against us, all of them petty to the point of absurdity. Finally a young planning officer from the local council, fed up with our neighbour's peevish sniping, began to read out, with a straight face, the next item on the agenda. The Whittakers, he announced, had applied for planning permission to build a go-kart track and a heliport on their land. Our neighbour jumped up, apoplectic, and began to rant and rave with such intensity the planning officer decided to let him in on the joke before he really did have a stroke. Most of the other folk at the meeting joined in the laughter, I was encouraged to see, and our neighbour gave us no more trouble. In fact he actually became quite friendly – well, almost.

What we resented most of all was the attitude of some local people towards our children, as though they were some kind of showbusiness 'freaks'. Inevitably this was reflected in the attitude of their companions at school. Eventually we felt obliged to take them out of the state schools and place them in expensive, private schools where at least they were not regarded as 'different', since the parents of their school friends couldn't care less how famous I was or how much money we had.

But you know, no sooner do you start building a wall around yourself than somebody comes along and tries to knock a hole in it. You plug a hole and somebody else tries to sneak in around an unprotected corner. It seemed as though every time we made a defensive move, such as putting the kids in private school, and congratulated ourselves on winning the war, something would happen to remind us we'd merely won another little battle.

It was the summer of 1974 and, since neither of us felt truly comfortable with live-in help, we'd bought a small cottage in the village for Nanny and her husband. In any case, live-in nanny or not, Natalie herself always got up to crying children in the night and every morning was in the kitchen by six thirty (she still is!). At that time, regular as clockwork, the post and the papers were delivered at seven – both by the same man. Since the kitchen lights were always on by then, he was in the habit of knocking once on the kitchen door and leaving post and papers on the doorstep. On this particular day he knocked persistently.

Assuming there was a package or something to sign for, Natalie opened the door and began a cheery greeting. The man's grim expression stopped her in mid-sentence.

'I'm sorry, Mrs. Whittaker' he said, waving a sheet of paper at her, 'but I found this pinned to your door. I think your husband should see it. It's disgusting!'

Natalie tried to take the paper from him, but he was reluctant to give it up. She explained that I had only returned home in the early hours of the morning and that she didn't want to disturb me until late. He finally agreed to give her the paper, but left with the advice, 'I should call the police to have a look at it if I were you!'

Convinced that it was just another scurrilous bit of scandal, Natalie gathered up the mail and papers and took them back into the kitchen before giving the sheet of paper a glance. When she did, she later told me, she felt physically ill.

There, expertly drawn, was a cartoon of me, nailed by my skin to a crucifix. To one side was a gravestone with a guitar propped beside it, and the words ROGER WHITTAKER – R.I.P. inscribed on it. The further message was that if I continued to sing, I would be killed. After the initial shock, Natalie put it carefully to one side out of sight, prepared the children's breakfast, then took the older girls to school. On her return, she put Jessica in her cot for her morning nap, and telephoned the local police.

When the police had left after taking Natalie's fingerprints, we still shrugged the whole thing off, feeling that the entire incident had been over dramatised. However, later that afternoon another policeman called to tell us that the note had been sent to London for analysis and, in the opinion of the experts, it constituted a very definite threat. The cartoon was too well drawn and deliberate and the wording of the message indicative of a fanatical and unhinged mind. We were aghast. Then came the questions.

'Had the dogs barked a lot in the night?'

'Yes.' They were always alert to every sound.

'Did you hear a car?' Again yes – being such a quiet lane, every passing vehicle was noticed. But we hadn't heard anything stop. That would have instigated even more hysterical barking from the dogs. Around and around we went, racking our brains for any clue.

As he left, the officer warned us that until they managed to get the culprit, we should be especially viligant. He was able to give us one good piece of news. They had managed to lift two unidentified prints from the letter and if by any chance the person concerned had any sort of record, they would at least be able to identify him – or her.

I was worried sick as I had to leave Natalie alone for two

weeks while I did some cabaret, so I arranged for Nanny and her husband to live in. They, as nervous and as jumpy as we, were not too happy. Finally they agreed, somewhat put at ease by the police promise to patrol as often as they could.

After a week, Natalie was able to tell me that the police had a pretty good idea who was behind the note, but that they couldn't prove anything as he had an unshakable alibi. He apparently hadn't left his house from early the previous evening until midday the next day, and we could pinpoint the hours in which the note had been nailed to the door.

Knowing it was probably somebody local made the tension even worse, and when I got back after the two weeks I found a very hollow-eyed Natalie. She had been unable to sleep, jumping at every sound. Now that I was home she visibly relaxed. That night when we went to bed, we began to laugh about the whole incident, cracking silly gags. Secure in each other's company, we began to nod off. Suddenly, we were very much awake, both sitting bolt upright clutching at each other as the most terrible banging came from outside.

'What was that?' whispered Natalie. 'Where did it come from?' Memories of Mau Mau came flooding back to me. One way they had of getting people out into the open was to attack defenceless animals, and the noises we had heard had come from the stable area.

'Oh my God, somebody is getting at the horses!' I moaned. 'I'm going out there.'

We had a heated argument in muted whispers, whilst in the pitch dark I tried to disentangle myself from Natalie's arms.

Before I go any further, I have to set the scene for you. It was a cold, misty, moonless night with water dripping relentlessly from the trees, owls mournfully hooting and the occasional fox barking. Hammer House of Horror couldn't have scripted it better! Even the dogs were frozen into silence and immobility, the hairs of their backs raised and their teeth bared as we crept downstairs. Natalie was silently crying as I set my plan of attack. In the darkness I would scout across the open ground to the stables with her watching my back. When I reached the stables, I would keep my back against the stable wall, only using my torch when I surprised the bastard!

'Let me call the police first,' Natalie begged, but I insisted that time was too short. I would be perfectly all right, I told her, totally unconvinced by my own words! With my heart in my mouth, armed with the heaviest poker I could find, I slipped out of the door as quietly as I could and headed towards the source of the noises. I hadn't gone twenty yards before Natalie lost sight of me in the gloom. Simultaneously the noises stopped. For a moment I hesitated. Was he listening and watching too? Every drip from the trees sounded like a pistol shot. Back at the house Natalie was preparing to loose the dogs and had suitably armed herself before leaving the doorway to call the police.

Desperately trying to recall the physical movements of tracking in the African bush, I crossed the open space as silently as possible finally reaching the solid security of the stable walls. After the banging, the silence was so loud that it seemed even the horses had stopped breathing – maybe they had! I slid around the building, my back firmly against the wooden wall of the stable. As I reached the corner I stopped and listened, hardly daring to breathe. Then, from only a few yards away, the banging exploded in my ears. Adjusting my grip on both torch and poker, I leapt around the corner and, flashing the beam in the direction I had pinpointed, let out a yell.

The words Natalie then heard me shout were not, 'Got you!' or 'Stand where you are!' or other arresting words, but 'Who let that bloody donkey out?' For there, with a metal bucket in his mouth which he was thumping on the concrete floor, was our long-eared Houdini – Monty!

Chaos! Natalie had released the dogs at the first sound of my voice, before realising what I was saying! They pelted towards me, snapping and snarling, yelping and yowling, searching for the invisible intruder. In hot pursuit, Natalie became entangled in her long nightdress, and went head first into the mud, as I sat on the cold ground beside a very bemused donkey, with tears of relief and laughter rolling down my face. When the pandemonium subsided, we rounded up the dogs, returned Monty to his stable, and, though splattered with mud, laughed all the way back to the house, deciding that our imagination really had got the better of us.

Later the police told us the real culprit was in their care. His alibi had been provided by his parents, who had misguidedly tried to protect him. We were not his first victims. What happened to him I do not know, nor do I want to, but it left me with a permanent dread of what might be lurking 'out there'.

*　*　*

Natalie was pregnant again! Who says lightning doesn't strike twice in the same place? During the dodgy early months of her pregnancy I tried to stay at home as often as possible or at least confine my tours to Britain. Then, when she was safely through the first few months and about six months gone, I went off to the Continent and beyond for five weeks. By the time I returned, she was in her final six weeks and very large indeed. 'It's going to be a boy,' I assured her, a forecast which, considering my track record in predictions, led Natalie to believe it was going to be another girl.

But I was right this time, wasn't I?

Joe Collins then persuaded me against my better judgment to return to the cabaret circuit outside of London for a few 'exclusive' dates. Knowing what some of those clubs could be like, I agreed on the condition there would be a No Strippers clause in my contracts. One of the clubs in particular had a highly questionable reputation for its brand of strippers but I was promised that there'd be none on the bill the week I was there. Since this would be Natalie's last chance to travel with me before the baby was born, she came along.

The rather doubtful club was my last stop on the tour. When we arrived for the first rehearsal Natalie told me Irene had advised her to get the cheque for the week *before* the last Saturday night show. That raised my hackles and did not augur well for the coming week. I got the feeling all would not be as it was supposed to be. Entering the cabaret room we were greeted by the club owner. He rushed towards us, smiling and rubbing his hands together unctuously. I decided I definitely would not buy a used car from this man.

'Oh Roger,' he said, 'you're early. Would you mind very much if we rehearsed the support acts first?'

'Not at all,' I assured him, and Natalie and I sat down to watch the other performers go through their routines. First on was an extremely large lady who pulled what appeared to be the contents of a junkyard onto the stage: an old vacuum cleaner, lengths of hose, saucepan lids and a washboard. These she proceeded to play. It was so painful that it was not even vaguely funny. To make matters worse, as soon as she opened her mouth with an explanation of what she was doing, it was obvious that 'she' was no lady but a man! A transvestite to open *my* show? I nearly disappeared under my seat. The owner's sixth sense must have picked up my vibrations because he hurtled down between the tables and plonked himself down next to us saying, 'Different, isn't she? My audiences love her. It's her fourth time with us!'

Beginning to question in my own mind just what sort of audience I was going to have, I asked who the next acts were.

'A wonderful comic!' was his reply. Now a wonderful comic can be a great act to follow, but a lousy comic (as he turned out to be) can be a killer to any singer's act. The comic finished his act with a glare in my direction that left me in no doubt that he felt he should be the star of the show.

'We're ready for you now, Roger,' said mine host. My musicians, who had floated in while the lady junk player had been rehearsing, started to haul their gear on stage.

'Is that all the support?' I asked. 'It's very short. Does it mean you want me to do an extra fifteen minutes?'

Without looking me in the eye, he mumbled, 'No. Don't worry, there is a stripper but she's already rehearsed.'

'What!' I yelled. 'You know there is a No Stripper clause in my contract.' He tried desperately to placate me as I marched to the stage to tell the boys not to bother setting up as we were leaving. Tearing along behind me, he kept saying, 'But she is most tasteful. Your audience will not be offended I can promise you.'

'Call Joe, Nats, and tell him I am not appearing here,' I said firmly.

More yelling and screaming and finally Joe, on the other end of the telephone, told me that although in the wrong, the club would probably sue me for non-appearance. Furthermore, the Agents Association would consider my refusal to appear as unwarranted because I had appeared with strippers in the past. I would be the loser all round. Reluctantly I had to agree to perform but seething with anger told Joe that it would be my last cabaret appearance in England. Finished! Never again!

Still with clenched jaws, I went backstage with Natalie half an hour before the show started to find everything in chaos. My female backing singer was refusing to share a dressing room with the 'lady'. She didn't mind the stripper, but she drew the line at a transvestite. The wife of one of the musicians had turned up – so had his girl friend! And somewhere in the hurly-burly a shout went up, 'Can anybody manage the lighting desk? The lighting engineer has collapsed, dead drunk!'

One of my bright musicians called out, 'Oh, Natalie can handle it!'

'No way!' shouted Natalie, backing off and trying to avoid the wife and girl friend who were physically assaulting each other. But there was nobody else, so ten minutes before the curtain was due to go up, Natalie tried to acquaint herself with the lighting console. The lighting booths in clubs were usually a diminutive black curtained-off area on the side of the stage – as was this one. A stage hand, seeing Natalie's condition, considerately found her a high stool to sit on. What they hadn't reckoned on was Natalie's 'bump' – lighting engineers very rarely being eight months pregnant. There was no way she could squeeze behind the desk. The resident band played louder and louder to drown the backstage riot as the stagehands manoeuvred a backdrop to allow the space for Natalie plus baby.

Show time – and miraculously the noise backstage petered out. The music started and Natalie frantically tried to follow the junk player and the comic who proceeded to move every which way on stage, not sticking to their rehearsed places.

Up until now, none of us had set eyes on the Tasteful Stripper, but as the comic took his bows there was a commotion around the back of the stage and a lot of heated discussion which could not have failed to have filtered through out front to the audience (who, incidentally, appeared to have enjoyed every moment of the previous performers' acts). Then, to everyone's consternation, one tall, fiftyish lady strode down the corridor, hotly pursued by a short, dark, greasy gentleman clutching a cassette player and a milking stool! Stripper? She was already halfway there! All she wore was a pair of black panties, a suspender belt, stockings and shoes and carried an immensely long purple feather boa!

Open-mouthed, we all gazed at this apparition as she grabbed the milking stool from the man and strode out on to the stage. This we had to see! Natalie, in her booth, hadn't yet glimpsed the next subject for her lighting skills, but was given the word by the stripper's assistant to throw up the main spotlight. Tinny music emanated from the cassette player heralding the start of the most outrageous series of bumps and grinds, with the few items of clothing disappearing in the first thirty seconds of her act.

Without so much as a G string and sitting astride the stool, that 'tasteful' lady did things with the feather boa that would have had her thrown out of any decent brothel! On several occasions the lighting failed to pick up the highlights of her performance as Natalie tried to control her confusion and laughter. In the wings we were all mesmerised, until, with a final flourish, the dreaded feather boa was flung in our direction. I swear it had a life of its own, for it seemed to wriggle its way towards us across the floor. I have never seen so many ogling fellows scatter to avoid that repulsive missile!

Fortunately, the lighting engineer recovered and managed to remain sober for the rest of our engagement. My girl singer shared changing rooms with the male musicians, but the battle between the wife and the girl friend went on all week and I never did get to know who won. Natalie secured the cheque for the band and myself in the afternoon of the last show but, true to form for that week, it bounced! She then decided that it was time to get home before the excitement meant that a bunch of weirdos had to act as midwives!

Natalie returned home but I went up north, and in the effort to keep busy during the day, played squash whenever possible. The lesson learnt in Holland that I should stop pretending I was an energetic twenty-year old was long forgotten. So it should not have come as any great surprise that, having been challenged by the local champion – ten years younger than I – I managed to injure myself quite badly. As I rushed to get a drop ball, I tripped over my opponent's leg and flew into the air to land on my left knee. I remember crying out, 'Ouch that hurt!' Then I looked down and saw that my left kneecap had disappeared around the back of my leg. Then the pain really hit! Now I know why 'kneecapping' is used as a hideous torture. I lay screaming like a banshee, hitting the floor with my fist until my drummer, Quinney, who was playing in the next court, came rushing over. My opponent didn't move, shock I suppose, but Quinney turned bright green and rushed out again. Later he told me he first made for the nearest bar to swallow a large brandy before calling an ambulance.

What followed I endured in a kind of red-tinted haze. The ambulance attendants put an airbag around the injured knee, but as the nitrous oxide cylinder was empty, there was no anaesthetic to relieve the pain. Every bump and jolt of the journey to the hospital was a living hell, but nothing compared with the pain maliciously inflicted by the female radiologist who grabbed my leg and twisted it to the angle she wanted! I don't think she was a fan! To add insult to injury, two young nurses took one look at the offending limb and commented that I had better be all right as they had tickets for the concert that night.

'I will, I will!' I moaned. 'If I ever get to see a doctor who can put it right.'

After what seemed like a lifetime, a lady in a white coat appeared, scanned my X-ray and announced that to do a proper job they would have to cut open the knee, replace my knee cap and stitch the torn tendons back into place. That was out of the question, so I begged her to just strap it up and let me get back to the theatre for the show that night.

This less drastic course of action was agreed upon, and an anaesthetist found who wafted me into blessed unconsciousness. When I awoke, I was instantly aware of the absence of pain, but in my dazed state saw white things floating in front of my face. When at last I was able to focus and interpret the mumble of words, I realised the white object was a hand clutching several pieces of paper.

'Can I have an autograph for Josie . . . and one for my aunt . . . and another for Sarah . . . .' I think I signed them but to be honest I can't really remember except that I know that when I finally was compos mentis enough for Quinney to take me back to the hotel, a large group of staff waved me goodbye, with a farewell message that I had better get some rest before the show as they had paid good money for the tickets and wanted their pound of flesh.

Encased in plaster from hip to ankle, I was unable to even put my socks on so Quinney moved into an adjoining room to become my nursemaid for the next six weeks. But that night I was on stage, albeit on crutches, to be greeted by raucous laughter from what I gathered was the medical contingent in the audience!

Unbeknown to me, Natalie was in a terrible state. When the clerk had asked the usual question, 'next of kin', the hospital, not Quinney, had telephoned her to let me know what had happened. However, what Natalie had heard when she answered the phone was, 'This is . . . (indistinguishable name) hospital. We regret to inform you that your husband has been involved in an accident, and . . . .' The line had then gone dead and they hadn't bothered to ring her back. Natalie was left shattered. Imagining the worst, she waited and fretted for hours until I was able to ring her to tell her exactly what had happened.

Maybe it was that shock that triggered Guy's early arrival. Two days later she telephoned me to say that although she had had a check-up with the family doctor that morning, and he had told her that she had another four weeks to go, *she* thought the baby was going to arrive any minute and therefore, as soon as she had given the girls their supper, she was going to drive herself to London and check into the clinic.

Her gynaecologist was away when she got there. It was a terrible November night and, although she was not in labour, his partner didn't want to risk her driving home again, so kept her in for the night. As I was already on stage, she left a message saying she would call me when she got home the next day.

I felt uneasy and couldn't sleep. At four in the morning, the telephone went off like an alarm. I knew it – and so had Natalie!

'She's in the theatre now. Please get here as soon as possible,' the nurse told me. With my gammy leg stuck straight out in front of me on the back seat of the cat, Quinney drove us at breakneck speed the hundred and fifty miles back to London. Natalie was just conscious when I dragged myself into her room, but in a pretty poor way. She just grasped my hand and whispered, 'Well, you've got your son!'

I suddenly realised that for the entire journey I hadn't given a thought to the sex of the baby, only that Natalie should be all right as the nurse's tone had sounded quite anxious. When Natalie had drifted off to sleep again, I got one of the nurses to take me to the nursery to inspect my heir. Another perfect, strong baby. I felt totally choked as I watched our new son screw up his tiny face and flex his fists.

For the rest of the morning I lay on the floor beside Natalie's bed, my leg throbbing incessantly, while the nurses fed me painkillers. When at last both of us were sufficiently recovered to talk properly, we expressed our mutual delight at having a son at last. When Natalie began to doze off again, I began planning all those cliché things most fathers dream of for their sons: the model railway, the football, a school with a first-rate rugby team . . . Later that day when the doctors told Natalie it would be unwise to try for any more children, we were happier still that this one had been a boy and we agreed at that moment to heed the doctors' advice.

Of all the children, Lauren was the most excited at the news. She was turning into a perfect tomboy, hating dresses and much preferring to grub around in the dirt playing football. Emily didn't mind either way, as long as she could participate in the mothering, and Jessica was too little to worry about anything other than vying for an equal share of the cuddles.

Our hands were really full now and so was the house. But what a gorgeous family!

Chapter 16

Something's going wrong with the singer and the song

THERE IS NO doubt about it, I was absolutely brainwashed by the success of 'The Last Farewell'. I'd like to believe that it wasn't my ego that was blown up out of all proportion but my commonsense that went haywire. I accepted every booking that came my way from just about any promoter anywhere in the world who dangled a carrot in front of me. And, since my schedules were planned as much as a year in advance, I agreed to squeezing in new concert tours and promotional appearances wherever there was a gap. If I had a single in the charts somewhere, the record company naturally wanted me to tour to promote it, and off I would go.

Now and again I would rush home, grab some sleep for a few days, then depart again. About all I had time for at home was a kiss hello and a kiss goodbye. After another breakneck tour of Germany, where I had several singles in the charts at the same time, I returned to London to launch a new British tour at the Albert Hall. The concert proved to be a tremendous success but somehow I wasn't elated as I should have been. I was tired. That last tour of Germany had been a killer. For the first time I wondered whether I was paying for my success at the expense of my health.

A post-concert party had been arranged at home for friends and business associates. It turned out to be a fun evening – but not for me. To Natalie's consternation, I excused myself after an hour and retired to bed, leaving her to entertain the guests. The party went on until about two in the morning. When Natalie crawled into bed beside me I was still awake, though thoroughly exhausted. Sleep just would not come. Somewhere around four, I dozed off, only to be awakened sharply by a piercing pain in my chest. I couldn't breathe. I shook Natalie awake but was so breathless I had difficulty explaining what I was feeling.

Natalie was so frightened her shaking fingers could hardly dial the emergency numbers. I don't know why I did it, but I got out of bed and staggered downstairs, where I collapsed unconscious.

I woke up in the cardiac unit of the hospital, hooked up to a battery of machines. For the next several hours I was poked and prodded by a platoon of serious-faced doctors until, around ten o'clock, Natalie was let in to see me, accompanied by one of the specialists.

'You're a very lucky man,' he pronounced. 'It's not your heart. Your diaphragm collapsed. How long have you been running around with this pneumonia?'

That pneumonia, I discovered, was the result of a 'flu I'd contracted on the German tour and ignored. Natalie and I were both immensely relieved that my heart was still ticking over nicely, nevertheless I was advised to go home and remain in bed for at least a week. A week! The news would spread panic through the British tour promoters. Six cancelled concerts! I took just a few days off and completed the rest of the tour, no smarter for the scare.

I was running so fast I nearly missed myself in passing. Back across the Atlantic, where I went to cash in on my chart rating, I found I had a small break in my Canadian tour so agreed to fit in a mini-tour of the States. I was rushed to Atlanta where I experienced my first attack of fan hysteria. I was greeted at the airport by a mob of screaming young people. It was flattering but truly unnerving. I'd never known such popularity before. I recalled that ten years earlier I'd appeared on a television show with The Beatles and John Lennon had confided to me his terror when faced with crowds of screaming fans. At that time he and all The Beatles had to set up diversions outside the theatre to throw the fans off the track so the group could escape. That was all right for them, I thought, in the Swinging Sixties, young chaps that they were, but here I was, nearing middle age, and having to fight my way through crowds to get to a radio station or a restaurant for a meal. My mind couldn't adjust to it all.

By the time I returned to Canada I was quite shell-shocked.

When I got to Vancouver, though, I was most fortunate in meeting two people destined to play an important role in my American career. One was John Ford, not the film director, but the man then in charge of record promotion for RCA. The other man was Chet Atkins, the quiet gentleman from Nashville, the most unassuming and natural superstar I've ever met. I was knocked out when he came to see me. I'd been a fan of his guitar playing since my earliest days in the business. To me he was a genius on that instrument and why on earth he should want to see me I couldn't fathom, but see me he did and gave my ego a tremendous boost by enthusing over my songs. He told me Floyd Cramer had recorded 'The Last Farewell' and before leaving said he hoped we'd be able to work together one day.

Ships that pass in the night, I thought, but secretly hoped that one day it actually might happen. To my mind Nashville was – and still is – the Mecca of the music world and to work with Chet Atkins there would be just about the finest thing musically that could ever happen to me. At the time, however, it was just a fond wish; Chet left town and I continued on my one-night stands of Canada.

John Ford provided me with most of the few laughs I had time for on that hectic tour. You'd meet him for breakfast one morning and he'd be dressed in blue jeans and plaid shirt and you knew he was off to sell country music. Next morning he'd be in a dark blue suit, white shirt and neat tie, and you knew that day he was selling classics. A wonderful chap and we struck up a friendship that has withstood the test of time.

As I reached the end of that tour I met a lady who unwavering faith in my music has done so much for me in the United States – Ethel Gabriel. Her name means little or nothing to the general public but in the corridors of power within the record companies she is a legend. Through Ethel I met Ed Preston, then head of RCA Canada, and Ethel's secretary, Susan Heilberg. Who would have dared predict then that one day Ed would become president of my own record label Stateside and Susan vice-president in the United States. Who indeed would have predicted that one day I'd have my own international record company!

All I knew then, or for that matter cared about, was that

there was a lot of work and a lot of money changing hands. The excitement in the air around me was electric.

On the other hand, Natalie was not impressed. In fact, she was pretty well fed up. On one of my flying visits home, arriving as usual like a whirlwind, she told me in no uncertain terms that on my rare appearances in the household I was becoming a pain in the neck, although her actual anatomical reference was rather lower down. She pointed out to me that she spent weeks, months even, organising the upbringing of the children and every other little detail of the family's day-to-day existence. Then I'd come home and in a couple of days throw everything into disorder, making waves where I had no business even sticking my oar in. I did not take to this lecture kindly. Actually, I thought she was being totally unreasonable. Was I not the father of these children? Why shouldn't I interfere?

But I had to agree that I was so wound up when I got home that by the time I got unwound it was time to leave again. We decided then and there that we should have a two-week holiday towards the end of the year – just the two of us, when we could relax away from business and act like husband and wife again.

When the time came we chose Barbados, with its sun and sand and sea, as the perfect place to unwind. My schedule was so tight that I had to fly in from Germany and meet Natalie at Heathrow to catch the flight to Barbados. As we hugged and kissed in greeting I quite casually told her that our European promoter would be joining us during our holiday. The word workaholic had not yet registered on my brain but I did notice that Natalie did a double-take and lost her smile. I couldn't figure out why.

In spite of the intrusion, we did manage a splendid holiday and returned to spend a family Christmas. Guy was beginning to walk and suddenly the house seemed too small for us. We loved that house so much we didn't want to move, so called in architects to design an extension. They submitted plan after plan until finally we had to recognise that any new building we attempted would ruin the architectural beauty of the place. The only alternative was to find a larger house.

Much to our pleasant surprise our search for a new home was brief. The first house we looked at, just a few miles from where we lived, took our breath away. It was built in the Queen Anne style, set in eight acres of magnificent gardens, offering all we needed by way of room, atmosphere, privacy and facilities. We sent in surveyors who reported that with the exception of rampant woodworm and ancient wiring and boilers, it was perfect.

We bought it.

As usual and as per schedule I was not to be around when the big move came, as I was off on a five-month world tour. But I wasn't worried. Natalie seemed to have everything under control. We knew that while the electricians and builders were working only part of the house would be habitable and she would have to cook meals on portable electric rings until the new kitchen was fitted – but she was cool, she could handle it. The day before the move I got into my car and drove off to begin the tour while Natalie set off to collect the children from school and go on to the new house to make sure the builders had everything ready for the following morning. When she got there she was met by a very worried builder.

John Cranwell, who had faithfully reconstructed our last home, was frantic. Early that morning one of the electricians working in the attic above what would be our bedroom had stepped on a beam and the whole thing had given way, tumbling him ten feet into the room below. Fortunately he'd only suffered a twisted ankle. Rather than worry Natalie about the 'ifs and buts' John had called in a structural engineer to assess the damage. As she arrived both John and this gloomy faced individual were standing outside gazing at the building. Trying to keep four small children from assassinating one another long enough to understand what the men were saying, she hauled them out of the car to go and explore. 'But not in the house!' yelled John. 'It's not safe.'

'What?' was Natalie's horror-stricken query. 'We're moving in tomorrow.'

'Not here, you're not!' announced doom-face.

Quelling the rising panic Natalie stood and listened to him. The beam had been one of four main beams holding the house together and all four were defective. The whole house would have to be pulled together with giant steel girders, which meant stripping the whole of the top floor. Then came the list of other faults he had discovered: dry rot in one wing of the house, all the windows had merely been filled to cover the rot in the frames. Twenty-four window frames would have to be made to order in view of the architectural style of the house. The boilers that we had been assured would last a few more years were, in fact, in danger of blowing up and the kitchen wing with two bedrooms and a bathroom overhead had been fire damaged at some point and would have to be demolished and rebuilt. With five different gangs of workmen the job could be finished in four months.

This was not the time to lose her cool so, packing the children off to Nanny, Natalie set about finding a hotel for the seven humans and assorted animals that made up our menagerie, but to no avail. She couldn't stay on where we were as the other people were due to move in only hours after we left, nor could she find storage at such short notice for all our furniture.

By this time it was six o'clock in the evening – eighteen hours before the move. John held his boys back and decided to make the three reasonable rooms over the stable block into temporary living quarters, working overnight to clear away forty years of rubble and dust and laying odd bits of linoleum over the rickety floors.

The following morning the move went ahead willy-nilly. All our furniture was off-loaded into the one and only habitable room in the new house. The children, nanny and housekeeper, together with all the animals, were ensconced in the stables. As one back wall in the house had been opened up with consequent concern over squatters and thieves, a camp bed was installed in the middle of the piles of furniture and for the next three months Natalie slept there alone, with torch in hand, until the heavy building work could be finished and the electricity supply reconnected. Halfway around the world I was getting reports of all this and the mounting bills that accompanied the nightmare. As to Natalie's state of mind, I could only hazard a guess. I suggested we sue for damages. Our lawyers agreed we would probably win a court action, but it could take years to settle and in the end would cost us as much as we might win. We just had to grin and bear it and accept that we had been well and truly 'done'.

The repairs on the house were finished just in time for my return at Christmas. I found Natalie in terrible shape, hollow-eyed and pale. She'd lost sixteen pounds. But with the coming of Christmas, when we decorated a huge tree in our beautiful drawing room and there were lots of presents for everybody and the sound of children's laughter in the house, the nightmare was forgotten. Only to be replaced by another one.

The season of peace on earth, goodwill towards men was over. The hate season began. Hardly had the new year been rung in before a few misbegotten souls in our new village began a vitriolic campaign against us. By comparison, the gossips and scandalmongers at our old village were rank amateurs. Don't ask me why it began. I really don't know. I can only say that we were deeply hurt and bewildered by the welcome of our new community. True, there were only three or four people involved, but in a small village that's a powerful group aligned against you.

Saddest of all, spurred on by the attitude of their elders, a few difficult and misguided youngsters launched their own campaign of vandalism and destruction; new young trees we planted were cut to the ground, gates were hacked to pieces with axes, the children's tree house was demolished time after time and the chicken run attacked so often we had eventually to get rid of all our stock. As fast as we repaired the protective hedge they cut their way through again. Finally, in desperation I had to erect the kind of steel fence you see around a military establishment with an electric wire running across the top.

The most wicked and vicious act perpetrated during that period involved our adored donkey, Monty. We had long since sold the horses, Natalie being far too busy to exercise and look after them, but Monty had come with us to our new home. The smaller children used to ride him and lovingly cleaned his tack and painted signs over his stable. However, his stable and paddock were behind a brick wall which blocked our view from the house. At first we kept finding his saddle lying in the damp grass, or Monty standing forlornly trying to shake off the bridle that had been wrongly put on. In an attempt to deter the would-be donkey riders we removed his tack to the house but one morning Natalie got up to hear distressed braying coming from the paddock, and flinging on her jeans and sweater rushed out. There stood our beloved Monty with blood running down his jaw! Somebody, we will never know who, had pulled wire through his mouth to make a 'bit' for a string bridle and, when it didn't work, had left him with the wire biting deeper and deeper into the soft sides of his mouth. Twenty-six stitches were needed to close the wounds. The greater damage was psychological, however. He would no longer let even our children near him; only Natalie could tend him in his nervous state. As we had nowhere nearer to the house to stable him, we had to let him go. Heartbreaking though it was, we managed to find a home for him where other donkeys were affectionately kept and the family prepared to overcome his fears. We still miss him.

Every time we tried to improve the property, we were deluged with complaints and anonymous tips given to the press, usually to the effect that I was breaking regulations. All these were without foundation, but upset Natalie nonetheless. Imagine trying to get tea for the children and suddenly there is a TV van full of reporters parked in your drive, refusing to move until they had their story. Even when sent packing by the police, they perched outside the main gate so that it was impossible to drive out the car without some loony leaping at you with a microphone in his hand!

We knew exactly who was behind all this and she and her cronies seemed to have nothing better to do with their time than sit and devise new ways of making our lives more miserable. Natalie at the time was quite seriously ill and her sense of humour running at an unusually low ebb. Her initial reaction was to contact legal advisers and have their mischief-making stopped by the courts once and for all. Once again, our solicitors were pessimistic, saying it would do us no good whatsoever with public opinion if we were to attack the 'poor little under-dog' however much in the right we were.

Seething with rage at one latest little snippet of malice to reach her ears, she again remembered her father's advice, 'Keep laughing! They simply don't know how to retaliate!'

A spark of an idea started her chuckling to herself. She would start her own false rumour in such a way that it would show the whole community just where all the malicious talk was coming from.

If those narrow-minded bigots thought having a singer living in the manor house was bad enough, how about an African chief with several wives? She got hold of a black comedian friend of ours who rubbed his hands with glee and busily set about gathering his 'wives' together. Natalie's plan was to erect large 'For Sale' signs all around the property, with 'Sold' slashed across them, on April Fool's Day. Then our friend, in full African garb, would wander around with his 'wives' following in his wake, viewing the outside of the property and jabbering about the improvements he would make for his large family. However, only two weeks before the intended caper, our friend rang to say he had been booked for an important date and wouldn't be able to carry out the charade, much to his regret.

Momentarily stumped, Natalie nearly dropped the plan. Then she came up with an even more subtle idea. The 'For Sale' signs would go up and through Clodagh, our secretary, who had a friend in the local estate agent's office, information would be planted and we would see how far it went. Her friend thought it a marvellous joke and promised to co-operate fully.

At dawn on April 1st, his team was out erecting the largest signs they could find, with 'Sold' slashed right across them, and we all sat back and waited. Everybody who was in on the joke was in our office near the main gate watching as by 8.30 a.m. little gaggles of people gathered, gesticulating and muttering amongst themselves at the sign. At five minutes past nine, a guffawing estate agent was on the phone to us.

'Got them! It worked like a dream. At nine o'clock on the dot my phone rang and it was your chief antagonist. She gave her name and demanded to know who the house had been sold to and for how much. I told her I was not at liberty to divulge the sale price, but that I did know that the purchaser was an Arab gentleman in the oil business. I could hear her gasp of horror.'

Delighted with his news, we waited for developments. Then, at lunch time when by tradition April Fool's jokes are supposed to be exposed, Natalie went down to the village shop. It was packed with people and, as she entered, a stony silence fell. One look at her attempt to keep a poker face told the shop owner all he needed to know.

'I knew it! I knew it! It was an April Fool! I wish you had let me in on it. I could have had a tape-recorder behind the counter and you would have had a memento of the occasion that would have had you laughing for the next twenty years!'

He had been witness to the most extraordinary scenes that Natalie took enormous pleasure in retelling to all of us at home. Within moments of that famous phone call, the gang of scandalmongers had gone from house to house in the village, spreading the word, and then proceeded to stake out the shops to catch any last member of the community and impart the dreaded news to them.

To drive the message home, Natalie got permission to put a large notice in the shop window which read, 'I do hope that you have all managed to laugh at our April Fool. We realise that in our business we are open to outrageous talk and gossip – but hope that you have managed to maintain your sense of humour as we have done over the years.' Nobody ever admitted they hadn't laughed and in fact we were flooded with letters from people, who formerly had been too timid to speak up. For the first time we found that we did have friends in the village. As you may have gathered Natalie was almost entirely on her own during our first two years in our new home, two difficult years battling against some very strange people for whom I feel more pity than anger. How little charity must be in their hearts, how little love in their lives, to engender such bitterness toward a family of neighbours whose only crime, it seemed to me, was to have a husband and father who was famous. *Mea culpa.*

When in the summer of 1977 a British television series was offered me, Natalie was delighted. At last I would be home for a couple of months. Alas, we found out that the studios were away down in the southwest of England. The only way the family would get to see much of me was for me to commute back and forth by private plane every chance I got. I'd been using private aircraft quite a bit, especially during my Canadian tours where they were the only practical way of hopping from city to city at odd hours and sometimes short notice. All that flying around in small planes had given me the itch to fly one myself and now at last the chance presented itself. The pilot I hired to fly me back and forth from home to studio also had an instructor's licence, so I used those weeks of commuting to take lessons. I spent every available hour learning how to fly and when I wasn't in the air or working I'd bury myself in my study learning all the other things one needed to pass the pilot's examinations. Perhaps needless to say, Natalie loathed all this; at last she had me in the country for two months but I might as well have been up the Amazon for all she and the children saw of me.

Getting that pilot's licence became an obsession with me. Nothing was more important. I got it all right and eventually went on to qualify as a pilot on twin-engine aircraft. Finally I bought my own plane.

Autumn arrived. One day, as I motored up the sweep of drive that led from the main gate to our house, I noticed idly how beautiful England was at that time of year. The previous summer we'd suffered a record drought (at least that's what Natalie told me) but now the garden was splendid, with variegated rows of brilliant flowers contrasting with the darker greenery of the herbaceous borders, the tall fir trees standing majestically in the broad expanse of lawn. There were lilies in bloom on the pond.

My mind was really elsewhere, however. I was preparing for a two-month Continental tour, excited as never before by the prospect of flying my own plane during most of it. Nagging me, though, gnawing away at the back of my mind like a ferret on a carrot was the painful knowledge that my relationship with Natalie was dangerously strained. I was also aware that it was no secret to our close friends and business colleagues. As far as the public and media were concerned we were still very much the perfect picture of a successful and happy show business family. We gave interviews to the glossy magazines and put on a happy face, but the twinkle was gone from Natalie's eyes. I knew it yet somehow perfidiously refused to know it.

Just two weeks after I left she rang me to tell me she was pregnant again. Against the doctors' advice and against all the odds, to be sure, but there it was. The baby was due in May. I was, as ever, over the moon. But the lights of my joy were dimmed by a remark that floated over the Channel to me. News of Natalie's pregnancy was greeted with surprise by one particularly bitchy friend. 'Really?' she said. 'How lovely!

And who's the father?'

Such was my reputation as an absentee husband.

* * *

Somewhere, sometime during those months of Natalie's pregnancy with Alexander I sang a lyric, 'something's going wrong with the singer and the song' and the song continues, 'there are none so blind as those who will not see.' Not original, that line. Better poets than I (notably Jonathan Swift) have said it. Was I subliminally writing about myself? Perhaps.

How do you get off the roundabout when it's travelling at such speed? How do you deal with people whose vested interest is in keeping you on that roundabout? I'd like to have a pound note for every entertainer who has at some point been faced with the same dilemma. Part of the answer is: maybe you don't want to get off. Maybe the thrill of the ride is all you've got left going for you. All around you there are people telling you you're the greatest, pumping your hand, patting you on the back, shoving contracts under your nose, reminding you of your obligations to your fans, to your promoters, to the record companies. Nobody reminds you of your obligations to your family or, for that matter, to yourself.

Unable to get near me, unable to penetrate that wall of people surrounding me, Natalie shouted down the phone to me one night, 'Don't tell *me* you're exhausted! Stop! Look at your date sheet when they dangle their latest carrot at you!'

She was becoming ever more frantic and bitter. 'You're killing yourself and us,' she said, pleading with me. 'Don't you realise that if you wear yourself out they'll drop you in favour of the next goose to lay a golden egg?'

There are none so deaf as those who will not hear, the poet also said.

I went straight from Germany to Canada without stopping at home. Deep down, had I the sense, or the courage, or the will to look, I was as miserable as Natalie. And I *was* tired, mentally and physically. But I drove myself, felt I had to keep going, my pride in my strength and my energy blinding me with this absurd, juvenile image I had of myself as some kind of superman. I had the disease, all right: I believed my own publicity.

Vaguely I was aware that Natalie was enduring a dreadful pregnancy; most of the time she was confined to her bed. I don't suppose I was home more than two weeks in that nine months. How could I have failed to respond to all those stilted telephone conversations, the degeneration of Natalie's ready wit, her honest laughter, into humourless, sarcastic badgering? When I bothered to think about it, which was rarely, I thought, well, my purpose in life is to provide my family with the best environment money can buy. And I'm doing all right. They've got everything they could wish for.

Of course I now know I was just kidding myself. I wasn't knocking my brains out for them. I was doing it for *me*.

I tried to arrange some time off around the week the baby was due but he arrived prematurely, about six weeks early. I was on a German tour and in fact in the middle of a concert when the news came through. I took no encores that night. My promoter had a change of clothes ready for me in the car and my private plane's engines were running when I got to the airport. Over Bremen at 29,000 feet an air traffic controller cut into my radio and asked the name of the pilot. When I identified myself he said, 'Congratulations – mother and son are doing nicely. Out!'

Alexander was in an incubator when I arrived and Natalie had not yet seen him. Semiconscious, she did manage to remark, mysteriously, that she'd like her arm back. Investigating, I discovered to my mortification that when she'd emerged from the anaesthetic she found herself being kissed, not by a loving husband but by a drunken promoter slobbering up and down her arm. For three weeks Natalie remained in hospital and when she came home she needed a full-time nurse for a month before she got back on her feet.

What I didn't know then but learned later was that our communication had deteriorated so badly Natalie hadn't bothered to inform me of the emergency that brought on the premature birth. Rushed to hospital to save her pregnancy she told Irene and the nanny, 'Don't bother Roger. He's too far away and it's not worth worrying him. If I lose the baby, then I'll tell him.'

I knew a bit about post natal depression so when Natalie appeared to be weepier than usual I put it down to the difficulty of the birth and the fact that her father was desperately ill. She had lost her mother when she was a little girl and he was all she had left, loving him perhaps more than anything or anyone on earth. Toby had suffered a stroke in the summer after several earlier heart attacks, one of which had been almost fatal. His deterioration now was due to the fact that after one of those attacks he had been unconscious for almost an hour.

The pressure on Natalie was becoming insupportable, not that I recognised it at the time. Following a difficult pregnancy and an even more difficult birth she now had to contend with a dying father who hovered pitifully in a twilight zone, unable to speak, tears of frustration streaming down his cheeks as he blinked responses to her questions. On top of all that she was trying to cope with the problem of a husband who seemed to have lost all interest in her love and in her wellbeing.

I was aware that Toby was approaching the end and I truly loved him, but I felt the best thing I could do for my family was remain as cheerful as possible and help Natalie's stepmother financially. They were sad days. That Christmas of 1978, when I returned home for a three-week break after another exhausting tour, all I wanted was to sleep and be left alone in peace. I was in no mood therefore for Natalie's announcement that she had booked a ten-day holiday for us in Spain, to begin after the Christmas celebrations. I was surprised, too, considering Toby's condition. However, quite sensibly, she said there was not much she could do for him, he was being well looked after, and she was on the point of collapse and needed a holiday. 'We both need this,' she said, 'to get to know each other again.'

I went through the motions of Christmas cheer in a daze, my laughter hollow, my smiling face a phony mask. I was overwhelmed with fatigue, my brain a sodden sponge, devoid of any thought, any emotion. I boarded our flight to Spain like a robot and sat there insensate. For three days at our sunny Spanish resort I did nothing but sit and read, absorbing not a word. I spoke to Natalie only when necessary and, in any case, we had nothing to say to each other. I hardly slept, lying awake in the darkness, my eyes open, haunted by some nameless anxiety. On the fourth sleepless night I got out of bed and began pacing up and down, up and down, like a prisoner in a cell. I couldn't breathe. I felt my heart was going to stop.

I shook Natalie awake. 'Get me home. I'm ill!'

We were on a chartered flight out early the next morning and that afternoon I was in my bed, inert, torpid, transfixed. I had never known such a state. I was a stranger to myself. I couldn't make contact with my brain or make the simplest decision. It was terrifying.

The doctor's diagnosis was complete exhaustion. He said I must remain in bed indefinitely, for as long as it took me to recover.

Heaven only knows what Natalie must have been feeling, how she was coping, for within hours of our return Toby fell into a coma and wasn't expected to live more than a few days.

For three weeks I was forced to rest while Natalie undertook a routine that would have crushed a weaker person. Living on three hours sleep a night, dealing with five children, an ailing husband and a dying parent, she tried to get her own shattered life into some sort of order. They say that behind every successful man there is a good woman. Thank God I had Natalie because not only did she manage to survive the dreadful situation at home, but she also took over the business.

By this time I was no longer just an entertainer, but a corporate body with international interests. I recorded in Britain for my own company, Tembo Records (a throwback to my Kenyan origins: tembo means elephant in Swahili). I also had a music publishing company and a production company. With me flat on my back, Natalie took charge. It came as quite a shock to a lot of people when she charged in, guns blazing. Many of them had been quite prepared to pick her creative brains down the years while studiously ignoring all her advice on my work schedule. Now they had to sit up and pay attention.

As the days of my illness passed by and I began to recover my senses, I came to understand that I had lost forever the woman I had married; too much had changed in our lives. That did not mean we were lost completely to each other but, if we were going to go on together, then we – or at least certainly I – would have to make adjustments. I dare say that in many respects this crisis point in our marriage – for it was just that – was not unique. The reasons behind the crisis might have been unique to us, but many a marriage reaches such a crossroads. The time comes for a re-examination of the relationship: who am I and who are you; not who we were when we met, or when we married but who are we *now*? I knew, without a doubt, that I wanted to go on with Natalie; the question in my mind was did Natalie want to go on with me? Or would she prefer to take the children and leave me holding onto a way of life that had become so precious to me and so meaningless to her.

One morning I noticed she'd begun smoking again after many years of abstinence. I tried, clumsily, to express my regret for my lack of consideration, for so many things that had gone wrong, explaining, excusing, pointing out the problems I faced. Once more I was blind and deaf, except to my own voice, to my own horizon. My obtuseness brought out in Natalie all those simmering emotions she'd kept bottled up for years. They bubbled over now and I caught the full heat of her anger.

'You've got problems!' she shouted. 'What about me? What about your children? They don't have a father. I don't have a husband, just some guy who floats in from time to time, uses the house as a hotel and drifts out again. What's the point of it all? Unless you change drastically I want a divorce!'

'You're not serious,' I said, shaken.

'You bet I am! We'd all be better off alone than putting up with the emotional strain of the odd occasion when you deem to grace us with your presence!'

That initial outburst out of the way she went on to point out to me just the sort of person I'd become, no holds barred.

'You and you alone are responsible for our present position. You're a grown man and you've been manipulated at every turn. Your whole future is in question as far as I'm concerned. You've got your whole life ahead of you. Do something about it. I'm going to spend as much time as possible with Pa.'

She left, leaving behind a very sober, anxious man. She was right. I now knew with awful clarity that all I wanted in life was for everything to be the way it had been before. The thing was, I knew that it could not be the same, that if anything was to be salvaged from what had been a wonderful relationship I would have to work for it. I would have to start from the beginning and prove myself and my love all over again.

In the midst of all this anguish, the telephone rang one day – the bell tolling for Toby. Natalie answered, then turned to me. 'I won't be back until morning. Dad just died.'

My heart went out to her, my sorrow deepened by the knowledge that at this most poignant moment she sought neither my support nor my comfort.

Strangely enough, once the worst was over, we began to rebuild our relationship. We tried to come to terms with the conflicting interests of my career and my family. Never again would I take Natalie for granted. Never again would I court disaster. My outlook on life underwent a dramatic change. Our first step was to establish that we both wanted each other. We agreed that two adults living together for the sake of the children was a nonsense. We had to love each other. I knew how much I loved her and needed her; the problem for me was to regain the trust she'd lost in my love. I accepted that this would take time and would have to be demonstrated.

At the same time, I knew in my heart of hearts that deep down she still loved me, although that love was submerged for the moment underneath several layers of anger and resentment. Why else, when I'd fallen ill, had she entered the arena on my behalf and fought so hard for my welfare? And she was fighting still, routing out the deadwood and the spongers and those others she knew so well who contributed nothing but damage to our personal relationship as well as to our businesses.

Her involvement – the jealous called it her interference – in my business was resented by many of those colleagues I had once prized as friends. Nevertheless I saw that she was making the right decisions – right for me, right for the business, right for *us*. Slowly, resolutely, talking to each other, working together, we rebuilt from the broken pieces of our relationship a marriage stronger in many ways than it had ever been before.

I discovered renewed happiness in my life at home. I savoured the release from the stresses of business. I vowed that never again would I be away from home for more than six weeks at a time and that all school holidays would find me at home with the children.

246

Chapter 17

There's a   hole   in the   side   of   Af —ri —ca

IF THIS WERE a film instead of a book you would now be seeing one of those corny old devices they used in black and white movies to indicate the passage of time: pages of a calendar flying off, weeks turning into months, months turning into years.

Our lives jogged along at a sensible pace; no overnight miracles, no waving of a magic wand and all our problems and troubles vanished for all time. We took two steps forward and one back, but we made progress. We made mistakes and we corrected them. We ran into business problems and we solved them. Together. That was the important thing; together. With one of my rare strokes of genius I even coerced Natalie into taking flying lessons. Not only did she learn to fly, she entered rallies and took up aerobatics! We now had something new in common.

In 1980, RCA in America asked me to come up with some musical ideas to aid the UNESCO Education for Handicapped Children Programme. Special schooling is needed for these children, especially in Third World countries. Remembering the enormous public response in the United Kingdom to my radio competition for lyrics, I proposed that RCA launch a competition along similar lines for children worldwide under fifteen, to write a lyric saying what they thought about their world. Under the banner, 'Children Helping Children' the competition got under way, with an international panel of celebrity judges including Yehudi Menuhin and Peter Ustinov. I agreed to put the winning entry to music.

What a selection I received! And what an insight into how children view the way adults run their world. It was amazing to learn how even the very young can see quite clearly where politicians go wrong.

One lyric finally stood out from the rest. 'I am but a small voice' said everything we were looking for. The winning writer, a delightful thirteen-year-old girl from the Philippines, Odina Batnag, was flown to New York with her family. At the press conference in the United Nations building, she charmed and enchanted the jaded, cynical press corps, then joined me at the Radio City Music Hall. Backed by the Harlem Boys Choir I did my best to do justice to the emotion and sentiments in her words, and I admit to being choked as her little figure, in traditional dress, joined me on stage. The audience stood and applauded and showed by their response that it understood.

From New York we flew off on a whirlwind tour of the States, then on to Europe to spread the word over there. Then came the message: could I return to New York? The B'Nai Brith had awarded me, together with Kenny Rogers, the Humanitarian Award. I was stunned.

In my hotel room I rehearsed and rehearsed my acceptance speech until I thought I had it right. All the lessons I had learned, especially that of being word perfect given to me by Keith Michell, went right out of the window when faced with so many dignitaries on that wonderful evening. Afterwards I suffered the agonies of what we call 'pillow bites' in our family – the mistakes you made that flood back just as you are dropping off to sleep – when I realised that I had only forgotten to thank the people of RCA! It was their idea to help UNESCO that led to my receiving that honoured award. So now, publically, my thanks to Bob Summers, Ethel Gabriel and all who in my utter nervousness I so shamefully neglected.

Until then I had been recording in Canada, but now RCA wanted me to be guided by an American producer and submitted a list of possible names. One leapt out of the page at me – Chet Atkins! I didn't even see the other names. My dream was coming true. Halfway through my first major tour of America he joined us in Boston to talk over projects. The rest is history. Natalie and I fell in love with Nashville and in particular with Chet and his wife, Leona. Two tours and three albums later it was Chet who started me off on a new project.

Deciding that 1982 should be a creative year with little or no touring, I invited Chet to stay with us on one of his rare trips to England, hoping that we might come up with something different.

After dinner one night we started an impromptu jam session. When Chet and Natalie had finished their raucous renditions of American folk tunes and collapsed into giggles, Chet breathlessly asked me to sing some of my African folk songs from my childhood, which I proceeded to do. After two or three numbers, he leaned forward and asked me to show him in slow motion just how I plucked my guitar, while he tried to follow on his. I had never really thought about my playing technique, having merely imitated the methods used by the Africans at home.

Totally bemused by the apparently inconsistent rhythms I used, Chet casually suggested that I should write some of my own African songs using those rhythms. It took a few days after his departure for the suggestion to sink home. What a great idea! But I would have to return to Africa to surround myself with the people and the atmosphere to revitalise my interpretations of the music. Then came another idea. Natalie had never been to my homeland and it would be the perfect opportunity to show her the background to the many stories I had told her. Then another idea: why not film her introduction to my homeland for television so that a much wider audience could enjoy and discover it with her?

Cautiously, I first mentioned my idea to Irene, whose reaction was instant and positive.

'Marvellous! Just what we've been looking for. Everybody is screaming for a TV special and a musical safari of Kenya would certainly be different!'

We calculated that we would probably need six weeks for the filming, followed by several months for the editing and recording of the music. With no more detailed plans than that, I decided to broach the subject to Natalie but, knowing how she felt about leaving the children without easy contact in case of emergencies, I was not confident about the outcome. Deep in the African bush is about as far out of touch as you can get, with only radio telephones in far flung lodges for communication with civilisation.

I decided that a beautiful restaurant and a gourmet lunch

would be the perfect setting to drop my bombshell – she never shouts so loudly in public!

'This is lovely,' she commented, as with full stomachs we finished the meal with coffee and a large cognac to complete the mellowing effects of good wine. As I casually told her of my plans, she glared at Irene who had come along to referee.

'I wondered why you fixed a working lunch here instead of our usual sleazy cafe,' she commented. Then came her 'what about the children?' questions. I had all that organised, I assured her. Apart from all the helpers at home, we would never be out of touch as I would be flying my own plane from each location to the next. The aviation authorities would know at all times our exact whereabouts. In an emergency she could be flown back to Nairobi and from there to home. Then I quickly enthused about the artistic merits of the project. She readily agreed about that, beginning to catch my excitement. Irene sat back in relief and then we allocated each other various tasks, not least finding a film crew at six weeks notice! I left Natalie and Irene with those 'minor' details as I disappeared into my own little shell of creativity.

Total chaos ensued! One film crew was found, only to back out at the last minute, leaving the ladies with only one week to find replacements. With my safety pilot, Peter Roberts, I pored over flight plans via Egypt, then to the Sudan, telling the authorities that there would be three extra passengers on board, as yet unnamed. The plans for the additional film crew's travel arrangements and technicalities in Kenya were safely in the hands of a Kenyan organisation, quite used to the madcap schemes of foreign film makers.

With only three days to go, a chief cameraman, assistant cameraman and sound engineer were found and, the night before departure, those three gentlemen met me for the first time, not in the best of spirits having been inoculated in every limb against all the infectious diseases that go with the wonders of Africa.

Dawn! G-SONG, my twin-engined Kingair, was packed to the roof with equipment. Natalie and the children waved us off at Stansted Airport, not very far from our home. Natalie was following three days later by scheduled airline, unenthusiastic about the prospect of a long flight in a small plane. To me, the flight itself was an adventure. Even the long hours of darkness and flying on autopilot were usefully filled as I talked over my plans with the film boys.

We landed in Nice to refuel, then went on to Heraklion (Crete) where we spent the night. The next day found us flying over Egypt, landing in Khartoum in the Sudan where we refuelled by prior arrangement, and then on to Nairobi.

Going back to your roots after twenty years can come as quite a shock to the system. As we were on final approach into Nairobi airport, my excitement was tainted with nagging fears that too many changes might have destroyed the Kenya I had known and loved.

You may imagine the thrill I felt, looking out of the pilot's cabin window, seeing my mother and father waiting to greet me. I would be a liar if I didn't admit that I glowed with pride at flying my own aircraft into the city of my birth, especially watched by the two people whom I loved with all my heart but who had expressed such doubts about my venture into the entertainment business.

Thank God Monty Ruben was there, too. Monty Ruben is one of Kenya's finest sons. He is one of those people who succeeds in forming bridges and smoothing paths as he goes along and somehow he managed to have all our equipment brought into the country without any of the expected problems.

To my delight I discovered that my Swahili had not deserted me and my memories of the African's attitude to certain things were still valid. For instance old age is treated with great respect in Kenya. One of their most respectful terms is 'Mzee', which means 'old man'.

As I was showing the customs officers around the aeroplane, the senior officer smacked me across the rump with his swagger stick in an attempt to pass me in the confined space. I immediately began speaking Swahili. He sat down and said, 'I'm sorry, Sir, I didn't mean to be disrespectful.'

'Don't worry about it,' I replied, 'for how could you be disrespectful to me when you are old enough to be my father.'

To give everybody time to get the feel of the country, I had arranged for the crew to stay in Nairobi while I spent some time with my parents, awaiting Natalie's arrival.

The beaming African faces at the airport, the chatter in

Swahili, the heat, was all as I remembered it. It was as though I had never been away, until the car topped the brow of a hill and I looked down on Nairobi itself. The skyline was totally unfamiliar, with skyscrapers thrusting upward all over the place. The city had become a modern metropolis similar to any large city anywhere in the world. Like a child I pointed out the changes to my parents as we drove along,

'Remember this . . . ?' 'Remember that . . . ?'

A lump caught in my throat when we came to one landmark that hadn't changed: my father's first shop with its 'WHITTAKER' sign still above the entrance. As we rounded the last bend, I saw the eucalyptus trees my mother had lovingly planted twenty-five years before now dwarfing the neighbourhood with heads a hundred feet high. Home itself had changed little except that the garden seemed richer in colour and life. My room was as I had left it. I unpacked and poked and pried into cupboards and drawers, discovering relics of my youth – old comics, my electric train and the once dreaded air-rifle. Talk about nostalgia!

That first evening we reminisced well into the night. I finally went to bed, going through the familiar routine of tucking in the mosquito net as though twenty years were yesterday and soon I drifted off to sleep to the lullaby songs of the cicadas and the night birds.

A dawn chorus of chattering monkeys woke me. Bursting with enthusiasm, I rushed into my father's study to start scribbling. I still had only the vaguest idea of what format the film would take, but the conversation of the previous evening had started the wheels turning in my mind and long before my parents emerged for breakfast, I had already composed a rough lyric to 'My Land Is Kenya'. During the next three days I drove my parents crazy as I dived back into the study with each new thought flashing through my brain. When the film crew arrived they said they wanted to film Natalie getting off the plane to capture her initial reaction, but I persuaded them that it would be a better idea to let her acclimatise herself in her surroundings before jamming cameras and microphones in her face.

I need not have worried about her reaction to Kenya. She was immediately intrigued by all she saw and bubbled over with excitement and questions as I conducted her on a brief tour of Nairobi, showing her our first home, my schools and finally my parents' present house. After a couple of hours' rest from the overnight flight, she joined us to go through the proposed film schedule and I relayed my plans to her. She could hardly wait to get out in the bush and discover for herself the country and the wildlife. However, a few minutes later a shriek from the bathroom told me that her transition from Europe to Africa was not going to be all that smooth. As we rushed to the door in consternation, she came dashing out, petrified.

'Now I know why I was wary of coming here!' she cried. 'There's a bloody great striped spider in the loo!'

The 'bloody great striped spider' turned out to be a harmless and extremely helpful mosquito spider who spends his brief life eating as many of the offending insects as he can.

We teased her so much that she decided then and there to suffer in silence, even if she had a coronary from encounters with what she called 'those horrible creatures'. I had forgotten she was an arachniphobe! She stuck to her word with only the set of her jaw from time to time indicating that yet another eight legged monster had made her acquaintance. Throughout the weeks that followed she never blinked an eye over the bugs and the swarms of flies that are in perpetual search of human and animal company in Africa.

The adventure was truly launched at 5.00 a.m. the following day, when our convoy of Land Rovers, packed to the roof with equipment and people, were waved off by my very dubious parents, who were quite convinced that Natalie would reappear in a few days in the throes of a complete nervous breakdown. I must confess to some trepidation on that score myself, but to the amusement of all it was I who over the days showed signs of nervousness whereas she became a converted bush-dweller practically overnight!

When I was a child I had run about in the bush without worrying because I had been brought up in that environment. However, twenty years of civilisation had left their mark. Elephants were suddenly an awful lot bigger than I remembered!

My Kenya friends had planned the trip carefully with the

aim of introducing Natalie and the film crew to African life in the wild step by step. We therefore began our trek with a visit to the famous Mount Kenya Safari Club, near the village of Nanyuki, an entrancing spot about as close to paradise on earth as you can get. Although just north of the equator, it is also several thousand feet up the slopes of Mount Kenya, on whose snowy peak the Kikuyu believe lives *Ngai* – God. The air is cool and sweet and at night it's cold enough to have a cedar-wood fire lit in your room. The aroma is delightful. From the Club we drove the few hours to Tree Tops, a must on every tourist trip. It's a crude wooden building set on stilts above an artificial water hole and salt lick, which is floodlit at night to make a 'moon' so that visitors can sit up till dawn and watch the parade of animals come to drink.

It wasn't what I would call 'natural' wildlife filming but it was a good way to start our trip. We remained overnight, then headed south to the great plains of the Masai Mara, glad to leave behind the tarmac roads and zebra-striped tourist mini-buses. As we rounded a hill, Natalie actually gasped: there below us, as far as the eye could see was a lush valley teeming with game – thousands of zebra, Thomson gazelle, wildebeest and giraffe, grazing peacefully. What we could not see from that distance, but I at least knew were there, were the predators, waiting silently and patiently in the tall grass. It was an impressive sight; one that I had all but forgotten. As the sun began to set, a huge yellow ball tinged with fiery red sinking below the far horizon, as if on cue a herd of giraffe ambled elegantly across the skyline, their silhouettes dark against the vanishing fireball. The film crew worked frantically in the fading light to capture the scene, one of the so many magnificent moments Kenya puts on display regularly.

We had to get going then for we were nearing the game park and one of the rules strictly adhered to within the park is that you cannot drive after dark with your headlights on. Guided by Terry Matthews and his wife Jeanne – childhood friends of mine – we headed for our camp site. Elephants were everywhere and more than once we would round a bend and come to an abrupt halt as a group of lumbering grey shapes hurried across our path. We were all pleased to see the end of the track, but our relief turned to dismay when we realised that we had to cross a ravine with a fast flowing river. We shouted for the boatman, who had been warned to expect us. Then came the problem of getting all the luggage, cameras and sound equipment across this obstacle course in what was now pitch darkness. Slithering and sliding down the bank by torchlight, Natalie whispered to me,

'Are there any hippos or crocs in this river?'

'Certainly,' I said, 'but I'm sure they wouldn't have a ferry where the animals rest at night.'

The following day I learned that this particular bend of the river was a favourite place of that large and very dangerous animal, the hippo, as was evidenced in daylight by deep hoofprints still welling with water.

Aided by a rope from the high bank on the other side of the river, we hauled our way across the remaining hundred yards to the edge of the camp. It had already been set up, with a welcoming fire blazing in the circle of tents, by the rest of the production team who had arrived in the afternoon. They had been quite worried about our late arrival as there had been a group of young bull elephants nearby earlier and, to the best of everyone's knowledge, they were still around. It is amazing how such large animals can 'melt' into the flimsiest undergrowth. By this time, however, we weren't paying too much attention as we were all exhausted after eight hours travelling.

Escorted by a Masai Askari armed with only a spear, Natalie and I found our tent and were soon feeling refreshed following a most welcome shower and change of clothes. A guard waited to escort us back but just as we were leaving the tent, Natalie heard rustling in the bushes only some five yards away.

'That's where the crew told me the elephants were last sighted,' she murmured nervously.

'Really?' said I, shining a torch in that direction and right into the face of a large tusker who threw up his trunk and screamed at us. The scream of an angry elephant is indescribable, making the hair on your head stand straight up! All I knew was that I yelled,

'*Run!*'

The guard needed no telling and was quickly yards ahead of us. Natalie, at the first note of that scream, had shot off like an

Olympic sprinter, and I wasn't far behind. Fortunately, it was only a warning bellow and he didn't follow, but my goodness did we grab that first drink offered us when we reached the circle around the fire! Terry, who had been a hunter for some twenty years before the banning of guns in the parks, told us that we'd done exactly the wrong thing and that we should have stood stock still. If the elephant had really meant business he would have covered the distance between us in two strides. We were still shaking an hour later and very, very carefully made our way back to our tent to sleep.

Sleep? Impossible. At about three o'clock in the morning, Natalie jumped into my bed. 'I'm in luck!' I thought, subsequently disappointed to discover the reason for her friendliness was that she had lifted the window flap to find out what the snuffling noise was in her left ear, only to come face to face with a hyena only inches away. The hyena had been more frightened than she and had fled into the darkness.

* * *

Each morning saw everyone awake and dressed by five-thirty. The most beautiful times of the day are definitely those first early hours, and the last few in the evening. It is impossible to sleep late as the bush comes alive with the first rays of dawn. Following a rushed cup of coffee we would be out and on the road finding locations or actually filming by six-thirty to wander back at about eleven when the heat became oppressive.

One morning, while having my coffee, I saw a movement out of the corner of my eye – two young elephants only a few yards from the first tent in our circle. I didn't like it. Natalie and I had become worried about our assistant cameraman, Peter, who appeared totally unconcerned by the proximity of the larger animals during filming and was rapidly becoming known as 'Dangerman'. On this occasion, it was his tent that was closest to the elephants. He was sitting outside it, changing film, obviously unaware of his approaching visitors.

'You'd better attract Pete's attention,' I whispered to Nats, 'and get him over here as fast as possible, while I get a couple of guards to drive off those elephants.'

As I didn't want to get into the elephants' line of sight, I went back into our tent, opened the rear flap and crept out to fetch the Masai. Natalie followed me and called out in the lowest tone possible.

'Peter!'

'What?' he yelled, looking at her.

'Ssh!' with a finger to her lips she went through a charade, trying to indicate that he should get back into his tent as quickly as possible. When he didn't get the message, she crept one tent closer and called again.

'This is an order! Go to the back of your tent and creep out around here. Now!'

Fortunately he did as he was told. Just as I arrived back with the guards and he sneaked over to our tent, the elephants reached where he had been sitting. Most of the time game will ignore tents and cars, but in that particular area the elephants and the buffalo were very unpredictable.

Peter and the rest of the crew at first ignored the advice given them but as the days passed they began to pay more attention. One of the rules of living under canvas in the bush is that when the fire dies down and everybody retires for the night you zip up the tent flaps and do not unzip them or leave your tent for *any* reason. As I said, most animals will ignore a tent but a human being wandering around the camp at night is fair game. One night Peter was disturbed by a snuffling noise outside his tent and disregarding the rules unzipped the flap to investigate only to find himself face to face with a buffalo! The animal was actually standing with its nose pressed to the canvas. Peter rapidly zipped up the flap again, grabbed his trousers, shook his companion awake, and the pair of them scuttled out of the back of the tent. Fortunately the buffalo did nothing but poke its nose around but it is an extremely moody and dangerous animal. It could have just as easily wandered around to the back of the tent in the time the two of them were getting dressed and consequently we could have had two very badly mangled – if not dead – camera crew.

Some of the filming was extremely boring, with passing shots endlessly taken and retaken. Many hours were spent just sitting, baking in the midday sun, the only cover often being our vehicles which turned rapidly into saunas. Thus far all the 'stars' of the film had been the animals. We had had very little contact with the Africans themselves until one of our drivers got into conversation with me during a break in filming. It turned out he was a Nandi, the same tribe that most of my ayahs had belonged to. I started to sing one of the songs they had taught me – much to his amusement. We hadn't seen a village for many miles but apparently deep in the undergrowth not far away was a Nandi village where many of his relatives lived. Before we knew it, he was organising his friends and relatives to come and sing for us. We had not planned on any night filming at that particular juncture, but did have a portable generator with us in case anything interesting occurred after dark.

That night, after a long day's filming, we showered and waited for the small group of Nandi singers to arrive. The generator was set up and a second fire lit some way from the camp. The problem posed by the generator seemed insurmountable. The sound engineer could not lose the humming, but thought we might at least get something. We waited and waited and were just about to start packing up when through the darkness came the sound of singing, and into the firelight stepped the most delightful sight I have ever seen. The 'small' group turned out to be about twenty singers in all, dressed in colourful costumes of every description, looking for all the world like medieval wandering mummers.

Behind them came the entire community of about two hundred men, women and children, all wanting to see and hear their relatives become film stars. It was impossible to organise them and I just told the film crew to keep rolling while I tried to control the enthusiasm of the audience. They sang and danced with natural humour and abandonment and I dread to think what some of the lyrics meant because every so often the audience would break up with laughter. It was a wonderful, spontaneous evening, ending with singers and villagers alike wandering off into the bush, still singing, smiling and waving.

We'd all been so involved in the filming that we'd been blissfully unaware that we'd had a further audience. Attracted by the noise, the elephants had gathered a hundred yards away and it was only when they followed in the wake of our Nandi friends that we realised they'd been there at all. Stan, our sound engineer, knowing how curious Peter was, had also deliberately avoided pointing out the large snake that had been attracted by the vibration of the generator and slithered to and fro amongst the milling feet of our extras.

After that marvellous experience we moved from place to place, sometimes many hundreds of miles apart, to find different tribes and different cultures. Sometimes we stopped in tourist lodges overnight where we could luxuriate in a hot bath and contact Nairobi for news of the children.

As we travelled I put music to all we encountered. However, thus far I had only recorded modern Kenya in song. My 'game plan' was to spend some time going back into Africa's history, to trace the origins of some of its songs and traditions. We decided the best place to find what I was seeking was the coastal region, where Islamic culture had played such an important part in the development of the continent. Even to me, who had seen it all before, albeit so many years past, the change of scenery from arid plain to palm-fringed beach was startlingly sudden.

Terry and Jeanne had chosen a tiny fishing village called Shimoni as our coastal base; from there we would be able to venture north and south into the ancient settlements that lined the shores of the Indian Ocean. In truth I wasn't entirely sure what I was looking for, but I hoped I'd recognise it when I saw it – or heard it.

Our base on that lovely coast gave Natalie the opportunity to indulge herself in what is perhaps her favourite pastime – deep sea fishing. Show Natalie a boat, the deep blue sea and a couple of fishing rods and she'll disappear into a world of her own. Actually, the prospect of such sport had been the bonus 'carrot' I'd offered her when convincing her to come along on this trip.

So, while Natalie went to do battle with the fish, I went to investigate the ancient, eerie ruins of Gedi, a long deserted Arab settlement. There were many legends about Gedi, all of them filled with mystery and I wanted to see this place for myself, experience its 'evil' atmosphere before putting the tales on film. When we got there, crew and I alike were struck by the ghostly menace of the ruins, giving credence to the strange stories I'd been told. Total silence reigned. Not a bird sang. Not an insect chirruped. No monkeys chattered in the branches of the acacia trees. There was no sign of any living thing at all. No one has ever explained the mystery of the Gedi ruins. Apparently one day it had been a thriving trading town and the next, as though by some magic, all form of human and animal life vanished.

Plague? Fire? War? Whatever the reason might have been there was no explanation for its current ghostliness; why had no animal life returned? Why this eerie, deathly silence?

Slavery along this section of the African coast had been an integral part of its trade and growth and was a detail of the story I wanted to tell. As we left Gedi to return to Shimoni I asked Terry to stop along a particular stretch of road to take a look at some caves we had been told about which had apparently been used as shelter for thousands of Africans waiting to be shipped out of Mombasa as slaves by their Arab captors.

The entrance to the caves was hard to find, being almost completely covered by decades of wild undergrowth. As we hacked our way in Terry gave warning; a brief sweep of his torch had picked out scuttling scorpions and tarantulas in the first few yards of sandy floor. Summoning up courage and treading carefully we ventured deep into the first cavern. We could tell from the echo of our voices that the caves stretched out like an open fan from the narrow entrance and must go on perhaps for miles. On we walked, our skins crawling at the sight of so many insects and snakes but for some time we found no evidence that the caves had ever been inhabited or used by humans. Then, as we rounded a bend, gruesome evidence stared us in the face: rotting wooden shackles lay in the dust alongside the shards of broken bowls and, as our torches probed the darkness ahead of us, they spotlighted human skulls and the scattered bones of broken skeletons. It needed little imagination to understand the terror and bewilderment of the poor souls who had been imprisoned here.

We left, emerging gratefully into the sunshine, deeply depressed. Nevertheless I told my crew that before we left the country I wanted to film that awful place. For the first time I met rebellion; nobody wanted to go back in there, not for another minute. But that night, in camp, I sketched out my ideas for a song that would tell the tale of Shimoni and the slave caves and convinced the crew that some good would emerge from our return. Go back we did and it was worth while, although none of us enjoyed the experience.

So engrossed was I in all I was doing that I never noticed the weeks passing until one day I was rudely brought back to reality by our continuity girl, who handed me a ticket to Berlin. Berlin? I'd completely forgotten that a year earlier I'd accepted a booking for one solitary but major television appearance there, and here I was with our time in Kenya running out yet with more to shoot: the last Gedi sequence and the grand finale we'd planned – a view of the African bush from a balloon. It was obvious I'd have to fly to Berlin, do the show and return. It was a nuisance but there was no other way. So we all returned to Nairobi, giving the production team a chance to view the 'rushes' and make sure we'd need no retakes. There was no point in Natalie going with me to Berlin so I sent her off to Terry and Jeanne to enjoy five days in the bush while I was away.

When I returned she gave me quite an earful of her adventures, which included being embraced by a hairy, bird-eating spider while in the loo, and finding herself in the midst of a battle between a pride of lions and an elephant herd defending a newborn calf from attack. The elephants won, incidentally.

We returned to Gedi to shoot the final sequences there, then piled back into my G-SONG early one morning to fly to where our balloons would be waiting for the aerial sequence I'd organised. We were all a bit uptight about this finale because we knew we'd have only one go at it; all depended on the winds and the hot air currents. Alan Root, my old school friend and now an eminent wildlife film maker, had made all the arrangements and our spirits lifted when we heard his cheery radio call from his own plane on his way to join us.

After landing at a ridiculously narrow and terribly short bush airstrip, we trudged to where the balloons were to be launched. Technically this was going to be the most complicated piece of film in the whole enterprise. It was planned that Stan, our sound engineer, would squat in the basket, under our feet and out of camera, while the camera crew followed in the second balloon. Timing was essential. The ropes for the second balloon had to be released *exactly* ten seconds after ours!

Natalie looked dubiously at the wicker basket and the gas being pumped into the massive striped balloon lying crumpled on the ground. But her fears were as nothing compared with Stan's. He was pea-green as he loaded his equipment into the bottom of the flimsy basket. The sun now appeared through the mist on the horizon and a shout from Alan gave us the five minutes to countdown. A mad rush followed as the camera crew checked and re-checked cameras and Alan's microphone was wired up. The Whittakers and the Roots climbed into the basket, trying not to trample on Stan, curled up in a ball at our feet.

Off! With the slightest 'whoosh' our ropes were released shooting us several hundred feet into the air. It was an incredible sensation to suddenly soar straight up. We were so spellbound we almost failed to hear a yell from the other basket, supposedly following. As we looked towards the sound we saw their launch – but one of the rope handlers was still dangling from the basket! We held our breaths: he released his hold and dropped from quite a height onto the ground. To hell with the film – was he hurt? But he got to his feet and with a cheery wave, wandered off. Breathing normally again, we settled down to watch the breaking dawn, and the panorama unfolding below us. Only the roar of the burners broke the stillness from time to time as Alan sought more height. At two thousand feet we levelled off and glided over the herds of animals, wondering whether the cameras were catching it all. Stan, of course, could see nothing. Due to the 'dangling man' the following balloon was quite a way behind, but try as he might, Alan couldn't slow us down. Then the wind shifted and abruptly we were rushing towards the Tanzanian border. Since none of us wanted to be guests of their government as illegal immigrants, we agreed to abandon our flight.

Far below we could see the speck of the Land Rovers following and Alan assured us they were only moments away 'in case of a bad landing!'

'What do you mean?' came a worried whisper from our feet. One look at Stan's face was all Alan needed to start a typical East African 'ribbing',

'Oh, don't worry, I have only crashed twice! Once with Jackie Kennedy – remind me to tell you about that!' Then casually, 'The basket may roll over and be dragged, so keep your arms well in and pad them with your sweater!' And a further comment: 'Oh yes! Be careful as you get out of the basket in case of wild animals . . .'

At this point we were descending rapidly and Stan had wound himself around his precious equipment, white as a sheet, his eyes tight shut.

At about two hundred feet Alan grinned at the quaking man at his feet, then went through an Oscar winning performance.

'Oh God! I think we're going to hit that tree!' he cried. There wasn't a tree in sight, but poor Stan didn't know.

'Whew! That was close, but I hope those cars manage to get over that ravine quickly as we have company. Look! Hyenas everywhere!'

I thought Stan would pass out. Seconds later we landed, so softly that Stan didn't even know we'd arrived until we scrambled out.

'You rotten lot!' he yelled after us as we rushed with our still cameras to catch the arrival of the other balloon.

We all compared notes, while Alan saw to the picnic brought along in the cars – a champagne breakfast in the bush. Total decadence! Tom, our chief cameraman, was in the depths of gloom, however. The other balloon had been so far behind that no close-ups had been possible.

'No problem!' said Alan, having done all this before. Quickly the other basket was uncoupled from the deflated balloon and hoisted onto the back of the lorry used to transport the balloons back to base.

Hurriedly, before the light changed too much, we scripted a close-up sequence, but as Alan, his wife and I clambered back into the basket, Natalie let out a yell and proceeded to go mad before our very eyes, slapping and contorting her body in every direction. Safari ants! She had been standing in a nest and now the little bastards were biting her every soft part!

'Tough luck!' we called. 'You can strip off in a moment when we've finished this sequence!'

Wincing and uttering some very unladylike oaths she joined us. We all laugh now when we watch that part of the film, with

Nats calmly acting out the balloon flight, listening intently to Alan's comments as to what we were supposedly seeing passing beneath us.

As soon as the cameramen called,

'Cut! It's a wrap!' she was out of the basket and into the bushes like a rabbit to strip off!

Peter, our pilot, having been born in Africa, was laughing louder than most at her predicament. His mirth abruptly turned to horror as he grabbed his crutch in pain – justice! – they had got him, too. But with no attempt to emulate Natalie's modesty, he disrobed in mid-run towards the river. Shouting with glee, all the other fellows stripped and joined him in the water, splashing and jostling like kids. The film was over and the party started!

That evening as we stood on my parents' lawn taking in the last rays of the sun, I vowed I would not stay away so long again. Later that night Natalie flew out and I was to follow the next day. Everybody involved in the filming was at the airport to see her off and there were few dry eyes as she walked towards the plane. Over the weeks, lasting friendships had been forged and many golden memories captured forever on film.

Chapter 18

Memories   come   creeping

LIFE COMES FULL circle, sometimes in the strangest ways. When I left Kenya back in 1962 I knew it would be many years before I'd return; but not in my wildest dreams could I have conjured up the actual circumstances of my homecoming. What an unforgettable experience that was, how wonderful once again to absorb the sights and sounds and smells of Africa, to see my parents, old friends, to wallow in the pleasures of the past. Nostalgia is like an anaesthetic: you experience no pain, only a beautiful haze. Anyway, when you grow older what matters to you is not the way it was, but the way you remember it.

After the warmth and sun of Africa, returning to the cold and wet of a British spring brought me down to earth with a bump. The film may have been 'in the can' but there was still a lot of cutting and editing to do and the recording of much important music.

During the course of our filming in Kenya the media had shown a lot of interest and when we returned we were inundated with requests for film clips, stills and interviews. I agreed with Irene that it was a good idea to keep the interest running and so let her book me on a number of chat shows. One of these, I was told, featured the various hobbies of the stars; since mine was flying and since I used my own plane in my business the idea evolved for me to be filmed in flight; this would become the opening sequence of the show. I would then go on to be interviewed. A good idea, I thought. It would be an easy show to do. I arranged therefore to fly into Northolt airport. On the appointed morning I waved goodbye to Natalie as she drove the kids off to school. From there she was going to our London office to do some work on the magazine we were then producing. 'See you after your taping!' she called out as she drove off.

At the airport near our home where I kept G-SONG tied down, I met the television production assistant who outlined the questions they would be asking. He told me they would be filming my landing, so you can be sure I made every effort to see that it was perfect. And it was. I taxied, parked, closed down the engines and opened the door. An official was there to greet me and behind him, his back to me, a man I took to be an engineer from his dress. Suddenly the official side-stepped and the 'engineer' turned around and thrust something into my hands.

'ROGER WHITTAKER . . . THIS IS YOUR LIFE!' cried Eamonn Andrews and a great cheer went up from the crowd that had surreptitiously gathered behind me.

Absolute and total shock. I didn't know what to say, how to respond. I just grinned stupidly and said,

'You caught me, Eamonn!'

The drive to the London studios found me still in a daze. All I could think of was: how on earth did Natalie keep it a secret? I thought I could read her like a book. Obviously I'd have to review my reading!

In the car, as he told me what was to follow, Eamonn appeared a trifle nervous. He told me then that Natalie had related to him a disastrous attempt at a *This Is Your Life* seven years earlier in Canada, and that I had jokingly warned her I'd divorce her if she ever tried to spring it on me again. Eamonn confided that he'd been convinced his surprise would be greeted by an angry, 'Not on your life, mate!' from me.

I can tell you that in the studio the 'star' of the programme is kept in isolation with not a clue to who is going to appear. I've never been so nervous in my life! Who was going to pop up? What were they going to say? What was *I* going to say? Would they drag in somebody from my past I'd forgotten – or, worse yet, would prefer to forget?

I can tell you, too, that I went through it all like a sleep-walker. Only four days later, when watching the tape of the show, did it all register.

Natalie, followed by our four eldest children, bounced onto the stage first, grinning from ear to ear. When I asked her how she'd managed to keep the secret she told me – and the millions watching – that until that very morning not even the kids had known. Instead of driving them to school, as they'd expected, she had diverted to London. Their change of clothes had been deposited at the studio by her on a previous trip. Alex, at three, was too little to appear, she said, but on the screen Eamonn then flashed a film clip of him singing and plucking on my guitar. I gulped hard to avoid embarrassing tears on television.

Still dazed I greeted guest after guest. My sister, who I hadn't seen for six years; old friends now scattered all over the world; friends from Kenya, who only a few weeks earlier I'd been living with – they, too, had kept the secret; Rolf Harris, my oldest friend in the business; Frank Carson, who gave me my first break; Joan Collins, Chet Atkins, my old university professor and even one of my first pupils from my teaching days in Africa. Had I really done so much, I thought?

Then a bonus surprise! From the wings came Brett and we talked briefly about the nine years he'd spent as part of the family. Truly a most poignant moment. He was now six foot four, with a handsome beard, and engaged to be married. As he took his seat I reckoned that was the end of the show, but no, sleepy little Alexander toddled out and flung his arms around me. Then the little ham blew kisses at the audience!

As the title music heralded the end of the show, we took the traditional walk to the front of the stage to wave goodbye – there, surrounded by my friends and family, I was suddenly overwhelmed by thoughts of where I was and how it had all begun. As a drowning man is said to see all life flash before his eyes, so did I, enveloped by the magic of the moment, see in a flash all that had happened to me. It was 'This Is Your Life Roger Whittaker' indeed.

Yes, there had been disappointment along with success; sadness along with the joy; some pain, but so much pleasure. I am the fortunate possessor of a treasure house of memories. I have been lucky enough to see many of my dreams come true and realise some good fortune well beyond my dreams. And I have been most fortunate of all to have a wife and children and many good friends with whom to share that good fortune and my happiness.

So far, so good!

CURRENT DISCOGRAPHY
ALBUMS

UNITED KINGDOM
TEMBO LABEL DISTRIBUTED BY I.M.S. POLYGRAM

THE SONGWRITER   *TMB 107/TMBC 107*
All numbers written solely by Whittaker except where otherwise indicated.
New World In The Morning/I'm Back/You Are my Miracle/All Of My Life/Call My Name/The Last Farewell (*Webster-Whittaker*) Durham Town/Come With Me/Surf (*Whittaker-Robertson*)/And Still The Sea/Why(*Whittaker-Stanton*)/Mexican Whistler/High/Image To My Mind/Hold On Tight/Oh No Not Me/I Don't Believe In If Anymore/I Was Born/The Seasons (Come And Go)/Smiler/Albany/So Long.

ROGER WHITTAKER IN KENYA   *812.949 –1/812.949 –4*
All numbers written solely by Whittaker except 'Did You Really Have To' where lyrics by T. G. Russell.
I'm Back/My Land Is Kenya/Shimoni/Good Old E.A.R. & H./Come With Me/Did You Really Have To/Make Way For Man/High/Come Back Again/My Land Is Kenya.

TAKE A LITTLE – GIVE A LITTLE   *TMB 101/TMBC 101*
Bitter And Sweet (I Will Follow You) (*Munro*)/Brave And Strong (*Munro-Kunze-Whittaker*)/Dover To Calais (*Munro-Murmann-Whittaker*)/Old Mother Nature's Garden (*Munro-Whittaker*)/Happy Everything (*Black-Stephens*)/Boogaloo Bossanova & Rock 'n Roll (*Munro-Murmann-Whittaker*)/Take A Little Give A Little (*Munro-Whittaker*)/Mary (*Munro-Kleinwort-Whittaker*)/So Far (Safari) (*Munro-Whittaker*)/Charlie Mahon (*Munro-Murmann-Whittaker*)/My Silver Eagle (*Heider-Munro-Whittaker*).

THE COUNTRY FEEL OF
ROGER WHITTAKER   *TMB 104/TMBC 104*

Changes (*Quinn*)/Honolulu City Lights (*Besmer*)/Ride A Country Road (*Whittaker*)/River Runs Still (*Quinn*)/I Can Hear Kentucky Calling Me (*B & F Bryant*)/When I Dream (*Mason-Theoret*)/Good Old E.A.R. & H. (*Whittaker*)/The First Hello, The Last Goodbye (*Robinson-Whittaker*)/I Can't Help It (If I'm Still In Love With You) (*Williams*)/Smooth Sailing (*Putnam-Throckmorton*)/Rocky Top (*B & F Bryant*)/Moonshine (*Whittaker-Petts*)/How Does It Feel (*Quinn*)/So Good To So Bad (*Silverstein/Goldstein*)/Everytime Is Going To Be The Last Time (*Whittaker*)/River Lady (*Adams*)/Don't Let Them Change (*Adams*)/Blue Eyes Crying In The Rain (*Rose*)/Bar Room Country Singer* (*Whittaker-Parkes*)/Red River Valley (*Trad: Arr. Whittaker*).

THE ROMANTIC SIDE OF
ROGER WHITTAKER   *TMB 105/TMBC 105*

It's Your Love (*Knowles*)/Before She Breaks My Heart (*Whittaker*)/Indian Lady (*Rankin-Whittaker*)/Time (*Whittaker*)/My World (*Browning-Spalding/Whittaker*)/Say My Goodbyes To the Rain (*Way*)/Here I Stand (*Bardotti-Baldan-Bembo-Thumpston*)/Summer Days (*Whittaker*)/Pretty Bird Of Love (*Whittaker-Giraud: Original French lyrics by Pierre Cour*/All The Way To Richmond (*Paxton-Welch*)/Let Me Be Your Sun (*Whittaker: Original French lyrics by Pierre Cour*)/New Love (*Adams/Robertson*)/Love Will (*Whittaker*)/Don't Fight (*Whittaker/Robertson*)/My Son (*Whittaker/Knowles*)/One Another (*Whittaker*)/For I Loved You (*Whittaker/Spitzer-Marlyn*)/I Am But A Small Voice† (*Ako'y Munting Tinig*) (*Whittaker: Original lyrics by Odina E Batnag*)/Tall Dark Stranger (*Whittaker*)/Newport Belle (*Whittaker*)/I Would If I Could (*Whittaker*)/See You Shine (*Whittaker*)/A Man Without Love (*Whittaker*)/Goodbye (*Whittaker*).

TIDINGS OF COMFORT AND JOY   *TMB 102/TMBC 102*

Ding Dong Merrily On High/God Rest You Merry Gentlemen/O Come All Ye Faithful/The Twelve Days of Christmas/In The Bleak Midwinter/The Christmas Song/Angels From The Realms of Glory/Mary's Boy Child/Away In A Manger/Have Yourself A Merry Little Christmas/The Holly And The Ivy/White Christmas/The First Nöel/The Little Drummer Boy/Sussex Carol/Hark The Herald Angels Sing/Infant Holy – Infant Lowly/Rocking/Winter Wonderland/Past Three O'Clock/Merry Christmas/Silent Night.

---

* Recorded live at the Cobo Arena, Detroit, Michigan, U.S.A.
† All royalties from this song are donated to UNESCO to aid handicapped children throughout the world.

HEART TOUCHING FAVOURITES *TMB 103/TMBC 103*

Red Roses For A Blue Lady (*Pepper-Brodsky*)/Somewhere My Love (*Lara's Theme from Dr Zhivago*) (*Jarre-Webster*)/Unchained Melody (*Zaret-North*)/Sentimental Journey (*Green-Brown-Horner*)/Scarlet Ribbons (*Danzig-Segal*)/Red Sails In the Sunset (*Kennedy-Williams*)/Eternally (*Parsons-Chaplin-Turner*)/Tenderly (*Lawrence-Gross*)/Stranger On The Shore (*Mellin-Bilk*)/I Love You Because (*Payne*)/Making Believe (*Work*)/It's Now Or Never (*Di Capra/Capurro/Arr: Schroder & Goud*)/Have I Told You Lately That I Love You (*Wiseman*)/I Can't Help It (If I'm Still In Love With You) (*Williams*)/Blue Eyes Crying In The Rain (*Rose*)/Red River Valley (*Trad: Arr. Whittaker*)/There Goes My Everything (*Frazier*)/Vaya Con Dios (*Russell/James/Pepper*).

SINGING THE HITS *TMB 106/TMBC 106*

Sailing (*Sutherland*)/Imagine (*Lennon*)/Evergreen (*Williams/Streisand*)/What A Wonderful World (*Alpert/Cook/Adler*)/Bright Eyes (*Batt*)/The Wind Beneath My Wings (*Henley-Silbar*)/Miss You Nights (*Townsend*)/Weekend In New England (*Edelman*)/Time In A Bottle (*Croce*)/Feelings (*Albert*)/Calypso (*Denver*)/Please Come To Boston (*Loggins*)/Your Song (*John-Taupin*)/I Can See Clearly Now (*Nash*)/Home Loving Man (*Macauley/Cook/Greenaway*)/She (*Aznavour/Kretzner*)/Send In the Clowns (*Sondheim*)/When I Need You (*Hammond-Sager*)/Too Beautiful To Cry (*Courage*)/Annie's Song (*Denver*).

THE BEST OF ROGER WHITTAKER *Reader's Digest Four Record Set*
RECORD ONE – Roger Sings Great Hits Of The 70s

Imagine/I Can See Clearly Now/Feelings/Fire And Rain/Home Lovin' Man/Miss You Nights/Moonshadow/Mammy Blue/Young Song/When I Need You/Sailing/Solitaire/Annie's Song/You've Got A Friend.

RECORD TWO—Romantic Memories

Sentimental Journey/Red Sails In The Sunset/Tenderly/Unchained Melody/Eternally/Scarlet Ribbons (For Her Hair)/Vaya Con Dios/Stranger On The Shore/A Taste Of Honey/By The Time I Get To Phoenix/You've Lost That Lovin' Feeling/There Goes My Everything/It's Now Or Never/I Love You Because.

RECORD THREE – Folk Favourites, Now And Then

Morning Has Broken/From Both Sides/Calypso/Streets Of London/Yellow Bird/Dirty Old Town/River Lady/Early One

270

Morning/The Ash Grove/Drink To Me Only With Thine Eyes/Foggy Foggy Dew/Scarborough Fair/Star Of The County Down/David Of The White Rock.

RECORD FOUR
Side One: Screen and Show Favourites – If I Were A Rich Man/Evergreen (Love Theme from *A Star is Born*)/Somewhere My Love (Lara's Theme from *Dr Zhivago*)/The Impossible Dream/Bright Eyes from *Watership Down*/Send In the Clowns/She.
Side Two: The Special Magic of Roger – New World In The Morning/You Are My Miracle/Durham Town (The Leavin')/Mexican Whistler/I Don't Believe In If Anymore/A Special Kind Of Man/The Last Farewell.

THE GENIUS OF LOVE   *TMB 108/TMBC 108*
The Genius of Love (*Mitchell/Reilly*)/Miss Lapotaire (*Scott*)/Your Voice (*Bogdanovs*)/Railway Hotel (*Batt*)/Destiny (I Was Meant To Be With You) (*Sneddon-McGinley*)/Jerusalem Goodbye (*Michalsky/Reshoft/ Whittaker*)/The Candle (*Whalley*)/Your Fool (*Hancock*)/One More Chance (*Page/Lang/George*)/Too Emotional (*Bogdanovs*)/Everybody's Got A Lonely Heart (*Michalsky/Reshoft/Whittaker*)/Only The Lonely (*Orbison/Melson*).

GERMANY
AVON LABEL DISTRIBUTED BY INTERCORD

TYPISCH
ROGER WHITTAKER   *INT 161.548/INT 461.548/INT 861.548*
River Baion (*Munro*)/Alle Die Jahre (*Munro/Tegge*)/Wenn Es Dich Noch Gibt (*Munro*)/Die Grosse Reise (*Munro*)/Deinen Tränen Trau Ich Nicht (*Munro/Mürmann*)/Tanz Heut Nacht Mit Mir (*Heider/Munro*)/Ich Bin Da (*Whittaker/Munro/Eberhardt*)/Margie (*Munro*)/Feierabend-Country-Sänger (*Whittaker/Parkes/Munro*)/Eine Stunde Ewigkeit (*Munro/Mürmann*)/Ich Pfeife Auf Alles (*Munro/Schaper*)/Goodbye Goodbye Goodbye (*Munro*).

ROGER WHITTAKER IN KENYA   *INT 161.554/INT 461.554*
Content as for U.K.

ROGER WHITTAKER: MEIN DEUTSCHES ALBUM

INT 161.508/INT 461.508/ INT 861.508

Goodbye Ist Goodbye (*Munro*)/Du Warst Niemals Eine Lady (*Munro/Mürmann*)/Calypso (*Denver/Kunze*)/Ruf Nach Mir (*Whittaker/Munro*)/Oh Martina (*Munro/Quintus*)/Der Tramp In Mir (*Munro*)/Seit Wann Ist Liebe Eine Sünde (*Munro/Mürmann*)/Einsamer Mann In Einer Fremden Stadt (*Macauley/Cook/Greenaway/Niessen*)/ Jeder Neue Morgen Ist Ein Abenteuer (*Munro*)/Dass Es Schön War Weiss Man Erst Viel Zu Spät (*Whittaker/Relin*)/Hör Mal Baby (*Munro*)/Boogaloo Bossa Nova & Rock 'n Roll (*Munro/Mürmann*).

EIN GLÜCK, DASS ES DICH GIBT

INT 161.552/INT 461.552/INT 861.552

Eloisa (*Munro*)/Sein Truck Fährt Weiter (*Munro/Kleinwort*)/Von Dover Nach Calais (*Munro/Mürmann*)/Saharaheiss – Alaskakühl (*Munro*)/Himmel Vorhanden – Engel Gesucht (*Munro/Kleinwort*)/ Abschied Ist Ein Scharfes Schwert (*Munro*)/Augen Wie Sterne (*Munro*)/Ich Denk'Oft An Mary (*Munro/Kleinwort*)/Charlie Mahon (*Munro/Mürmann*)/Hin Und Her Und Her Und Hin (*Whittaker/ Munro*)/Flasche Und Glas (*Munro/Eberhardt*)/Der Himmel Über Mir (*Heider/Munro*).

ZUM WEINEN IST IMMER NOCH ZEIT

INT 161.542/INT 461.542/INT 861.542

Lass Die Rosen Nicht Verblühn/Was Zehn Jahre Verbinden/ Highway-Zigeuner/Albany/NewPort Ist Die Welt/Zum Weinen Ist Immer Noch Zeit/Summer Sunshine City/Du Bist Der Tag/Grossvaters Stuhl/Lauf Nur Zu/Kinder Der Ganzen Welt.

GREATEST HITS IN CONCERT

INT 156.515/INT 456.515

New World In The Morning/Image To My Mind/Dirty Old Town/Mexican Whistler/New African Whistler/Chengalip/Image To My Mind/That's Life/What Love Is/Dream/Early One Morning/Durham Town/Image To My Mind/Morning Has Broken/Why/I Don't Believe In If Anymore/The Last Farewell/Skye Boat Song/Kilgarry Mountain.

ROGER WHITTAKER IN WIENER KONZERTHAUS

INT 181.500/INT 481.500

Here I Come (*Whittaker*)/Scarlet Ribbons (*Danzig-Cegal*)/Swiss Mountaineer (*Trad: Arr. Whittaker*)/Hound Dog (*Leiber-Stoller*)/Long Tall Sally (*Johnson-Penniman-Blackwell*)/Chengalip (*Whittaker*)/The

Rising Of The Lark (*Ceiriog*)/My Love Is Like A Red Red Rose (*Trad: Arr. Whittaker*)/Star Of The County Down (*Cathel-McGarvey*)/The Ashgrove (*Trad: Arr. Robertson*)/Ride a Country Road (*Whittaker*)/From The People To The People (*Whittaker*)/The First Hello, The Last Goodbye (*Robinson-Whittaker*)/A Special Kind Of Man (*Richards-Whittaker*)/The Last Farewell (*Webster-Whittaker*)/The Impossible Dream (*Leigh-Darion*)/Bridge Over Troubled Water (*Simon*)/By The Time I Get To Phoenix (*Webb*)/Proud Mary (*Fogerty*)/Yesterday (*Lennon-McCartney*)/You've Lost That Loving Feeling (*Spector-Mann-Well*)/Indian Lady (*Rankin-Whittaker*)/Yarmouth Quay (*Adams-Robertson*)/Demon Rum (*Smith-Smith*)/River Lady (*Adams*)/The Last Song (*Smith*)/If I Knew Just What to Say (*Logier*)/Canada Is (*Hyde-Robertson*).

THE ROGER WHITTAKER
CHRISTMAS ALBUM   INT 161.505/INT 461.505
Hallelujah It's Christmas (*Whittaker*)/Mighty Like A Rose (*Trad: Arr. Robertson*)/Christmas Song (*Robertson-Whittaker-Adams*)/Country Christmas (*Adams*)/D'Arcy The Dragon (*Adams-Robertson*)/The Governor's Dream (*Whittaker-Robertson*)/Momma Mary (*Whittaker*)/Guten Abend, Gute Nacht (*Brahms Lullaby*)/(*Trad: Arr. Whittaker*)/Home For Christmas (*Adams-Robertson*)/A Time For Peace (*Adams-Robertson*)/Christmas Is Here Again (*Whittaker*)/Tiny Angels (*Taylor-Whittaker-Robertson*).

WEINACHTEN MIT
ROGER WHITTAKER   INT 161.553/INT 461.553/INT 861.553
Süsser Die Glocken Nie Klingen/O Du Fröhliche/Morgen Kommt Der Weinachtsmann/Gloria (Heilige Nacht Auf Engelsschwingen)/Ihr Kinderlein Kommet/O Tannenbaum/Kling Glöckchen Kling/Leise Rieselt Der Schnee/Am Weihnachtsbaum Die Lichter Brennen/Alle Jahre Wieder/Von Himmel Hoch, Da Komm Ich Her/Es Ist Ein Ros'entsprungen/Kommet Ihr Hirten/Stille Nacht, Heilige Nacht.

THE VERY BEST OF
ROGER WHITTAKER   INT 161.550/INT 461.550
River Lady/Albany/Dirty Old Town/I Don't Believe In If Anymore/Yarmouth Quay/Elizabethan Serenade/From The People To The People/The Last Farewell/Image To My Mind/Let Me Be Your Sun/Ride A Country Road/Indian Lady/Durham Town/Guten Abend, Gute Nacht.

DU GEHÖRST ZU MIR   *INT 161.555/INT 461.555/INT 861.555*
Schatten Und Licht (*Munro-Kunze*)/Die Nacht Von Marseille (*Mussig-Munro*)/Leben Mit Dir (*Munro*)/Treulos (*Munro*)/Wenn Das Herz Narben Hat (*Munro-Kunze*)/Lieben Sie Brahms, Madame? (*Munro-Kleinwort*)/Fernweh (*Munro-Kunze*)/Tage Wie Tropfen (*Munro*)/Für Ein Leben Zu Zweit (*Munro*)/Lass Dich Fallen (*Munro*)/Es Wird Nacht (*Munro*)

LOVE DREAMS   *INT 161.551/INT 461.551*
Annie's Song/Miss You Nights/You Are My Miracle/Time In A Bottle/All Of My Life/Feelings/Love Lasts Forever/Evergreen/When I Need You/Here I Stand/Send In The Clowns/Angels of Love/She/Every Time Is Going To Be The Last Time.

THE ROGER WHITTAKER
 PORTRAIT   INT 156.516/INT 456.516
All numbers written solely by Whittaker except where otherwise indicated.
Ride A Country Road/Disillusioned Fool (*Delany-Whittaker*)/Hold On/And Still the Sea/Idle Dreamer (*Kofsky-Whittaker*)/Tall Dark Stranger/The Last Farewell (*Whittaker-Webster*)/The First Hello, The Last Goodbye (*Robinson-Whittaker*)/The Seasons Come and Go/The Kind of Guy Who'd Help You See It Through (*Harper-Whittaker*)/So Long/Image To My Mind/I Don't Believe In If Anymore/Oh No Not Me/Summer Days/Pretty Bird Of Love (*Cour/Whittaker/Giraud*)/Mother Mine Sleep On/From The People To The People/Indian Lady (*Rankin-Whittaker*)/Before She Breaks My Heart/My World (*Spalding-Whittaker*)/Let Me Be Your Sun (*Cour-Whittaker*)/Time/Durham Town.

ROGER WHITTAKER:
SENTIMENTAL JOURNEY   *INT 136.500/INT 436.500*
Zhivago's Melody (*Jarre*)/Unchained Melody (*Zaret-North*)/Scarlet Ribbons (*Segal-Danzig*)/Red Sails In The Sunset (*Williams-Kennedy-Grosza*)/Vaya Con Dios (*Russell-Pepper-James*)/Tenderly (*Lawrence-Gross*)/Sentimental Journey (*Brown-Homer-Green*)/Eternally (*Parsons-Chaplin*)/It's Now Or Never (*Di Capus-Schroder-Gold*)/I Can't Help It If I'm Still In Love With You (*Williams*)/Red River Valley (*Traditional*)/There Goes My Everything (*Dallas-Franzier*).

CANADA

RELEASE ON THE TEMBO LABEL   DISTRIBUTED BY R.C.A.

ROGER WHITTAKER   *TM 1010/TMK 1010*
Everytime Is Going To Be The Last Time/All Of My Life/Hold On/Pretty Bird/Image To My Mind/From The People To The People/The Seasons (Come And Go)/A Rose Called Isobel/On No Not Me/Don't Let 'Em Change/And Still The Sea/So Long.

THE MAGICAL WORLD OF
ROGER WHITTAKER   *BTM 4000/BTMK 4000*
Google Eye/Nasty Spider/Boa Constrictor – Slitheredee/Winkin', Blinkin' And Nod/Whistle Stop/The Fox/Unicorn/Puff The Magic Dragon/Yellow Bird/Big Rock Candy Mountain/Blues For Lauren Marie.

LIVE IN CANADA   *TM2 5000/TM2K 5000*
Contents as for Germany GREATEST HITS IN CONCERT

REFLECTIONS OF LOVE   *TM 1853/TMK 1853*
It's Your Love/Before She Breaks My Heart/Indian Lady/Time/A Day In The Life Of A Lucky Man/Here We Stand/Summer Days/The First Hello, The Last Goodbye/All The Way To Richmond/New Love.

A TIME FOR PEACE   *BTM 4001/BTMK 4001*
Content as for Germany ROGER WHITTAKER'S CHRISTMAS ALBUM

RIDE A COUNTRY ROAD   *BTM 4005/BTMK 4005*
Ride A Country Road/Disillusioned Fool/Remember Love/River Lady/The Kind Of Guy Who'd Help You See It Through/She Wrote A Little Song/One Of These Days/Sweet Sight/Going Home/Cactus.

THE BEST OF ROGER WHITTAKER   *TMT 2255/TMK 2255*
The Last Farewell/New World In The Morning/I Don't Believe In If Anymore/All Of My Life/The First Hello, The Last Goodbye/Mon Pays Bleu (Durham Town)/Before She Breaks My Heart/It's Your Love/River Lady/Here We Stand/Dirty Old Town/Summer Days.

FOLKSONGS OF OUR TIMES   *TMT 2525/TMK 2525*
The Ashgrove/Down By The Sally Gardens/Eriskay Love Lilt/Foggy, Foggy Dew/My Love Is Like A Red Red Rose/She

Moves Through The Fair/David Of The White Rock/The Rising Of
The Lark/Star Of The County Down/Greensleeves/The Lewis Bridal
Song/Drink To Me Only.

IMAGINE   *TM2 6000/TM2K 6000*
Imagine/When I Need You/Weekend In New England/Sailing/Miss
You Nights/Annie's Song/Evergreen/Wonderful World/Love Lasts
Forever/Peace Train/Feelings/If I Knew Just What To Say/Your
Song/Home Lovin' Man/Time In A Bottle/Lying Eyes/I Can See
Clearly Now/Calypso/Solitaire/Send In The Clowns.

LIVE FROM THE PEOPLE   *BTM 4002/BTMK 4002*
Here I Come/Scarlet Ribbons/Russian Whistler/River
Lady/Yarmouth Quay/From The People To The People/Proud
Mary/Hound Dog/Long Tall Sally/You've Lost That Lovin'
Feeling/Swiss Mountaineer/Demon Rum/Special Kind Of Man/The
Last Song.

MIRRORS OF MY MIND   *TMT 3501/TMK 3501*
Call My Name/Goodnight Ruby/Please Come To
Boston/Wishes/Carry Me (Dreams On A Roof)/You Are My
Miracle/Family/Kentucky Song Bird/I Knew You Sunset/Blow
Gentle Breeze/It Takes A Lot.

VOYAGER   *TMT 3518/TMK 3518*
I Was Born/Paper Bird/See You In The Sunrise/Here I
Am/Lighthouse/Sail Away/Yele/I'll Be There/Love Is A Cold
Wind/All Of My Life/Song For The Captain/On My Own Again.

ROGER WHITTAKER WITH LOVE   *TMT 3778/TMK 3778*
Love Will/Don't Fight/My Son/One Another/For I Loved You/I Am
But A Small Voice/Tall Dark Stranger/Newport Belle/I Would If I
Could/See You Shine/A Man Without Love/Goodbye.

MES PLUS GRANDS SUCCÈS   *TMT 1016/TMK 1016*
Une Rose Pour Isabelle/Après La Guerre/Berceuse Pour Mon
Amour/Le Mistral/Bonne Nuit Maman/Laisse-Moi
T'Aimer/Siffleur Méxicain/MammyBlue/La Ballade De
L'Amour/Un Éléphant Sur Mon Balcon/Les Yeux Bleus/Verse Le
Vin Leila/Hello! Bonjour! Happy Day!/Le Dernier Adieu/Siffleur
Africain/Mon Pays Bleu.

LES CHANSONS DE MA VIE   *BTM 4004/BTMK 4004*
Isabelle Et Caroline/Une Fille Qu'A Un . . . Tu Vois/Tu Es Un

Chat/Bulles de Savon, Bulles De Soleil/Le Mistral/J'Habite Une Étoile/L'Enfant A La Rose/Vieux John Est Mort/La Jarretière D'Élisa/Ma Vie Est Là/Daisy O Daisy/Mon Pays Bleu/Ma Geisha/Marchand De Couleurs.

MEIN DEUTSCHES ALBUM — *TMT 3519/TMK 3519*
Contents as per Germany.

LES TEMPS DES AMOURS — *TMT 1020/MK 1020*
Les Temps Des Amours/Donne-Moi Un Baiser/Tu Es Ma Mélodie/Attends-Moi/Les Filles De Rimouski/Louisiane/Je N'Ai Qu'Une Chanson/Quand Je T'Aimais/Dieu Alors/Je M'En Vais.

TAKE A LITTLE – GIVE A LITTLE — *TMT 4325/TMK 4325*
Content as per U.K.

TIDINGS OF COMFORT AND JOY — *TMT 4327/TMK 4327*
Ding Dong Merrily On High/The Christmas Song/Rocking/The Twelve Days of Christmas/The First Noel/The Holly And The Ivy/White Christmas/The Little Drummer Boy/Angels From The Realms Of Glory/God Rest You Merry Gentlemen/Mary's Boy Child/Past Three O'Clock/We Wish You A Merry Christmas/Silent Night.

ROGER WHITTAKER IN KENYA — *TMT 4322/TMK 4322*
Contents as per U.K.

ROGER WHITTAKER –
GREATEST HITS, VOL. TWO — *TMT4323/TMK4323*
Stranger On The Shore/Albany/Annie's Song/Barroom Country Singer/Love Lasts Forever/I Am But A Small Voice/You Are My Miracle/Too Beautiful To Cry/Yellow Bird/Evergreen/My Love, Cape Breton And Me/Ride A Country Road.

THE WIND BENEATH MY WINGS — *TMT4321/TMK 4321*
Too Beautiful To Cry/Albany/Together/The Wind Beneath My Wings/England/Hold On Tight/Give Her Thorns/My Love, Cape Breton And Me/Let Me Be Your Sun/Goodbye To The Rain.

RCA RELEASES

A SPECIAL KIND OF MAN — *A YL1 3946/A YK1 3946*
Why/Moonshine/No Blade Of Grass/A Special Kind Of

Man/Paradise/He Starts Below/What Love Is/Candy Cloud/ Mexican Whistler/Morning, Please Don't Come/My Kind/The Last Farewell.

I DON'T BELIEVE IN IF ANYMORE   *AYL1 4177/AYK1 4177*
I Don't Believe In If Anymore/Emily/Flap Flap/Finnish Whistler/ The Book/Mistral/I Should Have Taken My Time/Lullaby For My Love/Festival/Halfway Up The Mountain/Sugar My Tea/Swaggy.

NEW WORLD IN THE MORNING   *AYL1 4178/AYK1 4178*
New World In The Morning/Both Sides Now/Early One Morning/San Miguel/Water Boy/Those Were The Days/Durham Town/Good Morning Starshine/This Moment/Sunrise, Sunset/Whistle Stop.

EN SPECTACLE AU QUEBEC   *KPL1 0027/KPK1 0027*
Le Mistral/Une Rose Pour Isabelle/Siffleur Africain/L'Été Est Mort Ce Soir/Apres La Guerre/I Believe/Siffleur Méxicain/La Ballade de l'Amour/Mon Grand-Pere Irlandais/Berceuse Pour Mon Amour/Mammy Blue/Mon Pays Bleu.

ROGER WHITTAKER'S GREATEST HTS *KPL1 0118/KPK1 011*
The Last Farewell/Durham Town/Whistle Stop/Mammy Blue/Song For Erik/Special Kind Of Man/New World In The Morning/I Don't Believe In If Anymore/Mon Pays Bleu/Mexican Whistler/Why/ Canada Is.

LA BALLADE DE L'AMOUR   *KYL1 0413*
Le Marchand de Couleurs/Mammy Blue/Une Rose Pour Isabelle/Bulles de Savon Bulles De Soleil/L'Été Est Mort Ce Soir/Ma Geisha/Mon Grand Pere Irlandais/Bateau de Papier/Love Time Rag Time/Le Vin Le Diable Et L'Amour/Je Suis Un Pop Song/La Ballade de l'Amour.

MON PAYS BLEU   *KYL1 0425/KYK1 0425*
Mon Pays Bleu/Plus Haut Sur La Montagne/Un Elephant Sur Mon Balcon/Flap Flap/Vous Pouvez Toujours Essayer/Un Enfant Nous a Souri/Le Mistral/Berceuse Pour Mon Amour/Festival (Brazilian Whistler)/Swaggie (Australian Whistler)/Le Siffleur Finlandais (Finnish Whistler)/Un Monde Est Né.

SONGS FROM THE HEART   *DMD2 067/DMD2T 067*
Red Roses For A Blue Lady/Lara's Theme (Somewhere My Love)/
Stranger On The Shore/I Can't Help It If I'm Still In Love With
You/Eternally/Sentimental Journey/Red Sails In The Sunset/Have I
Told You Lately That I Love You/Annie's Song/Sailing/Making
Believe/Tenderly/Unchained Melody/I Love You Because/Scarlet
Ribbons/Blue Eyes Crying In The Rain/It's Now or Never/There
Goes My Everything/Vaya Con Dios/The Last Song.

WORLD'S MOST BEAUTIFUL
CHRISTMAS SONGS   *CSPS 2659/16SP 2659*
Contents as per UK TIDINGS OF COMFORT AND JOY except no 'In the
Bleak Midwinter' or 'Sussex Carol' and 'O Tannenbaum' in place of
'Rocking'.

THE GENIUS OF LOVE   *TMT 4329/TMK 4329*
Contents as per U.K.

U.S.A.

THE GENIUS OF LOVE   *AFL1 5803/AFK1 5803*
The Genius of Love (*Mitchell/Reilly*)/Miss Lapotaire (*Scott*)/Your
Voice (*Bogdanovs*)/Railway Hotel (*Batt*)/Jerusalem Goodbye
(*Michalsky/Reshoft/Whittaker*)/The Candle (*Whalley*)/Your Fool
(*Hancock*)/One More Chance (*Page/Lang/George*)/Everybody's Got a
Lonely Heart (*Michalsky/Reshoft/Whittaker*).

THE LAST FAREWELL
AND OTHER HITS   *AQL1 0855/AQK1 0855*
New World In The Morning/Both Sides Now/Halfway Up The
Mountain/Water Boy/The Last Farewell/I Don't Believe In If
Anymore/Good Morning Starshine/Sunrise, Sunset/Whistle Stop.

REFLECTIONS OF LOVE   *AFL1 1853/AFK1 1853*
It's Your Love/Before She Breaks My Heart/Indian Lady/Time/A
Day In The Life Of A Lucky Man/Here We Stand/Summer
Days/The First Hello, The Last Goodbye/All The Way To
Richmond/New Love.

FOLK SONGS OF OUR TIME   *AQL1 2525/AQK1 2525*
Contents as per Canada.

THE ROGER WHITTAKER CHRISTMAS ALBUM
ANL1 2933/ANK1 2933

Contents as per Germany.

MIRRORS OF MY MIND
AQL1 3501/AQK1 3501

Contents as per Canada.

VOYAGER
AQL1 3518/AQK1 3518

Contents as per Canada.

ROGER WHITTAKER WITH LOVE
AQK1 3778

Contents as per Canada.

WHEN I NEED YOU
AYL1 3911/AYK1 3911

When I Need You/Weekend In New England/Annie's Song/Lyin' Eyes/Time In A Bottle/Home Lovin' Man/Miss You Nights/Solitaire/She/Your Song.

A SPECIAL KIND OF MAN
AYL1 3946/AYK1 3946

Why/Moonshine/No Blade of Grass/A Special Kind of Man/Paradise/He Starts Below/What Love Is/Candy Cloud/Mexican Whistler/Morning, Please Don't Come/My Kind/The Last Farewell.

LIVE IN CONCERT
CPK2 4057

Contents as per Germany GREATEST HITS IN CONCERT.

NEW WORLD IN THE MORNING
AYL1 4178/AYK1 4178

Contents as per Canada.

THE WIND BENEATH MY WINGS
AFL1 4321/AFK1 4321

Contents as per Canada except 'Sweet Young America' instead of 'Albany' on Side One.

IMAGINE
AYL1 4658/AYK1 4658

Imagine/Wonderful World/Sailing/Love Lasts Forever/Feelings/Calypso/If I Knew Just What To Say/Peace Train/Your Song/I Can See Clearly Now/Evergreen/Send In The Clowns.

ROGER WHITTAKER'S GREATEST HITS
AYL1 4743/AYK1 4743

You Are My Miracle/Albany/Annie's Song/Barroom Country Singer/Too Beautiful To Cry/I Am But A Small Voice/Yellow Bird/My Love, Cape Breton and Me/The Wind Beneath My Wings.

THE BEST OF ROGER WHITTAKER   *AYL1 5166/AYK1 5166*
Contents as per Canada.

TAKE A LITTLE – GIVE A LITTLE   *NFL 8047/NFK1 8047*
Take A Little Give A Little/Bitter And Sweet (I Will Follow You)/
More Than Anything/Happy Everything/Now The Pain Begins/Mean
Woman/Chicago Girl/Dover To Calais/My Silver Eagle.

SUFFOLK MARKETING RELEASES
ALL TIME HEART-TOUCHING FAVOURITES*SMI1 40/SMIC 40*
Contents as per U.K.

WORLD'S MOST BEAUTIFUL
CHRISTMAS SONGS   *SMI1 53/SMIC 53*
Contents as per Canada.

ALL MY BEST   *DML1 0637/DMK1 0637*
The Last Farewell/The First Hello, The Last Goodbye/Mexican
Whistler/Dirty Old Town/Summer Days/All Of My Life/I Don't
Believe In If Anymore/Elizabethan Serenade/Lullaby/New World In
The Morning/Kilgarry Mountain/Mammy Blue/Hello, Good
Morning, Happy Day/Oh No Not Me/Time/Before She Breaks My
Heart/Image To My Mind/Durham Town/Skye Boat Song.

AUSTRALIA AND NEW ZEALAND
R.C.A. RELEASES

SONGS TO REMEMBER   *VAL1 0371/VAK1 0371*
Durham Town/Wonderful World/Got To Head On Down The
Road/Send In The Clowns/Dirty Old Town/Bright Eyes/New World
In The Morning/Time In A Bottle/Calypso/I Don't Believe In If
Anymore/Feelings/The Last Farewell.

TIDINGS OF COMFORT AND JOY   *VPL2 6693/VPK2 6693/1*
Content as per U.K.

ROGER WHITTAKER IN KENYA   *MAL1 0005/MAK1 0005*
Content as per U.K.

GIVE A LITTLE – TAKE A LITTLE   *VPL1 6686/VPK1 6686*
Content as per U.K.

ROGER WHITTAKER: *VPL1 6664/VPK1 6664/*
ALL TIME FAVOURITES   *and SFL1/SFK1 01008*
Lara's Theme/Unchained Melody/Making Believe/Scarlet Ribbons/

Red Sails In The Sunset/Red Roses For A Blue Lady/Red River Valley/Vaya Con Dios/Blue Eyes Crying In The Rain/Love You Because/It's Now Or Never/Have I Told You Lately That I Love You/I Can't Help It/Both Sides Now/Sentimental Journey/There Goes My Everything/Eternally/Tenderly/Stranger On The Shore.

ROGER WHITTAKER LIVE WITH SAFFRON *SP2 231/SPK1 231*
New World In The Morning/Image To My Mind/Dirty Old Town/Mexican Whistler/New African Whistler/Chengalip/Image To My Mind/That's Life/What Love Is/All I Have To Do Is Dream/Early One Morning/Durham Town/Image To My Mind/A Day In The Life Of A Lucky Man/This Moment/Ride A Country Road/Berceuse Pour Mon Amour/Image To My Mind/Morning Has Broken/Why/I Don't Believe In If Anymore/The Last Farewell/Skye Boat Song/Kilgarry Mountain.

ROGER WHITTAKER LIVE *VAL2 0468/VAK2 0468*
Here I Come/Scarlet Ribbons/Swiss Mountaineer/Hound Dog/Long Tall Sally/Chengalip/The Rising Of The Lark/Star Of The County Down/The Ashgrove/Ride A Country Road/From The People To The People/The First Hello, The Last Goodbye/A Special Kind of Man/The Last Farewell/The Impossible Dream/Bridge Over Troubled Waters/By The Time I Get To Phoenix/Proud Mary/ Yesterday/You've Lost That Loving Feeling/Indian Lady/Yarmouth Quay/Demon Rum/River Lady/The Last Song/If I Knew Just What To Say/Canada Is.

CHANGES *VAL1 0466/VAK1 0466*
When I Dream/Changes/Honolulu City Lights/Smooth Sailing/I Can Hear Kentucky Calling Me/How Does It Feel/Moonshine/Rocky Top/River Lady/Bar Room Country Singer.

AUSTRALIA
R.C.A. RELEASES

A TIME FOR PEACE *VAL 0241/VAK1 0241*
Contents as per Canada.

THE WIND BENEATH MY WINGS *VPL1 6643/VPK1 6643*
Content as per U.S.A.

NEW ZEALAND
R.C.A. RELEASES

RIDE A COUNTRY ROAD *RDL 1701/RDLC 1701*
Ride A Country Road/Disillusioned Fool/Remember Love/River

Lady/Cactus/She Wrote A Little Song/The First Hello, The Last Goodbye/One Of The Days/Sweet Sight/Going Home.

FEELINGS   *VLP2 6583/VPK2 6583*
Feelings/Wishes/Imagine/I Can See Clearly Now/Home Lovin' Man/Calypso/Call My Name/Wonderful World/Sailing/When I Need You/Solitaire/Annie's Song.

THE MAGICAL WORLD
OF ROGER WHITTAKER   *VAL1 0239/VAK1 0239*
Google Eye (*Lauder-Milk*)/Nasty Spider (*Taylor*)/Boa Constrictor/ Slitheredee (*Silverstein*)/Winkin', Blinkin' and Nod (*Simon-Field*)/ Whistle Stop (*Whittaker-Hayes*)/Little Dreamer (*Knowles-Nuttall*)/The Fox (*Trad: Arr. Whittaker*)/Unicorn (*Silverstein*)/Puff The Magic Dragon (*Yarrow-Lipton*)/Yellow Bird (*Luhoff-Keith-Bregman*)/Big Rock Candy Mountain (*Trad: Arr. Whittaker*)/Blues for Lauren Marie (*Whittaker-Barkwood*)/Bottle Tops (*Harper-Blakely*).

SOUTH AFRICA
GALLO RECORDS RELEASES

MY FAVOURITE LOVE SONGS   *DGL845/6*
Content as per Canada ALL TIME HEART TOUCHING FAVOURITES

TAKE A LITTLE, GIVE A LITTLE   *ML4761/MC 4761*
Content as per U.K.

LIVE WITH SAFFRON   *DGL 813/4*
Content as per Australia/New Zealand.

SCANDINAVIA
TEMBO   LABEL : DISTRIBUTED   BY   POLYGRAM   RECORDS   A/S

ROGER WHITTAKER IN KENYA   *Export 812.949-1/812.949.4*
Content as per U.K.

TAKE A LITTLE, GIVE A LITTLE   *TMB 101/TMBC 101*
Content as per U.K.

KENYA
TEMBO LABEL : DISTRIBUTED BY POLYGRAM RECORDS LTD

Content and numbers as per SCANDINAVIA